Routledge Revivals

A History of the Public Library Movement in Great Britain and Ireland

Originally published in 1932, *A History of the Public Library Movement in Great Britain and Ireland* is concerned with the rise and progress of the public library as it stood at that time. The establishment and growth of the public library may be viewed as part of the great social movement for the spread of knowledge among the poorer classes which took place in the late eighteenth century and the early years of the nineteenth century. This movement was characterized by the establishment of various educational agencies, which are covered in this book, along with the introduction of the Public Libraries Act passed in 1850 and other legislation that followed.

A History of the Public Library Movement in Great Britain and Ireland

John Minto

First published in 1932
by George Allen & Unwin Ltd

This edition first published in 2025 by Routledge
4 Park Square, Milton Park, Abingdon, Oxon, OX14 4RN

and by Routledge
605 Third Avenue, New York, NY 10017

Routledge is an imprint of the Taylor & Francis Group, an informa business

© 1932 John Minto

All rights reserved. No part of this book may be reprinted or reproduced or utilised in any form or by any electronic, mechanical, or other means, now known or hereafter invented, including photocopying and recording, or in any information storage or retrieval system, without permission in writing from the publishers.

Publisher's Note
The publisher has gone to great lengths to ensure the quality of this reprint but points out that some imperfections in the original copies may be apparent.

Disclaimer
The publisher has made every effort to trace copyright holders and welcomes correspondence from those they have been unable to contact.

A Library of Congress record exists under LCCN: 32026880

ISBN: 978-1-032-89894-0 (hbk)
ISBN: 978-1-003-54520-0 (ebk)
ISBN: 978-1-032-89903-9 (pbk)

Book DOI 10.4324/9781003545200

A HISTORY OF THE PUBLIC LIBRARY MOVEMENT

IN GREAT BRITAIN AND IRELAND

by

JOHN MINTO, M.A., F.L.A.

LIBRARIAN OF THE SIGNET LIBRARY
EDINBURGH

LONDON
GEORGE ALLEN & UNWIN LTD
AND THE LIBRARY ASSOCIATION
1932

FIRST PUBLISHED IN 1932

All rights reserved

PRINTED IN GREAT BRITAIN BY
UNWIN BROTHERS LTD., WOKING

GENERAL INTRODUCTION TO THE SERIES

The publication of a systematic series of practical and authoritative Manuals of Library Work, which shall survey Library polity and practice in their latest aspects, is a requirement of which administrators, librarians, and students alike have long been conscious, and is much overdue.

In the Library world not the Great War alone, with its aftermath of new conditions, but also the Library Act of 1919, have marked the termination of one long epoch and the commencement of a new and yet more prosperous era. The removal of the crippling limitation of the penny rate at once paved the way for a renaissance of the Library Movement, and remarkable extensions and innovations, both in buildings and in service, have ensued. The great work of the Carnegie Trustees in fostering the development of urban Public Libraries has now been largely diverted into fresh channels, and County and Rural Library Systems now cover the country from Land's End to John-o'-Groats. The public demand and appreciation of Libraries have increased enormously, and, in response, old methods have been revised and new ones introduced. The evolution of Commercial and Technical Libraries and the development of Business and Works Libraries would amply suffice to indicate this spirit of progress, but, during the last decade or

THE PUBLIC LIBRARY MOVEMENT

so, the entire field of Library service has been subjected to review and experiment, and little, either in administration or routine, remains entirely unchanged.

It will, therefore, be sufficiently obvious that the old textbooks relating to Library practice can no longer serve, and that there is a real need for new manuals, written by persons of experience and authority, and treating of the new conditions in a full and thoroughly practical manner. It is this void that the series of Library Manuals is designed to fill, and the fact that these volumes are to be issued by Messrs. George Allen and Unwin Ltd. in conjunction with the Library Association, should afford adequate proof of the qualifications of the authors to treat of the subjects upon which they will write. If sufficient support is forthcoming the series will be made comprehensive and complete.

The volumes will be supplied with bibliographical references throughout, and will be illustrated where necessary. No effort will be spared to make the series an essential tool for all those who are engaged in Library work, or who intend to embrace Librarianship as a profession. To students they will be invaluable. The uniform price of 10s. 6d. net will be adhered to so far as possible, so as to bring the Manuals within the reach of all.

WM. E. DOUBLEDAY
General Editor

PREFACE

In the preparation of this work I have received much assistance from many of my colleagues in the Library Association. My thanks are specially due to Sir John Ballinger, Mr. W. E. Doubleday, Sir Herbert Lewis, Mr. S. A. Pitt, Mr. H. D. Roberts, Mr. G. E. Roebuck, and Mr. E. A. Savage, who generously allowed me to make use of certain of their published and unpublished papers. To the chairmen and secretaries of the various branches and sections of the Library Association and kindred associations I am indebted for information readily granted concerning these bodies.

I desire also to thank Mr. R. W. Chapman, of the Clarendon Press, for according me permission to quote extracts from articles in the *Dictionary of National Biography* on prominent men in the library profession.

Mr. James Hutt very kindly gave his consent to my publishing in an appendix the very useful conspectus of the Libraries Acts which he prepared for use in connection with his lectures at the Aberystwyth Summer Schools.

Mr. E. A. Savage, Hon. Secretary of the Library Association, has helped me throughout with wise counsel and advice. In addition to contributing the

THE PUBLIC LIBRARY MOVEMENT

biographical notices of James Duff Brown and Sir John Y. W. MacAlister, he has read the work in MS, and has also read the proofs.

A list of the main works consulted will be found in Appendix I.

JOHN MINTO

CONTENTS

CHAPTER		PAGE
	PREFACE	9
I.	INTRODUCTORY	13
II.	THE SPREAD OF EDUCATION, AND THE RESULTING DEMAND FOR READING MATTER—THE CIRCULATION OF POPULAR LITERATURE—FORERUNNERS OF THE PUBLIC LIBRARY—EARLY MUNICIPAL FOUNDATIONS, PAROCHIAL LIBRARIES, ITINERATING LIBRARIES, SUBSCRIPTION LIBRARIES, MECHANICS' INSTITUTES	15
III	THE NEED FOR LIBRARIES FREELY OPEN TO THE PUBLIC—THE MINUTES OF EVIDENCE AND REPORTS OF THE SELECT COMMITTEE ON PUBLIC LIBRARIES	47
IV.	THE REPORTS OF THE COMMITTEE	71
V.	THE PUBLIC LIBRARIES ACT, 1850	80
VI.	EARLY ADOPTIONS OF THE ACT	96
VII.	SUBSEQUENT AMENDING LEGISLATION	99
VIII.	FURTHER AMENDING AND CONSOLIDATING LEGISLATION	114
IX.	REMOVAL OF THE RATE LIMITATION	125
X.	RECENT LEGISLATION	145
XI.	PUBLIC LIBRARY PROGRESS AND POLICY	149

THE PUBLIC LIBRARY MOVEMENT

CHAPTER		PAGE
XII.	THE LIBRARY ASSOCIATION	162
XIII.	TRAINING FOR LIBRARIANSHIP	208
XIV.	BRANCH AND DISTRICT ASSOCIATIONS AND SECTIONS	234
XV.	OTHER LIBRARY ASSOCIATION ACTIVITIES	259
XVI.	COUNTY LIBRARIES	272
XVII.	COMMERCIAL AND TECHNICAL LIBRARIES	280
XVIII.	LIBRARIES FOR THE BLIND—HOSPITAL LIBRARIES—CHILDREN'S LIBRARIES—SCHOOL LIBRARIES	289
XIX.	PROMINENT WORKERS AND BENEFACTORS	301
	APPENDIX I. LIST OF SOME BOOKS CONSULTED	343
	APPENDIX II. CONSPECTUS OF THE VARIOUS ACTS OF PARLIAMENT RELATING TO PUBLIC LIBRARIES, MUSEUMS, AND GYMNASIUMS. COMPILED BY JAMES HUTT, M.A., F.L.A.	345
	INDEX	353

A HISTORY OF
THE PUBLIC LIBRARY MOVEMENT

CHAPTER I

INTRODUCTORY

The story of libraries is as old as the story of civilization itself. In Mesopotamia the researches and excavations of Botta and Layard in the middle of last century at Kuyunjik (Nineveh), the ancient capital of the Assyrian kings, and the more recent excavations of British and American expeditions at Nippur, Kish, and Ur of the Chaldees have demonstrated the existence of large collections of clay tablets, some of them dating back to three thousand years before the Christian era.

These inscribed tablets contain records of religious ceremonies, civil and political events, trade documents, etc., and for their preservation were housed in the temples of the gods and in the palaces of the kings. As they were arranged and catalogued, and made available to such of the King's subjects as were able to make use of them, they may be described as the earliest public libraries known to us.

In Egypt also the libraries of her ancient kings were large and important, containing not only the records of royal transactions and important events

THE PUBLIC LIBRARY MOVEMENT

of civic interest but also the sacred books of the Egyptian religion and commentaries thereon, as well as medical works and works of the imagination. Perhaps the most famous of these libraries is that of Rameses II at Thebes. According to Diodorus Siculus, this library bore an inscription which he interprets as ψυχης ιατρειον, the dispensary, or surgery, of the soul. But to trace the development of libraries from these early collections of clay tablets and papyri through the centuries to modern times is not our object here. This has already been done by various hands and by none more graphically or succinctly than by Sir Frederic Kenyon in his admirable little book on *Libraries and Museums* in Benn's Sixpenny Library. We are concerned only with the rise and progress of the public library as we know it to-day in Great Britain and Ireland.

CHAPTER II

THE SPREAD OF EDUCATION, AND THE RESULTING DEMAND FOR READING MATTER—THE CIRCULATION OF POPULAR LITERATURE—FORERUNNERS OF THE PUBLIC LIBRARY—EARLY MUNICIPAL FOUNDATIONS, PAROCHIAL LIBRARIES, ITINERATING LIBRARIES, SUBSCRIPTION LIBRARIES, MECHANICS' INSTITUTES

The establishment and growth of the public library may be viewed as part of the great social movement for the spread of knowledge among the poorer classes which took place in the late eighteenth century and the early years of the nineteenth century. This movement was characterized by the establishment of various educational agencies, some account of which may here be briefly given.

Sunday Schools which, in their beginnings, were not exclusively religious institutions, and were not confined to children, were the result of the pioneer efforts of Robert Raikes, printer in Gloucester (1780), of the Rev. Rowland Hill in London (1784), of Hannah More, Sydney Smith, and others. Secular subjects were taught in these schools, and evening classes were sometimes held during the week as part of the system. The formation of the Sunday School Union in 1803 gave a powerful impetus to the movement in England. It provided for "the training of teachers, the grading of classes, and schemes of lessons suitable to the various stages of the scholars' mental growth."[1]

The establishment of two important societies, the National Society for the Education of the Poor (1811) and the British and Foreign School Society (1814), carried forward the educational movement for the greater part of the nineteenth century. The moving spirits of these two societies were the Rev. Andrew Bell, D.D., and Joseph Lancaster.

The monitorial system which was used in the schools of both these societies had been developed in France in 1790. Both Bell and Lancaster claimed to have been the first to use it, but the system is much older than either, and is to be found fully described by John Brinsley in his *Ludus Literarius* published in 1612. Bell, who was a native of St. Andrews and educated at that University, took Orders in the Church of England and went to India in 1787, where he became superintendent of the Madras Orphanage for the sons of soldiers. Finding difficulty in obtaining the services of qualified teachers, he adopted the plan of conducting the school by the aid of the pupils themselves, which proved fairly successful. On his return from India in 1797, he published a pamphlet entitled *An Experiment in Education made at the Male Asylum at Madras*. It attracted comparatively little attention till the system was adopted by Joseph Lancaster, a Quaker, and used in the many schools which he founded

[1] *Chambers's Encyclopædia* (Article on Sunday Schools).

THE SPREAD OF EDUCATION

throughout the country on the so-called Lancasterian System.

On the establishment of the National Society's Schools, Bell was appointed general superintendent, and their number rapidly increased to over twelve thousand.

Bell, who died in 1832, bequeathed a sum of £120,000 for the purpose of founding educational establishments in St. Andrews and other towns in Scotland.

When the British and Foreign School Society was established in 1814, Lancaster took a prominent part in its activities, and was for long its leading spirit. These two societies practically dominated the administration of education in England until, under the pressure of public opinion, Parliament began to take it up. After the Reform Bill of 1832 the first grant in aid of education was made by Parliament. This grant, and subsequent grants, were made for the building of schools, and participation in the grant was conditional upon the raising of half the cost of the building by local contributions. In all cases an application for a grant in aid had to be made with the approval of one or other of those two educational societies. This condition gave rise to a long and embittered ecclesiastical controversy as to the control of education, not wholly extinct even at the present day.

The natural result of the spread of education was the creation of a demand for reading matter, which the very few existing libraries that were freely

THE PUBLIC LIBRARY MOVEMENT

accessible to the public were quite unable to supply. As is usual, however, the demand stimulated supply, and there were not wanting many enterprising publishers willing to cater for the needs of those who, having been taught to read, were eager to make use of their newly acquired accomplishment. There sprang up a mass of reading matter—one can scarcely apply the term literature to a great deal of it—in the form of cheap, popular magazines and journals.

The earliest of these,[1] *Chambers's Journal* (originally entitled *Chambers's Edinburgh Journal*), was started on February 4, 1832, by the brothers William and Robert Chambers, "to take advantage of the universal appetite for instruction which at present exists." Their enterprise was well rewarded, for their venture at once proved popular, and in a year or two reached a circulation of 80,000. *Chambers's Journal* outlived all its contemporaries, and maintains a vigorous life as a centenarian at the present day. In addition to the *Journal*, the firm of W. & R. Chambers also issued at this period of its history a number of works designed for popular instruction, e.g. *Chambers's Information for the People*, *Chambers's Educational Course*, *Papers for the People* (12 vols.), *Chambers's Miscellany* (20 vols.), *Chambers's Cyclopædia of English Literature* (2 vols., 1844; [5th ed.] 3 vols. By D. Patrick, 1901–3), and, later, *Chambers's Encyclopædia* (1859–68), frequently revised, current edition, 1922–27.

[1] Hammond (J. L. and B.), *The Age of the Chartists*.

THE SPREAD OF EDUCATION

Chambers's Journal was followed within a few weeks by the *Penny Magazine* of the Society for the Diffusion of Useful Knowledge, edited by Charles Knight, which lived until 1845. It was illustrated, but, unlike *Chambers's*, it contained no fiction. A continuation in 2 vols. entitled *Knight's Penny Magazine* was published in 1846. The Society also published the *Penny Cyclopædia* in 27 vols. and three supplementary vols. (1833–58), edited by George Long and others; *The Library of Entertaining Knowledge*; and *The Library of Useful Knowledge*— all of which were very popular in their day.

The *Saturday Magazine* (1832–44), issued by the Society for Promoting Christian Knowledge (S.P.C.K.), which included a certain amount of religious matter, did not survive quite so long as the *Penny Magazine*, which was entirely secular.

After the reduction of the stamp duty on newspapers in 1836 from 4d. to 1d., a number of journals entered into competition with *Chambers's* as periodicals for the family circle. The most important of these was the *Family Herald* (established 1842), which had, and continues to have, a wide circulation. It contained many romantic tales as well as "useful information and amusement for the million," domestic hints, amusing anecdotes, and biographical sketches of famous men of all times, with articles on the etiquette of good society, and similar information. A popular feature was a section devoted to "Answers to Correspondents."

In 1849 Eliza Cook founded and edited *Eliza*

Cook's Journal, to "give her feeble aid to the gigantic struggle for intellectual elevation now going on." It was a magazine of a very serious and instructive character, and contained, every week, one of the poetess's well-known moral poems, as well as some fiction of a didactic character. Owing to ill-health, she was obliged to discontinue its publication in 1854.

John Cleave, the Chartist, who had taken an active part in the agitation for an unstamped Press, and who before the duty was reduced had been issuing his *Weekly Police Gazette* and *Journal of News, Politics, and Literature* in defiance of the stamp laws, found that evasion of the duty at 1d. had become more difficult than it had been at 4d., was obliged to raise the price of his *Police Gazette* from 2d. to $3\frac{1}{2}$d., and was unable to make it pay its way as a stamped newspaper. He accordingly started *Cleave's London Satirist and Gazette of Variety* in 1837, the title of which was afterwards changed to *Cleave's Penny Gazette of Variety and Amusement*, and its character altered to introduce more fictional matter. He announced his intention of keeping it free of politics, but that did not prevent him from satirizing in cartoons all political parties and the current abuses of the time. It proved very popular, containing as it did articles advocating the opening of museums on Sundays, temperance, etc., with much information on household matters, natural history, gardening topics, etc. The fiction section frequently consisted of extracts from

THE SPREAD OF EDUCATION

Dickens's works, and sketches written in imitation of his Pickwickian style, which were a common feature of similar periodicals of the time. Later, the *Gazette* contained many thrillers of the blood-curdling terrorist school.

Edward Lloyd, founder of *Lloyd's Newspaper*, started in 1841 his weekly *Companion to the Penny Sunday Times and People's Police Gazette*, which outdid all its rivals in the publication of tales of terror and highly coloured sentiment, and was embellished with crude illustrations of exciting incidents in the stories. Two years later the popularity of the *Companion* led him to publish a *Weekly Penny Miscellany* and *Lloyd's Penny Atlas and Weekly Register of Novel Entertainment*, both of which were widely circulated. Lloyd also issued in penny parts a large number of novels and romances of a style similar to those in his weekly magazines.

In the evidence given before the Select Committee on Public Libraries in 1849 it was suggested that much of this class of fiction was of an immoral and anti-social character, and that the establishment of public libraries where literature of a better sort would be provided for the people was very desirable. When we consider the long hours of work which were then universal, the bad conditions under which it was very often carried on, and the comparatively few opportunities of social relaxation other than those the public-house provided, we can readily understand the craving on the part of the labouring classes to have their minds occupied with

THE PUBLIC LIBRARY MOVEMENT

the reading of tales which made them for a time at least forget the sordidness of their lot.

We have stated that the existing libraries were unable to meet the demands of the public for books to read. Let us see then what the available facilities for reading were other than the cheap periodicals referred to above. The principal libraries available were the early municipal foundations, parochial libraries, subscription libraries, and mechanics' institutes.

Early Municipal Foundations

In the early part of the seventeenth century the desire to help their less-fortunate brethren led a few wealthy and philanthropic men to present or bequeath their collections of books to municipalities with a view to their preservation for the free use of all.

A public library was established in the Free Grammar School of Coventry in 1601, the initiative being probably taken by Dr. Philemon Holland, "the translator-general of his age." A separate library room was provided in the school. This library existed until 1913 or 1914, when the valuable residue was sold by the governors of the school, much to the dismay and indignation of the citizens when the facts became known. The original donation book of the library, with a list of the first donors, is now in the Cambridge University Library, the authorities of which had the good sense to purchase what Coventry had stupidly sold.

EARLY MUNICIPAL FOUNDATIONS

Probably this public library and that of Norwich were the earliest municipal public libraries in England.

The municipality of the city of Norwich in 1608 set apart three rooms, "parcel of the sword-bearer's dwelling," and fitted them up for the reception of a library in the south porch of the New Hall (now St. Andrew's Hall). The rooms were to serve the additional purpose of lodgings for preachers coming from a distance to preach in the city. The sword-bearer had to find "bedding, lynnynge, and other necessaries for their lodging." The Mayor, Sir Thomas Petters, set a good example, which was quickly followed, by heading the list of gifts to the new library with fifteen volumes.[1] This early library now forms part of the Norwich Public Library.

In 1615 a city library was opened at Bristol through the munificence of Dr. Toby Matthew, Archbishop of York, and Robert Redwood, a public-spirited citizen. This library, like that at Norwich, was afterwards incorporated in the Bristol Public Library. In 1623 Sir John Kederminster established a parochial free library at Langley Marish in Buckinghamshire. Leicester has had a city library since 1632, and the famous library of Sir Humphrey Chetham was, under the terms of his will, made freely accessible to the inhabitants of Manchester in 1653. The great difficulty in preserving the continuity of these early libraries has

[1] Article by Albert D. Euren, Editor of the *Norwich Mercury*, in *Book Auction Records*, Vol. 10, 1913, p. xxiv.

THE PUBLIC LIBRARY MOVEMENT

been the want of provision for their maintenance and the lack of funds for their growth. The Chetham Library is believed to be the only library in England with a continuous history since its foundation, freely accessible to all. It will readily be understood that these few and scattered libraries could, of necessity, do little to meet the needs of the reading public of England.

PAROCHIAL LIBRARIES

The parochial libraries, many of which were established in the eighteenth century mainly through individual benevolence, were intended principally for the use of the clergy, but were accessible also to persons of respectability when furnished with an introduction. Dr. Thomas Bray (1656–1730), author of *Catechetical Lectures*, Rector of Sheldon (1690–99), had been selected in 1696 by the Bishop of London as his commissary to Maryland in the settlement of the Church there, but, in going round the country to solicit contributions for missions, he was met with refusals on the plea that the needs of the people at home were more pressing, and that they would rather contribute to help the home clergy by establishing libraries for their use than send out missionaries or libraries to the colonies. This argument appealed to him, and he devoted himself with characteristic energy to a scheme for the establishment of parochial libraries in England and America. Out of this scheme grew the Society for Promoting Christian Knowledge (1698–99)

PAROCHIAL LIBRARIES

and the Society for the Propagation of the Gospel (1701). Bray sailed for Maryland in 1699, but returned to England in 1706 as Rector of St. Botolph Without, Aldgate, where he laboured till his death on February 15, 1730.[1] After Bray's death a number of the friends whom he had gathered round him formed a society called "The Associates of Dr. Bray" to carry on his work, and a large number of additional parochial and lending libraries were founded. The Bray Libraries are still being carried on by "the Association of the late Dr. Bray and his associates for theological libraries for the clergy and lay members of the Church of England" from the S.P.G. headquarters at Tufton Street, Westminster.

In at least one case, that of Beccles, in Suffolk, the parochial library "made the commencement of a town library," but, for the most part, though founded by charitably disposed persons, these libraries fell into disuse and neglect, no provision having been made for adding to them.

In addition to the parochial libraries of England most of the cathedrals and larger churches had attached to them libraries which were accessible to properly introduced persons, although they were primarily intended for the use of the cathedral or diocesan clergy. In Durham, Manchester, Peterborough, and York such freedom of access was readily obtainable.

A system of parochial, presbyterial, and synodical

[1] *Chambers's Encyclopædia.*

libraries was established by the General Assembly of the Church of Scotland in the early eighteenth century for the use of the ministers, schoolmasters, students and other inhabitants of various parishes throughout the Highlands and Islands of Scotland. The inception of this scheme was largely due to the Rev. James Kirkwood, for some time minister of Minto, Roxburghshire, who afterwards became Rector of Astwick, Bedfordshire, and subsequently was appointed by the S.P.C.K. their corresponding member for Scotland.

In 1699 Kirkwood published anonymously his famous pamphlet "An Overture for Founding and Maintaining of Bibliothecks in every Paroch throughout this Kingdom, humbly offered to the consideration of this present Assembly." The pamphlet is of extreme rarity, but is of importance in the history of the public library movement. A copy of it was discovered in a volume of tracts in the Wigan Public Library by the late librarian, Henry T. Folkard. It was exhibited at the Glasgow meeting of the Library Association in 1888 by William Blades, who was desirous of ascertaining its authorship. Professor W. P. Dickson, Curator of the Library of Glasgow University, then President of the Association, compared it with the only other known copy belonging to Professor John Ferguson, which was bound up with another anonymous pamphlet by Kirkwood, bearing internal evidence of its authorship. Professor Dickson was able, in a letter to the *Library Chronicle*, Vol. 5,

1888, p. 116, to show that the two pamphlets were by the same hand. The 1699 pamphlet was privately reprinted in 1899, with introductory remarks by William Blades, giving an account of both pamphlets, and a short biographical notice of the author. A fuller account of the two pamphlets is given in an article entitled "Highland Libraries in the Eighteenth Century," by the Rev. Professor Donald Maclean, in the Records of the *Glasgow Bibliographical Society*, Vol. 7, 1923, pp. 36–43.

Kirkwood's scheme of 1699 was rather ambitious, and some of his proposals were too impracticable to be put into force, but it showed Kirkwood to have been a man of ideas a long way in advance of his time. Professor Maclean, in the article above mentioned, says his scheme "fairly entitles its author to the title of 'Father of Free Libraries.'"

After enumerating the difficulties experienced by students in obtaining the books required for their studies, including the lack of funds for their purchase, distance from towns where they are printed, and so forth, he declares that "complete and free libraries are absolutely necessary for the improving of the arts and sciences and for advancing of learning amongst us," and goes on to elaborate his plan. It included the giving in of all his own books to the parish library by every minister, where they were to be catalogued and valued, "so that on removal to another parish he, or on his death, his heirs, shall have first call on the stipend of the parish to the amount so valued." A union catalogue of all the libraries was to be made, printed, and circulated to each library. Each library was to have one copy at least of every valuable book extant, the parish librarian, who would be either the Reader or the Schoolmaster, was to find caution for the faithful keeping of the books and to lend only to responsible persons within the parish. There was to be a bookbinder in every presbytery provided with a house and all the tools of his trade, and given a small yearly stipend, or, alternatively, the librarian or the minister's servants might be taught bookbinding. Each library was to be standardized by having the same method of arrangement of the books upon its shelves, so that ministers or students, if removed to another parish, should know exactly where to find a book in the library. A fund for buying and printing books, both new and old, English and foreign, was to be established by levying a month's cess on heritors and ministers in each parish, and each library was to get a copy of every book printed. The month's cess he reckoned would amount to 72,000 pounds Scots yearly. The printing of all these books and the binding of them would form a considerable manufactory and would maintain many people at work; students would not have to spend their money in purchasing foreign works or in travelling to foreign universities. Gentlemen would be allured to spending their time in reading and so prevented from gaming and drinking. The manufactory would in a short time carry away the whole trade of printing from

PAROCHIAL LIBRARIES

all the rest of Europe. It would be honourable to this country to be the first and only nation for a while to have this regular and useful plenty of books, learning would flourish, and "these libraries in two or three hundred years would be so full and compleat that the most famous and magnificent libraries in the world shall not outdo the meanest library in any paroch of this Kingdom for numbers of valuable and useful books." He winds up by saying: "I hope that what hath been said will be sufficient to persuade all lovers and encouragers of learning that this founding and promoting of bibliothecks in every paroch throughout this Kingdom is both necessary and easie, advantagious and honourable, our interest and our duty."

Although there is no record in the Acts of the General Assembly of Kirkwood's "Overture" having been considered by that body, he returned to the charge in 1702 with a second pamphlet, already referred to. It is entitled "A copy of a letter anent a project for erecting a library in every Presbytery or at least County in the Highlands, from a reverend minister of the Scots nation, now in England, to a minister at Edinburgh, with reasons for it, and a scheme for erecting and preserving these libraries." He set to work to collect funds and books for his project through the S.P.C.K., and in *A Memorial Concerning the Disorders of the Highlands*, published in Edinburgh in 1703, reference is made to "Mr. Kirkwood and others in London having lately collected upwards of twelve thousand merks in

THE PUBLIC LIBRARY MOVEMENT

books and money for erecting libraries in these places."

In 1704 the General Assembly took the matter up, and on the 29th of March in that year passed "An Act anent libraries in the Highlands" to the following effect: "The General Assembly taking to their consideration that there is a project sett on foot by some piously enclined persons in this and the neighbour nation of England for erecting libraries in the Highlands of this Kingdom, and that good advances have been made therein, do declare their approbation of that design, and appoints a letter of thanks to be written to the Society in England for propagating Christian knowledge, and to others who have given assistance in this matter; empowers the commission to apply to the Lords of the Treasury for their assistance in order to the bringing down of the saids books from England, and transmitting the same to the places underwritten at which they are to be fixed in this Kingdom." A list of places where libraries were to be established is added.

In 1705 a second "Act concerning the libraries for the Highlands, Islands, etc.", was passed, appointing a committee of management, and allocating anew nineteen presbyterial libraries and fifty-eight parochial libraries.

In 1706 a third "Act concerning the libraries" contained additional instructions to the committee as to the manner in which they were to distribute the libraries, urging them to send books where

PAROCHIAL LIBRARIES

they are most needed. Rules were drawn up for the borrowing of books. No person was to be allowed to borrow more than two books at a time, each book was to have its price marked against it in the catalogue, and a deposit of one-quarter more than its value had to be made by the borrower as a security for its safe return. No book was to be kept longer than six weeks, and a half-yearly inspection had to be made of the libraries within its bounds by each presbytery. All Protestants were to have access to and use of the libraries, and no difference in opinion was to preclude them from the same. This condition clearly shows the public nature of the libraries.

In the same year, and again in 1709, the Assembly instructed letters to be written to Mr. Kirkwood, Dr. Bray, and other ministers in England, thanking them for their care and liberality in procuring the libraries.

In 1709 the Assembly passed another "Act for erecting public libraries in presbyteries" in order that at least one library should be placed in each presbytery, and recommending that such of the presbyteries as had not received any of the books sent from London should contribute among themselves in order to lay a foundation for a library at each presbytery-seat, and to procure voluntary contributions from the several parishes for this purpose.

It is evident that the libraries in the Highlands suffered from depredations during and after the

Rebellion of 1715, for we find the Assembly in 1720 instructing the Agent for the Church "to concur in a process of spuilzie of the presbyterial and two paroch libraries taken away out of the manse of Alness," and ordaining the expenses as far as concern the said libraries and the minister of Alness's damages to be borne out of the public money. It is clear, too, that the libraries were suffering from neglect, as is evidenced by the repeated instructions of the Assembly during the years from 1720 to 1740, to synods and presbyteries to report on the state of the libraries, after calling upon ministers and presbyteries to account in that matter, "failing which they will be complained of to next Assembly." The Commission of the Assembly were ordered to prepare a full statistical report on the libraries, and to instruct those who had received libraries, and had not increased them, to send them to the agent of the Church for redistribution to new presbyteries, particularly to those in remote places. "The public libraries continued in being till about 1826,[1] when, according to the *Moral Statistics* of that year, 'very few of them were then known to exist.' Apart from political upheavals and social changes, two striking but opposing factors were chiefly responsible for their disappearance. Moderatism, on the one hand, cultivated its soul on romantic literature and had little use for such books

[1] The library sent to Inverness is still extant and can be seen in the session-house of the High Church, Inverness. Rev. Professor Maclean's article on Highland Libraries in *Records of the Glasgow Bibliographical Society*, Vol. 7, 1923, p. 43.

PAROCHIAL LIBRARIES

as the libraries supplied. On the other, there was an outburst of Gaelic sacred and popular poetry after the '45.' Along with these a rapid increase in the translation of theological, catechetical, homiletical, and devotional books into Gaelic rendered libraries no longer so necessary, and they accordingly fell into disuse."

In 1708 Parliament passed an "Act for the better preservation of parochial libraries in that part of Great Britain called England" (7 Anne, c. 14). The main object of the Act was to secure the continuance of the libraries, but as it did not make financial provision for their maintenance, its effect was negligible. The Act states that such libraries had been founded by the charitable contributions of well-disposed persons. It provided for the making of catalogues, the recording of donations, and for regular inspection; and the responsibility for carrying out these duties was laid upon the clergy of the different parishes. In England and Wales, as well as in Scotland, these parochial libraries were primarily intended for the use of the poorer clergy, but as they were not regularly kept up to date by the addition of new books they fell into disuse and decay.

Itinerating Libraries

The scheme of itinerating libraries established in East Lothian in 1817 by Samuel Brown, Provost of Haddington, is interesting as a pioneer effort at forming a system of circulating libraries for a

THE PUBLIC LIBRARY MOVEMENT

county area. Provost Brown's ideal was to have a library within a mile and a half of every inhabitant of the county, if possible. His plan was to station a division of fifty volumes as a minimum in every village and hamlet where someone to act as a librarian could be found. Each collection contained in general about one-half to two-thirds of purely religious works, the remainder being books of history, biography, and science. The average cost of providing each collection "complete with bookcase, catalogue, labels, advertisements, and issuing-books" (i.e. record of issues) was £10. The divisions were stationed at each centre for a period of two years, at the end of which time a general exchange took place. The maximum number of centres in operation at any period in the history of these libraries was fifty, the area covered being twenty miles by fifteen. The original stock was provided by the founder himself with the aid of a few subscribing friends. The main centre was at Haddington, and other centres were established at Dunbar and North Berwick. A scheme of subscription was started whereby subscribers of 3s. per annum (afterwards increased to 5s.) had the privilege of first loan of new books for a period, after which they went into general circulation. Up to 1832 the books in each depot were issued to borrowers without charge, but in that year a charge of one penny per volume was made during the first year, and no charge during the second year, of the stay of the collection at a centre. The number of centres

ITINERATING LIBRARIES

gradually declined owing to the difficulty experienced in finding persons sufficiently enthusiastic to act as librarians and to keep up the interest in the libraries. The persons volunteering were generally teachers, shopkeepers, or others keenly interested. Provost Brown's scheme was copied elsewhere. In 1825 he was requested to take over the superintendence of similar libraries which had been founded in Edinburgh, Leith, and the neighbourhood, where there were twenty-one centres besides a number of stations for new books at various seminaries in Edinburgh. He sent a number of similar libraries to Jamaica, Canada, South Africa, and St. Petersburg, to be managed by missionaries in these places.

In recounting the history of these early foundations of libraries through the philanthropic efforts of charitably disposed persons we have noted how the enthusiasm of the founders had carried their schemes to a successful outcome, but that owing to the absence of any permanent institution responsible for their continuance and growth they had fallen into decay through inanition. We have noted, too, that in some cases where a library had been founded by a generous donor with an endowment probably sufficient to maintain it in a state of efficiency in the donor's day, for want of voluntary successors possessing an enthusiasm equal to his own and lack of sufficient funds to meet changed conditions these libraries too became more or less stagnant. It would seem to be the case that the enthusiasm of the

THE PUBLIC LIBRARY MOVEMENT

voluntary needs to be supplemented by the permanence of the statutory.

In his admirable presidential address to the Library Association at Blackpool in 1928, Dr. A. D. Lindsay, using the case of the Central Library for Students (now the National Central Library) as his text, emphasized the value of co-operation between statutory bodies and voluntary associations. His remarks were so much to the point that we take the liberty of quoting them at some length.

"This co-operation," he said, "is indeed the life and soul of the adult educational movement, and, for that matter, of most of the hopeful social movements of our time. Men used to debate (they still debate) whether this or that social activity should be carried on by the State or some kind of statutory authority on the one hand, or by voluntary organizations on the other. What we are coming to see is that all fruitful social activity—education above all—needs both. Education is an affair of the spirit, and of such it is always true that 'the wind bloweth where it listeth.' The things that really matter there cannot be listed or regimented or satisfactorily forecast. They elude rules and all kinds of administrative routines. The greatest achievements of the spirit are sporadic and unforeseen. They come up and down the country, in the most unexpected places, when two or three are gathered together—and sometimes in the most expected places they will not come. It is my experience, and I am sure it is yours, that at the back of all real achievements in

ITINERATING LIBRARIES

education or learning one finds a few individuals whose enthusiasm, and direction, and inspiration, are the real source of life. But, for all that, the spirit of social movements needs a body—a sound, well-constructed, healthy body—as much as the mind of the individual needs a body. Without the stability and continuity which good administration alone can give—without assured ways and means—without adequate equipment—how short-lived and ineffectual, for all their enthusiasm, such voluntary movements are apt to be! Not that organization and efficient administration can ever supersede voluntary effort; that was the old theory, that the experiments of voluntary effort were taken over *en bloc* by the statutory authority when they had proved a success. That is clearly wrong. No great work is ever done unless it can go on inspiring an ever-renewing voluntary effort. But neither can any real lasting work be done unless the enthusiasm of voluntary effort gets embodied in institutions, and is helped by a structure of administration and equipment which will preserve the gains of the past—which will prevent enthusiasm having to waste itself in beginning again each time from the beginning—which will by co-ordination and organization make the achievements of all the heritage of each."

SUBSCRIPTION LIBRARIES

Probably the most successful type of library established prior to the rate-supported public library was the public subscription library. Most towns of any importance possessed these libraries from the third decade of the eighteenth century onwards.

As early as 1725 Allan Ramsay, the poet, started the Edinburgh Circulating Library in his shop in the Luckenbooths, which became the haunt of all the prominent citizens of the town. This is the earliest recorded circulating library in Scotland. Sir Walter Scott states that as a young man he read in it with great avidity. The project, however, did not meet with universal approval, for in the Rev. Robert Wodrow's *Analecta*, Vol. 3, p. 515, occurs the following passage: "This profannes is come to a great hight, all the villanous profane and obscene books and playes printed at London by Curle and others are gote doun from London by Allan Ramsey, and lent out, for an easy price, to young boyes, servant weemen of the better sort, and gentlemen, and vice and obscenity dreadfully propagated. Ramsay has a book in his shope wherein all the names of those that borrow his playes and books, for two pence a night, or some such rate, are sett doun, and by these wickedness of all kinds are dreadfully propagat among youth of all sorts." It is plain that Wodrow had no first-hand knowledge of Allan Ramsay's library, for he goes on to say that his informant was my Lord Grange, who persuaded the Town Council to demand an inspection of the borrowers' book, but that Ramsay, having got wind of the threatened inspection, had concealed all the

SUBSCRIPTION LIBRARIES

incriminating literature, and nothing came of it. The library, which passed through the hands of several booksellers, was ultimately sold at auction in 1832.

In spite, however, of the strictures of the critics of circulating libraries as disseminators of undesirable literature, these institutions have carried on until the present day, and have met the needs of a large proportion of the population. As adjuncts to a bookseller's business they have proved useful, enabling him to carry on his business in the days before the net-book agreement came into force, when many booksellers were obliged to stock all sorts of side-lines to "keep their heads above water."

Of subscription libraries other than those carried on by booksellers, there are many which were founded in the eighteenth and nineteenth centuries in the larger towns under the names of Lyceum or Athenæum, some of which are still flourishing. The earliest circulating library in London was established about the middle of the eighteenth century. The first in Birmingham was opened by Hutton in 1757. The Liverpool Lyceum was founded in 1758 and is still in active operation. Warrington formed a library in 1760, which afterwards became part of the Warrington Museum and Library, the first to be established in England under the Museums Act of 1845. The Leeds Library was established in 1768, and the Bristol Museum and Library in 1772, which now forms part of the Municipal Reference Library. Other English proprietary

THE PUBLIC LIBRARY MOVEMENT

libraries have been established at Leicester, Liverpool (Athenæum, 1798), Manchester, Nottingham, and elsewhere.[1]

The most important subscription library of the present day is the London Library in St. James's Square. It was founded by a number of eminent scholars and public men, primarily at the suggestion of Thomas Carlyle, and was opened for use in May 1841. Carlyle, when he went to London to work in the British Museum, found that he could not carry on his studies in that busy hive of literary industry, and, as he could not borrow books from it for home reading, he started the project of forming a lending library on a large scale. It was "designed to contain books in all departments of literature and philosophy and in all languages, its chief distinguishing features being the privilege enjoyed by subscribers of having books at their homes both in London and in the country." This ideal has been consistently followed since its inception, and by steady accretions of books, and by the issue of author and subject catalogues, which are models of their kind, the library has been kept well up to date.

MECHANICS' INSTITUTES

The fullest account of the rise and early progress of those valuable institutions which played so important a part in the adult education of the working-classes during the nineteenth century is given in James Hole's *Essay* on their history and manage-

[1] *Encyclopædia Britannica*, 11th ed., *s.v.* Libraries.

MECHANICS' INSTITUTES

ment, which gained the Society of Arts' prize, and was published by Longmans in 1853. The beginnings of the movement are also well recounted in Lord Brougham's *Practical Observations upon the Education of the People Addressed to the Working Classes and their Employers*. This pamphlet first appeared as an article in the *Edinburgh Review* in 1824 and was published in 1825, passing through no fewer than twenty editions within that year. It is of special value as coming from the pen of an active participant in the movement. It is dedicated to George Birkbeck, M.D., whose lectures to Glasgow mechanics, delivered on Saturday evenings during his occupancy of the chair of Natural Philosophy in the Andersonian Institution in that city, may be said to have been the germ of the mechanics' institute movement. To illustrate his lectures at the institution Dr. Birkbeck required scientific instruments, and had to get them specially made. He thus came into contact with the mechanics who made such instruments. He was so struck with their eagerness to understand the uses and underlying principles of the instruments they were making for him that he decided to establish a class for their instruction. This was known as the mechanics' class. His lectures to them began in 1800, and by the time that he left Glasgow in 1804 they had proved so popular that he was accustomed to have audiences of 700 or more eager students. The lectures were continued by Dr. Andrew Ure, his successor in the chair, and in 1808 a library

THE PUBLIC LIBRARY MOVEMENT

was formed for the use of the mechanics, and its management was entrusted to a committee chosen by themselves. The attendance at the lectures gradually fell off, they were given at wider intervals, and the members of the library committee had a feeling that their interests were not being properly looked after by the directors of the Andersonian Institution. A controversy arose between this committee and the directors as to the ownership of the library. The mechanics wished to be recognized as an independent body and to have the library declared their property. The directors of the Andersonian not unnaturally failed to see eye to eye with them in their contentions, and the result was that a large number of mechanics seceded from the lectures of the Andersonian Institution and formed the Glasgow Mechanics' Institution for the promotion of the arts and sciences, which was opened on November 5, 1823, being the first of its kind bearing the title of mechanics' institute to be established in the United Kingdom. Dr. Birkbeck was nominated the first honorary patron. The lecturers were to have no voice in the management, but were to have the free use of the library. The principal course of lectures was on chemistry and mechanics, and the fee for a full course was ten shillings. The library was available to all students, and after attending five full courses students were entitled to life membership on payment of half a crown annually. The books purchased for the library were to be mainly scientific, but works on

MECHANICS' INSTITUTES

general literature were also added. The institution was reorganized in 1879, and in 1881 the name was changed to College of Arts and Science. In 1886 the Glasgow Technical College was established and the College of Arts and Science was amalgamated with it. In 1912 this became the Royal Technical College.[1]

It was not until the year 1821 that the example of Glasgow in providing lectures to mechanics was followed in Edinburgh. On the initiative of Mr. Leonard Horner and others a prospectus was circulated in the month of April amongst the mechanics of the city announcing the commencement in October of courses of evening lectures twice a week on mechanics and chemistry, with the opening of a library of books upon the subjects available for home reading as well as in the library. The terms of admission were to be fifteen shillings a year for both lectures and library. A statement was then issued to the public at large announcing the establishment of a School of Arts, with particulars of the plan, and inviting subscriptions. By September over 200 mechanics had entered their names as students, and the financial support of subscribers was such that the directors were able to open the school in October as announced. The library began with about 250 volumes restricted to the subjects of the lectures. It gradually grew, largely by donations, as there was no separate fund for its maintenance, and by 1836 the annual issues had reached

[1] Burns (C. D.), *History of Birkbeck College*, p. 19.

THE PUBLIC LIBRARY MOVEMENT

over 3,000 volumes. Classes in geometry and higher arithmetic were also formed by the mechanics themselves for their mutual instruction under the monitorial system. The name of the school was altered in 1851 to the Watt Institution and School of Arts in memory of James Watt of steam-engine fame. It is now the Heriot-Watt College.

Another school of arts which grew out of the scheme of itinerating libraries founded at Haddington by Provost Brown in 1817 was established there by some tradesmen in 1821, and lectures were delivered for several years. The need of books covering the subjects lectured upon led to the formation of a library, the scope of which was afterwards widened to include general literature. It is understood that the books of the itinerating libraries, or such of them as were still available for circulation, were incorporated in this library, which as a subscription library was continued until 1853, when it was merged in the Haddington Town Library.

A mechanics' institution was formed in Edinburgh by and for working-men to give instruction in such subjects as were not dealt with at the School of Arts, e.g. history, music, poetry, phonography, etc., but it was brought to a premature close owing to the alleged breaking of the regulation that religious subjects were not to be discussed, through the delivery of an historical lecture by a Unitarian minister, and the consequent breaking away of a large number of the students.

All of these institutions just mentioned had

MECHANICS' INSTITUTES

lectures as their basic feature, but others, e.g. the Mechanics' Apprentices Library at Liverpool, established in July 1823, were libraries only. The Edinburgh Mechanics' Subscription Library founded in 1825, "to embrace every department of British Literature," had a long and successful career.

In November 1823, following upon an article in *The Mechanics' Magazine* in the preceding month from the pen of its editor, J. C. Robertson, a meeting was held in London, presided over by Dr. Birkbeck, and as a result the London Mechanics' Institution was founded. It was formally opened in January 1824 with an inaugural address by Dr. Birkbeck, who was appointed its first president. In 1862 the title of the Institution was changed to the Birkbeck Literary and Scientific Institution, and the scope of its teaching was enlarged. In 1907 the title was again changed to Birkbeck College, now a constituent part of the University of London.

After the formation of the London institution, Dr. Birkbeck took an active part in the establishment of no fewer than six similar institutions in London in the following year, and he was frequently called upon to deliver addresses at the opening of others throughout the land. His friend, Henry Brougham (afterwards Lord Brougham), who had been closely associated with him in all these activities, greatly helped the progress of the movement by the publication of his *Practical Observations*, already referred to. So rapid was the spread of these institutions that by 1849 it was reported that at least 400 were in active operation in the United Kingdom, and by 1863 some 700 similar institutions had been established. They were for the most part voluntary associations of mechanics and working-men formed for the purpose of providing their members with technical and general knowledge by means of lectures, classes, reading-rooms, and circulating libraries. They were almost invariably managed by committees of the members themselves, and they provided instruction and recreation for thousands; but the main hindrance to their success as adult educational institutions was the great deficiency in the elementary education of the students themselves. The use of the name "Mechanics' Institute" also, as applied to these subscription libraries, was rather unfortunate from the point of view of their development as public libraries, inasmuch as it deterred many of the better educated class from becoming members, under the mistaken idea that membership was confined to the mechanics or artisan classes. Although this was true of some of the earliest institutes, it was far from being the case with many others. When rate-supported libraries began to be established, the library of the Mechanics' Institute not infrequently became the nucleus of the public library stock. The amount of good they did in their day in the way of providing reading for the masses is incalculable. Many a man who made his way in the world before free education became universally compulsory owed much of his success to the mechanics' institute of his native town.

CHAPTER III

THE NEED OF LIBRARIES FREELY OPEN TO THE PUBLIC—THE MINUTES OF EVIDENCE AND REPORTS OF THE SELECT COMMITTEE

Having given some account in the last chapter of the spread of education, the growth of a demand for books, and the limited number of accessible libraries available for those desirous of cultivating the habit of reading and study, and having endeavoured to show that the main difficulty in maintaining these libraries in a state of efficiency lay in the lack of permanent provision for their upkeep and growth, we come now to the period when this difficulty was to be overcome through the establishment by Act of Parliament of public rate-supported institutions under popular local management.

The first point that strikes one in considering the earliest efforts to establish a system of public libraries locally controlled under parliamentary sanction is the opposition that was encountered by its promoters, notwithstanding the modest nature of their proposals. The second point at which nowadays we wonder is the grudging and niggardly nature of the financial support that was to be accorded to the libraries.

To understand this opposition and parsimony it

needs to be remembered that in many quarters the idea still prevailed that it was a dangerous thing to give education to those who were then described as the lower orders of society. Education it was feared would give them ideas above their station, and it was necessary that they should be kept in their place, lest they get to know too much. The fear was expressed, as we shall see when we come to treat of the opposition in Parliament to the Bill, that the libraries, particularly if lectures were to be given in them, would be converted into schools of agitation and sedition.

The main source of our information in regard to the history of these efforts is to be found in the "Report of the Select Committee appointed on the best means of extending the establishment of libraries freely open to the public, especially in large towns in Great Britain and Ireland."

The Minutes of Evidence

The appointment of this Committee was made on the motion of William Ewart, M.P. for the Dumfries Burghs, on March 15, 1849. Its first meeting was held on March 30th, when Mr. Ewart himself was appointed Chairman. The first meeting for the taking of evidence took place on April 19th, Mr. Edward Edwards, assistant in the Department of Printed Books of the British Museum, being the first witness called. Mr. Edwards, who had for a number of years taken a keen interest in public libraries in this country, on the Continent,

THE MINUTES OF EVIDENCE

and in America, had collected a great deal of information on the subject. His statistics were first published in the *Transactions* of the Statistical Society of London in 1848 and followed upon an article of his which had appeared a year earlier in the *British Quarterly Review*, entitled "Public Libraries in London and Paris."[1] The attention of Mr. Ewart having been drawn to these articles, he at once moved for the appointment of the Select Committee above referred to. The recommendations of the Committee led to the passing of the first Public Libraries Act, 1850. The statistics which Edwards had collected with so much labour over a series of years were freely placed at the disposal of the Committee. In giving his evidence he laid emphasis on the paucity of public and semi-public libraries in this country as compared with the large numbers established on the Continent of Europe. He produced plans of Paris, Vienna, Berlin, Dresden, Munich, Copenhagen, Rome, and Florence showing the libraries in each city, along with a map showing the relative provision of books in libraries publicly accessible in the principal states of Europe as compared with their respective populations. (Map and plans are reproduced in the Report.) The map showed that Holland and the British Isles had the fewest libraries, the latter having only a little over half a book per inhabitant, while in the smaller German states, where public libraries were numerous, four and a half volumes per person were available. He

[1] Ogle (J. J.), *The Free Library*, 1897, p. 11.

THE PUBLIC LIBRARY MOVEMENT

stated that "nearly every European State was in a far higher position, both as to the number and extent of libraries accessible to the public, and, generally, as respects the accessibility of such libraries as do exist," and that this had been so for a very considerable period. He referred to the frequent complaints that authors in this country had made on this score, and instanced the case of Gibbon, who, when attacked by critics for his imperfect citation of authorities, said that "for the want of a good public library he was often obliged, at great expense, and with great difficulty, to send for books from abroad; sometimes for large and expensive works, in order to verify a single citation. He found himself in a much better position when residing in Switzerland and in France than when residing in this country." Even in the case of the British Museum it was much less accessible in the days of Roscoe and Isaac Disraeli than it should have been. Long delays often occurred in obtaining books.

Asked to give his definition of the term "public" as applied to libraries, he said, "I would take it as embracing, first of all, libraries deriving their support from public funds, either wholly or in part, and I would further extend it to such libraries as are made accessible to the public to a greater or less degree."

With regard to the accessibility of continental libraries, in the majority of cases—in, say, twenty out of every twenty-five—anyone could go into a

THE MINUTES OF EVIDENCE

public library and ask for a book; in other cases some sort of introduction or guarantee of respectability was required. With regard to this country he believed that "Chetham's Library at Manchester is the only library where there is avowedly no restriction upon admission." The only formality required there was that the visitor was requested to write his name and address in a register book. The other libraries, about thirty in number, were more or less publicly accessible, although the admission was to be considered a matter of grace and favour, they being mainly university and college libraries, or libraries belonging to societies such as the Dublin Society in Ireland, and the Faculty of Advocates and the Society of Writers to the Signet in Scotland.

Mr. Edwards also gave statistics regarding public libraries in the United States of America, including not only the State libraries, but also those belonging to universities, corporations, and learned societies. The State libraries, supported by legislative grants, were accessible for lending purposes to all persons bringing satisfactory introductions, and the society libraries and the university libraries to the members of these institutions, and to persons introduced by them. On the Continent of Europe the provincial libraries were supported by municipalities for the most part. A great many of the town libraries in France were formed in localities where formerly monasteries were situated, by the appropriation of the monastic libraries, whilst in this country the monastic libraries were either destroyed or very greatly injured at the Reformation, as is recorded in Leland's *Collectanea*. "Another reason for the fewness of public libraries in this country has been the isolation of such bequests or foundations as have occurred. They were left without any sort of general control or supervision" and few additions to them were made. He instanced the Cotton Library, made public in 1700, which, for the first sixty years of its life, had but one donation made to it, but since its incorporation with the British Museum several important collections had been bequeathed or presented. Nearly one-half of the contents of the British Museum had been acquired as donations or bequests. Particulars were also given by Mr. Edwards as to the origin and accessibility of Sion College Library near London Wall, Dr. Williams's Library in Redcross Street, and Archbishop Tenison's Library in St. Martin-in-the-Fields. The public and semi-public libraries available in Scotland and in Ireland were then reviewed, with an account of their foundation, extent, accessibility, and the amount of funds available for their maintenance. With regard to those libraries which were entitled to the copyright privilege of obtaining on demand a copy of every book published in the ordinary course, or which received a Treasury grant in lieu thereof, Edwards felt that being in receipt of public money they should give free access to members of the public in return for it, to the extent at least of allowing the

THE MINUTES OF EVIDENCE

public to read in the libraries. "There should be an entire revision of the conditions on which Treasury grants are accorded, requiring that accessibility should be made an indispensable condition of such grants, and that the libraries receiving them should be placed under some definite supervision and responsibility." He thought that it would be very desirable also "that any existing libraries, which are disposed to place themselves under the inspection, for example, of the Committee of Council on Education, which is perhaps the body most analogous to that Ministry of Public Instruction which I hope we shall have some day, should be enabled to do so"; and in case of their own resources being deficient, that they should obtain some grants under the Committee of Council in aid of those resources. He thought too that such aid should especially be afforded with regard to the preparation of catalogues, "upon which the utility of libraries entirely depends, scarcely any of the existing libraries having now any resources at all by means of which catalogues can be printed and published."

When asked by the Chairman, "By what means do you think the formation of new public libraries in this country might best be promoted?" he replied, "The first means I can recommend would be the extension of the Museums Act, the object of which was to levy a rate for the establishment of museums, proceeding upon a requisition or resolution of a definite proportion of the ratepayers assembled in public meeting, such rate not to exceed a halfpenny in the pound upon the rental of the district." This Act, introduced by Mr. Ewart and Mr. Brotherton, was passed in 1845, but was not taken much advantage of, mainly, he believed, because no provision had been made for bringing a parliamentary grant in aid of local contribution as is done in educational matters.

He was strongly of opinion that libraries should be open in the evening. "It would enable the working-classes of the population to get access to the public libraries, who, unless some such change is introduced, must continue to be debarred from access to them; and I think it would also, in many cases, be of great advantage to professional men, and even to men whose profession is literature." He instanced the library of Ste-Geneviève in Paris and the library of Strassburg, where such a plan was in use with great benefit.

In concluding his evidence on the second day of his examination, Mr. Edwards gave it as his opinion that much good would result from having a system of periodical inspection, by, say, the Committee of the Privy Council dealing with educational matters, of all institutions connected with literature and the arts to which the country contributes in the way of annual votes. An account should be rendered and a statement made by a Minister on the part of the Government to the people. He believed that such a statement would not be rendered many years in succession without an increase of the contributions

THE MINUTES OF EVIDENCE

in aid of those purposes, and it would excite increased co-operation in many quarters.

Further evidence was submitted by M. F. P. G. Guizot, who had served France, both as Minister of Public Instruction and as Prime Minister, on the public libraries of France. His evidence showed that in almost all the public libraries every one who came to read was admitted, books were lent to every one who was a known person in the town or who came with a recommendation. That was the general practice in France. He corroborated Mr. Ewart's evidence as to the greater accessibility in general of public libraries in France as compared with this country.

Mr. Van de Weyer, Minister of H.M. the King of the Belgians, gave evidence as to Belgian libraries to the effect that in Antwerp, Brussels, Bruges, Ghent, Louvain, Liége, any person without any letter of introduction or authorization could go into the public library and be supplied with a book on asking for it. These public libraries were supplied with Government publications.

Professor W. Libri, of Pisa, who had had extensive experience in examining libraries in Italy, under special commissions from the Italian Government, was examined at considerable length. He, too, emphasized the greater accessibility of libraries in Italy than in this country, no letter of recommendation or introduction being necessary for access to the public or university libraries. This was not applicable to the Vatican Library, where there were many restrictions, particularly in the matter of copying manuscripts. Official copiers had to be employed and paid. Authors were obliged to give copies of their works on publication to the public libraries of the State in which they lived. Practically every town in Italy had its municipal library freely open to the public. As in France, all the religious corporations were abolished under the domination of Napoleon and many of the municipal libraries were formed from their collections of books.

M. Libri, fearing that the evidence he had given under examination might have suffered from his imperfect acquaintance with the English language, afterwards addressed a letter to Mr. Ewart setting forth the points which he wished specially to emphasize. It is a very valuable document, containing important historical information on the libraries of France and Italy then existing, and embodying the views on the constitution and management of libraries, metropolitan, provincial, and municipal, of one whose varied experience entitles them to be examined with attention and respect. His opinion "that in every great country there should be at least one library in which one may expect to find, as far as it is possible, all books which learned men, men who occupy themselves upon any subject whatever, and who cultivate one of the branches of human knowledge, may require to consult," has long been accepted as axiomatic. He called attention to two principal points, which in a large library ought to precede all others, namely cataloguing and

THE MINUTES OF EVIDENCE

classification. He deplored the state into which the Bibliothèque Nationale in Paris had fallen from want of room and of assistants to catalogue and arrange the books as added. This had led to a frightful state of confusion, very considerable losses, and inconveniences of all kinds, to put an end to which efforts for a long time past had been used in vain.

The Rev. H. Christmas, Librarian of Sion College, the Rev. Philip Hale, Librarian of Archbishop Tenison's Library, Mr. Richard Cogan, Librarian of Dr. Williams's Library, Mr. Thomas Jones, Librarian of the Chetham Library, Manchester, were also examined as to their respective libraries, their condition and accessibility. Mr. George Dawson, M.A., a lecturer, well acquainted with the libraries of the mechanics' institutions in the manufacturing towns in England and Scotland, gave evidence as to these libraries, showing that, apart from works of fiction, the great demand by the readers was for political and historical works. Many of the working-men were very well read. In Birmingham, for example, he said he could produce five or six working-men whom he should be happy to have examined against almost any of the middle classes in the place. There were very good subscription libraries in Manchester, but the cost of the subscription was beyond the means of the working-classes. The schools of design in these towns were very much used by the artisans, but they had difficulty in obtaining books relating to

THE PUBLIC LIBRARY MOVEMENT

their subjects of study. "For the last many years," he said, "in England everybody has been educating the people, but they have forgotten to find them any books. In plain language, you have made them hungry, but you have given them nothing to eat; it is almost a misfortune for a man to have a great taste for reading, and not to have the power of satisfying it." In the rural districts, with which he was also well acquainted, there were a number of parochial and village libraries, but they were under the influence of men connected with the towns and of clergymen who were too apt to make the libraries largely theological, and the libraries were not popular on that account. The basis of these libraries should be the very best books, the highest quality of literature that the country possesses. The working-classes were greatly interested in political subjects, and books on those subjects were eagerly sought for and read, historical books and books of travel were in demand, and poetry was much read. Debating societies were increasing in number, but these were apt to be mischievous without a good deal of reading on the part of the members, and the supply of books was limited pretty much to what the mechanics' institutes could provide. In Birmingham there were some families now beginning to put a shelf or two of books in their kitchens, but the great hindrance to the demand for books was the inability of many either to write or read. "We have eight millions in the country who cannot write yet." When asked if he could suggest any

THE MINUTES OF EVIDENCE

plan for extending libraries in the country, he said he could not unless they could get a rate for their establishment; but that, if the libraries were free, considerable accessions would be made by way of donations, particularly if it were known that Government would give a grant in proportion to the sum subscribed locally. He would put the libraries under the Town Councils. He was sure that "as you increase the duties of the Town Councils, and invest them with higher functions, you will have better men elected to the Town Council."

Mr. Thomas Maitland (Kirkcudbright), Solicitor-General for Scotland, afterwards a Judge of the Court of Session, Lord Dundrennan, was asked to give information on the subject of the Advocates' Library, Edinburgh. He stated that although the library belonged to the Faculty of Advocates it had always appeared to him to possess one very important character as a public library, in so far as it enjoyed a public right in the shape of the privilege of Stationers' Hall of receiving a copy of every publication. He could not imagine that the privilege was intended to be given simply for the use of a body of private barristers. "Though the library is the property of the advocates practically it is the property of the public, for there is no library in Great Britain where the access given to the public generally is more liberal than in the Advocates' Library. Strictly speaking, an order is required to obtain admission to it, but that has fallen into desuetude. Every person of respectable appearance

THE PUBLIC LIBRARY MOVEMENT

applying for access to books or manuscripts is supplied with them, and is allowed to consult them with such facilities as our limited building affords. The great defect in the administration of the Advocates' Library, in my opinion, is the extent to which it has been converted into a common circulating library. Apart altogether from the books obtained from Stationers' Hall, the injury to the library has been quite incredible. All the ordinary readable books, for which there is a great demand, are now reduced into a state and condition so bad that it is perfectly disgraceful. As the library is the private property of the Faculty, it may at first sight appear difficult to find grounds for legislative interference with it. But I must own that the possession of the privilege of Stationers' Hall gives, in my view, a very sufficient ground for such interference. It could never have been the intention of the statute to give that privilege to injure authors and publishers, by immediately converting the books so given to the ordinary purposes of a circulating library. The intention must have been, as it ought to have been, to place them in a library of deposit to be used and consulted to any extent within the walls of the library, but above all to be preserved...." He considered it inconsistent with the proper preservation of a great library to lend out the books; the parties had much better go to the library. He would make great exertions to give every accommodation in the library, such as is given in the British Museum, that is a better

THE MINUTES OF EVIDENCE

system of preserving the character of a national library, and such, he thought, ought to be the character of the Advocates' Library. He was in favour of having the library open in the evening as late as nine o'clock. He thought it would be desirable to follow up the results of education by giving facilities to the people to have books, by the establishment of libraries not only in large towns but also in country districts.

Mr. Henry Stevens, formerly Librarian at Yale College, an American bibliographer, gave evidence on the libraries of the United States stating that they were small but very numerous. The want of large public consulting libraries, like those of Europe, was much felt by students in the United States. Most of the existing libraries were virtually open to everybody, and grants for their support were in many cases made by the State. Nearly all the libraries were lending libraries. The working-classes used them to a great extent.

Mr. J. F. Marsh, Town Clerk of Warrington, was examined as to the establishment of the museum and library there. They had rented a building for its accommodation temporarily, which was opened on November 1, 1848. They had received donations of books to the number of 1,200 volumes. The nucleus of the library was a proprietary library formed in 1760 which had been allowed to decay. It was open every Wednesday and Saturday from 10 to 4, and from 6 to 9.30 in the evening. No charge for admission was made, but they had promises of annual subscriptions of upwards of £70, and upwards of £650 had been subscribed for the erection of a museum. The halfpenny rate produced £80 a year.

Mr. Samuel Smiles, author of *Self Help*, gave evidence upon the Yorkshire Union of Mechanics' Institutes, pointing out that the mechanics' institutes in the large towns, generally speaking, were not institutes of mechanics; they were for the most part institutes of the middle and respectable classes; a class superior to working-men, and a small proportion of working-men receiving comparatively high wages, support these institutions. All those institutions have libraries attached to them which form a bond of union for the institution, which has classes and lectures as part of its activities. A taste for reading had sprung up and was rapidly extending, encouraged by the numerous cheap publications then issuing from the Press. Other institutions such as Mutual Improvement Societies and The Odd Fellows were forming libraries for the working-classes. The books were obtained largely by donations, as the workers themselves could not afford to purchase them to any extent. Many of the books given as donations were dull, heavy, and unattractive, but if public libraries were formed open to all and furnished with sufficiently attractive books it would tend to foster the increasing desire for education amongst the working-classes. The chief value of such libraries would be in their being lending libraries. He believed that a very efficient

THE MINUTES OF EVIDENCE

method of extending and supporting public libraries would be to give pecuniary aid in proportion to the contributions raised in the districts. A local interest in the working of the libraries would thus be assured.

Mr. Smiles afterwards wrote a letter to the Chairman in which he spoke highly of the system of itinerating libraries in use in East Lothian, stating that it was his conviction that that system, efficiently worked, would do more, in connection with elementary instruction, to elevate the character and improve the tastes of our town and country population than almost any other system that he knew of. The system, however, required constant supervision and the exercise of considerable judgment. It would be a judicious economy to pay for such service, and to make it worth the while of a man of energy and judgment to devote his time and labour to the superintendence of the itinerating libraries of a district.

Mr. Charles Meyer, German Secretary to the Prince Consort, gave evidence upon the libraries of Germany, and certified that the information given by Mr. Edwards in his evidence about German libraries was correct. There was scarcely a town of 12,000 inhabitants that did not possess a public library. These were supported partly by ancient funds, partly by the contributions of the State, and partly by subscriptions. He emphasized the desirability of having special libraries connected with manufactures and commerce in the large towns.

THE PUBLIC LIBRARY MOVEMENT

Mr. J. B. Langley, Stockport, gave evidence upon the mechanics' and scientific institutions in different parts of England with which he was well acquainted. He stated that there were about 400 of these institutions in England and Wales alone. The libraries were an essential part of these institutions, without which they would cease to exist.

Mr. Eugene Curry, of the Ordnance Survey of Ireland, reported upon the Irish libraries and the valuable manuscripts they contained. Provincial libraries were scarce in Ireland. He did not know any act of the Government that would be so prudent, nor be followed with such beneficial results as the establishment of good libraries in the provincial towns and in Dublin.

Mr. William Jones, Corresponding Secretary and Superintendent of the Religious Tract Society, gave the result of his experience of the circulation of books by that Society. Between 5,000 and 6,000 libraries had been granted in Great Britain and Ireland since the Society began its grants in 1832. The grants were limited to the publications of the Society, the number of volumes granted varying from 100 to 200 in each library. The libraries were placed in different districts, wherever persons were found willing to superintend them, and to pay part of their cost. The Society found that the books were more valued if the parties receiving them gave a portion of their value, generally half the published price. In this way they had distributed libraries among schools, churches, and chapels,

THE MINUTES OF EVIDENCE

manufactories, etc. They were now seeking to form more libraries in Ireland. He believed it was the case that there were seventy-three towns in Ireland in which there was not a single bookseller's shop.

Mr. Joseph Brotherton, a member of the Committee, gave information concerning the Salford Library and Reading Room, showing that it contained about 3,200 volumes. It was open every evening, except Sunday, from six to ten o'clock. It was a subscription library, vested in trustees, the subscription being 1s. per quarter, admitting to the reading-room, evening classes and lectures. An average of about fifty volumes was lent out every night to about 274 subscribers.

Mr. William Lovett, Manager of the National Hall in High Holborn, the headquarters of an association for the promotion of the political and social improvement of the people, gave particulars of the institution and its classes and library. He also gave information about the London coffee-houses, some 2,000 in number, many of which had libraries connected with them as well as providing periodicals and newspapers. They were much frequented by the working-classes and had had a very beneficial effect upon the habits of the people. Judging by the gradual increase of these libraries, he believed that public libraries would be greatly appreciated by the working-classes.

Mr. E. R. P. Colles submitted information concerning the public libraries of Dublin, in particular that of the Royal Dublin Society, which he stated

THE PUBLIC LIBRARY MOVEMENT

was more readily accessible than the British Museum. Books were lent out, but only to members of the Society. The Society was established in 1731 for the promotion of husbandry and other useful arts in Ireland, and there were about 800 members. He was of opinion that it was undesirable to use the library as a lending library. Libraries on a large scale such as that library should be considered as libraries of deposit; the public use of such libraries would be increased by not lending. He gave particulars also as to the accessibility of the King's Inn Library, Marsh's Library, and Trinity College Library.

Mr. S. W. Waley gave evidence on the provincial libraries of France, based mainly on his knowledge of the library at Boulogne, which is supported by an annual grant from the town. The French Government gives copies of its own publications to the provincial libraries, and also encourages the publication of works of an expensive and valuable character by subscribing for a number of copies and distributing them among the public libraries in Paris and the provinces.

Mr. John Imray, a Scottish civil engineer, was examined as to his knowledge of parochial and village libraries in Scotland. They were formed generally by donations from landed proprietors, clergymen, etc., and were usually kept in the church vestry or the schoolhouse. Interest in the libraries was well maintained for a year or two, but as there was no scheme for adding to the collections,

THE MINUTES OF EVIDENCE

when the original stock was read, interest ceased. He suggested that there should be some central depot from which these libraries could be recruited, and that they might with advantage be exchanged from one parish to another on the plan of the itinerating libraries in the South of Scotland. He also gave evidence as to the institution of Ragged Schools and libraries in London with which he had had a good deal to do, and which were much taken advantage of by street-sellers and others of the very poor.

Mr. C. R. Weld, Librarian of the Royal Society, gave information on the Society's library and the means of access to it which was freely accorded by the Fellows. The catalogue of the Library was kept well up to date. This was not the case at the British Museum, where delays occurred in obtaining books because they had not yet been added to the catalogue.

Mr. Edwards was further examined as to the complaints that had been made by readers at the British Museum of being unable to get books recently published. He admitted that the complaints were well grounded. The blame rested with the Chancellor of the Exchequer, the Treasury grants being insufficient to provide a large enough staff of transcribers, with the result that books were not entered into the catalogue quickly enough, and so could not be supplied owing to the rule that every reader must find the book he desires in the catalogue before asking for it. The demands of the Trustees for additional funds for cataloguing pur-

THE PUBLIC LIBRARY MOVEMENT

poses had been modified by the Chancellor of the Exchequer. He did not think that the Reading Room of the Museum should be a place for loungers to amuse themselves by turning over new books, but it was quite possible that persons having studious pursuits might need to get access to new books at the Museum, and they ought to get them there. The question was put to him: "Do you not think that both objects would be best accomplished by regarding the British Museum primarily as a depository for national literature, and as a place for research and study, and combining with that institution the establishment of distinct and accessible libraries for the public in other places and under other circumstances?" He answered: "I most entirely think so, and I hope that the labours of this Committee will result in the creation of such additional libraries, and then I think the question with respect to new books would stand upon a wholly different footing as far as the Museum is concerned." He feared that many books had been three years in the Museum before finding their way into the catalogue. He then gave particulars of the official regulations for admission to a number of German libraries, as bearing out the evidence he had already given at former sittings of the Committee. He afterwards submitted statistics concerning parochial and clerical libraries in this country founded by Dr. Bray and his Associates, most of them founded between 1704 and 1790. He also mentioned the parochial and presbyterial libraries

THE MINUTES OF EVIDENCE

founded by the General Assembly of the Church of Scotland in the Highlands and Islands from 1704 onwards. He further submitted statistics of cathedral libraries in England and diocesan or cathedral libraries in Ireland.

He thought that these parochial and cathedral libraries could be made useful to the public by giving them some permanent means of support by grants from a public fund, the amount of the grant to be dependent upon the amount of local subscriptions. Power also should be given to the libraries to exchange books. He was of opinion that "it would be a very desirable thing if something of a topographical character were given to these libraries, so that in every part of the country there should be at least one library containing a large collection of books relating to that part of the country, to its history and antiquities, and it would be essential that good catalogues of the libraries should invariably be printed and published." He advocated what we should now describe as a union catalogue for libraries like the cathedral libraries which contain very much the same books. These catalogues might be compiled on the method adopted for the French naval libraries, which indicated by a simple reference in how many libraries copies of a particular book are to be found. Mr. Edwards was next examined as to the nature and form of catalogues which he considered should be provided. He thought it was very important that in every large public library there should be a depart-

THE PUBLIC LIBRARY MOVEMENT

ment of catalogues of other libraries, and gave his views as to whether alphabetical or classified catalogues were to be preferred, and as to some methods of cataloguing. He advocated the formation of special libraries suited to the wants and pursuits of particular localities, to which he felt sure there would be many willing contributors who, having made special collections, would be glad to see them preserved for the public use.

Mr. Brotherton detailed the steps which had been taken for the establishment of the public library at Salford, and said he believed that other towns would follow their example. In order to give permanence to these libraries, the property should be vested in the Town Council, a permanent corporate body. All public institutions such as libraries should be exempt from local taxation.

Mr. G. A. Hamilton gave evidence on the state of education in Ireland, and particulars of the libraries in the country. Education had greatly advanced in Ireland recently, but there was great penury of public libraries.

Mr. Ewart laid before the Committee a statement sent to him by Mr. William Chambers, the publisher, regarding a public library recently established at Peebles, and a letter from Mr. Thomas Harkness, Commissary Clerk, Dumfries, upon agricultural libraries and farmers' clubs formed in several counties of Scotland. These had been found of great utility in providing information to farmers which had led to a distinct improvement in husbandry.

CHAPTER IV

THE REPORTS OF THE COMMITTEE

FIRST REPORT

The Report of the Committee founded upon the foregoing evidence was submitted to the House of Commons on July 23, 1849. It laid stress upon the greater number and accessibility of public libraries on the Continent of Europe and in America compared with this country, pointing out the disability under which literary men laboured here from the want of similar institutions to which they could resort in prosecuting their studies; and, as a consequence, finding it necessary either to collect their own instruments of literary labour or to go abroad to work in the libraries of foreign nations.

A list of the libraries possessing the privilege of receiving a copy of every work on publication, and of those enjoying an annual grant from the Treasury in lieu of the above privilege, which was withdrawn by Act of Parliament in 1836, was given. The Committee expressed the opinion that "in the absence of any valid reason to the contrary, these libraries thus privileged were bound to make some requital to the public by throwing their literary treasures (so far as they reasonably can do so) open."

The spread of education had wrought a great

improvement in national habits and manners, and this had been assisted by the successful efforts made in many directions to provide reading facilities for the people by the establishment of libraries to which they might resort. "There can be no greater proof of the fitness of the people to profit by these institutions than their own independent efforts to create them." The libraries connected with mechanics' institutes throughout the country, and with the coffee-houses in London, were instanced. "The great practical education of an Englishman is derived from the incessant intercourse between man and man in trade, and from the interchange and collision of opinion elicited by our system of local self-government; both teaching him the most important of all lessons, the habit of self-control. But it would be wise to superadd to these rugged lessons of practical life some of the more softening and expanding influences which reading and which thought supply."

In Scotland "a respect for education and reading, long fostered by the ancient and excellent system of instruction by means of parochial schools, is hereditary in the people." In many districts libraries had been formed, "but these tendencies to the acquisition of knowledge deserve further development, both by the formation of libraries in towns and the dissemination of village libraries throughout the rural population of Scotland."

"Amid the reasons in favour of the establishment of public libraries," the Report goes on to say,

THE REPORTS OF THE COMMITTEE

"we must not omit to consider the great extension which has been given, of late years, to the system of 'Lecturing' throughout the country. This has created a desire among the hearers to pursue, by means of books, the study of the subjects lectured upon. Students in the provinces are constrained to make an occasional pilgrimage to London to seek for a solution of their difficulties from the shelves of the British Museum. There can scarcely be a stronger proof than this of the necessity for creating provincial public libraries."

In considering the method by which public libraries could best be established and maintained the Committee thought that the general want was not so much the want of books and objects to be deposited, as of a depository for the reception of them. "It was probable that if buildings devoted to the purposes of a library or museum existed, and if the institutions for which they were erected were firmly and inalienably secured in some fixed and lasting society or corporation, and exempted from the burden of local taxation, the materials to fill these buildings would easily, and in many cases voluntarily, be supplied."

"There should be, in all countries, libraries of two sorts: libraries of deposit and research; and libraries devoted to the general reading and circulation of books." It had been suggested by Mr. Edwards in his evidence that the duplicates in the British Museum might be used to constitute a lending library; and that the triplicate copies might

THE PUBLIC LIBRARY MOVEMENT

most usefully be presented to provincial libraries. The Committee were disposed to agree with that suggestion. They earnestly recommended the question to the consideration of the Government, as well as that of having public libraries open in the evening, as was done in certain French libraries.

Government grants to libraries were recommended by many witnesses, and the Committee supported the recommendation as a far less objectionable appropriation of the public money than many other unopposed modes of expending it.

The Committee further recommended that power be given by Parliament enabling Town Councils to levy a small rate for the creation and support of town libraries. The association of libraries with museums seemed a most obvious and desirable alliance and the Museums Act of 1845 might be extended to include libraries. Topographical museums should be found in all chief provincial towns, "where history may find a faithful portraiture of local events, local literature, and local manners; and art and science a collection of all objects illustrative of the climate, soil, and resources of the surrounding country." Special libraries illustrative of the peculiar trade, manufactures, and agriculture of the place should be formed. The Committee were convinced that the first step in the formation of libraries was to establish a place of deposit, a local habitation for the books, and measures should be taken for securing the property in the Town Council of the place, or in some fixed

THE REPORTS OF THE COMMITTEE

and perpetually renewable body. Donations would then abundantly supply the books, as had been the case in the British Museum and other libraries at home and abroad.

It was the opinion of the Committee that much of the future character of our agricultural population, social, moral, and religious, would depend upon the extension and due formation of village libraries. These libraries would also convey much valuable information on the subject of emigration, it being essential that the people about to emigrate should be supplied with exact and ample information in town and country libraries about the countries to which they were going, and about the mode of reaching them.

On the general question of the establishment of libraries the Committee recognized certain general principles, viz. that they should be based on a firm and durable foundation; that they should be freely accessible to all the public; that they should be open during the evening; and that they should, as far as possible, be lending libraries. The last consideration they regarded as of great importance. "Many men, in order to derive the fullest advantage from books, must have them not only in their hands but in their homes. A great public library ought above all things to teach the teachers; to supply with the best implements of education those who educate the people, whether in the pulpit, the school, or the Press. The lending out of books, therefore, which is a general characteristic of foreign

THE PUBLIC LIBRARY MOVEMENT

libraries, should be an essential element in the formation of our own. Nor, to such classes as those we have just described, and to the labouring classes, is the opening of libraries during the evening a point of less importance.... Precautions should be taken to secure every library against fire. Not only should the building, if possible, be fireproof, but the shelves and the furniture should be of iron."

The Committee referred to the fiscal regulations in the matter of the importation of books and the heavy duties that importers had to pay. The paper duty, too, was oppressive upon trade, interfering with labour, and restrictive of literature. The advertisement duty was another impediment to the extension of libraries and the circulation of books as it was to trade and labour generally.

The Committee expressed their thanks to all who had given evidence, and especially to Mr. Edwards of the British Museum, and in conclusion declared that:

"Your Committee feel convinced that the people of a country like our own—abounding in capital, in energy, and in an honest desire not only to initiate, but to imitate, whatsoever is good and useful—will not long linger behind the people of other countries in the acquisition of such valuable institutions as freely accessible public libraries. Our present inferior position is unworthy of the power, the liberality, and the literature of the country. Your Committee believe that, on such a subject as this, inquiry alone will stimulate improvement. Even

THE REPORTS OF THE COMMITTEE

while they are concluding their Report, they observe with pleasure, that, in addition to the library already formed at Warrington, the creation of a large public library has been planned and accomplished in the public-spirited borough of Salford. It will be a source of extreme satisfaction to your Committee if the result of their labours shall be, still further to call out, to foster, and to encourage among their countrymen that love for literature and reverence for knowledge of which, during the course of their inquiries, they have had the gratification to trace the spontaneous development."

SECOND REPORT

A second Report by the Select Committee re-appointed on February 14, 1850, with the addition of Lord Seymour, dated August 1, 1850, was submitted. This Report dealt mainly with the British Museum and its accessibility and administration as compared with continental libraries. It appears that doubts had been expressed as to the accuracy of the statistical and other details given in the evidence contained in the 1849 Report. Returns on foreign libraries were accordingly procured from our ministers abroad through H.M. Secretary of State for Foreign Affairs. These Returns, and the further evidence which was led, were printed along with the Report, additional Returns from practically every foreign country being printed in 1851 and 1852.

THE PUBLIC LIBRARY MOVEMENT

Mr. Edwards was again examined by the Committee, and, when asked if he thought it desirable that the British Museum should be extended and opened in the evenings, he gave it as his opinion that "a better plan than extending the Reading Room of the British Museum would be to provide new libraries for general resort, open to all comers, and to regard the British Museum Library as a library for the higher class of students, for purposes of research and erudite study, and so to meet both requirements." General libraries should be established in different parts of London. "That is a great want, and a want for which I hoped the labours of this Committee would result in providing some supply." M. Libri's evidence was to the same effect, viz. that it should never be attempted to use as a popular library the large libraries intended in the first instance for a superior class of readers.

Mr. Antonio (afterwards Sir Anthony) Panizzi, Keeper of the Printed Books (afterwards Principal Librarian) of the British Museum, also gave lengthy evidence on the British Museum and its free accessibility as compared with continental libraries. He was not in favour of lending books from the Museum, nor of having it open in the evening. The experiment of keeping open from four until seven o'clock during the summer months was tried, but the attendance was not sufficient to warrant its continuance.

The Committee in this second Report say:

THE REPORTS OF THE COMMITTEE

"Your Committee are of opinion that the evidence which they have received shows the expediency of establishing in this metropolis other public libraries of a popular character, by which the British Museum would be relieved from a numerous class of readers who might be equally well accommodated elsewhere. They think that the establishment of such libraries would receive great assistance from the munificence of private persons, whenever the insufficient means for literary study in this metropolis shall have been more generally brought under the notice of the public."

The Report concluded by stating that "Your Committee see no reason to vary the general conclusion arrived at by the Committee in the last session of Parliament, respecting the main object and scope of their inquiry—that this country is still greatly in want of libraries freely accessible to the public, and would derive great benefit from their establishment."

CHAPTER V

THE PUBLIC LIBRARIES ACT, 1850

Meantime, on the same day, as it happens, on which the Select Committee was reappointed (February 14, 1850), Mr. William Ewart introduced in the House of Commons his "Bill for enabling Town Councils to establish Public Libraries and Museums." In doing so, he said there was scarcely any country in Europe so inadequately provided with public libraries as England. Generally speaking, on the Continent the rule of accessibility was universal. In Italy and Germany no great town was without a library. Here there was only a sort of small public library in Manchester; but there were none in Glasgow, Leeds, Sheffield, and other great manufacturing towns; whilst in Amiens, Rouen, Lyons, Marseilles, and other towns in France the working-classes resorted in numbers to the fine public libraries that were open to them. The Americans had made far greater advancement in the matter than the people of this country had. In every state of the Union there was a library kept up by the State, and accessible to the public, and from them the people derived immense benefit. His Bill was a brief one. A few years ago his friend the member for Salford (Mr. Brotherton) and himself had introduced a Bill enabling Town Councils to establish public museums of art and science. It

THE PUBLIC LIBRARIES ACT, 1850

was carried unanimously and had proved of considerable advantage to the public. The proposed Bill would consolidate the two Bills and enable Town Councils to found both museums and public libraries. The Museums Act gave power to levy a rate of one halfpenny in the pound. That principle he had adopted to allow Town Councils to purchase land and erect buildings and furnish them out of the proceeds. The property would be vested for ever in the Town Council, thus securing perpetuity. The Museums Act restricted the power to towns of 10,000 inhabitants. He thought it better to extend the power to all municipal bodies whatsoever. He proposed to abolish the charge of one penny per person admitted to the museum which was allowed by the Museums Act. It was a useless impediment. His Bill would not give the Town Council power to purchase books; they relied upon books being supplied by the donations of individuals. There arose the question, Was it called for? It was. It had even been anticipated by the town of Warrington, which had taken advantage of the Museums Act to establish a library as well as a museum. In Salford, too, the Town Council had placed at the disposal of the public a large building which was in their possession, and although it had been in existence as a library only six months they already had 5,000 books in it. One advantage of the museums would be that they would be illustrative of the local and natural history of the places in which they were established. The promoters of the Bill merely asked that these popular institutions might be legally founded by the people, supported by the people, and enjoyed by the people.

Mr. Brotherton (Salford) seconded, and leave was given for its introduction by Mr. Ewart, Mr. Brotherton, and Mr. G. A. Hamilton (Dublin University).

In moving the Second Reading of the Bill on March 13th, Mr. Ewart said he had already explained its objects in detail on introducing the measure. The simple object of the Bill was to give a permissive power to Town Councils to levy a small rate for the establishment of public libraries and museums in all municipal towns. The Bill was founded on the recommendation of a Select Committee which sat last session, and also on the expressed wishes of several towns which had petitioned Parliament on the subject. The Museums Act enabled Town Councils in towns having a population of 10,000 inhabitants and upwards to levy a small rate to establish museums of art and science for the benefit of the public; and all that the present Bill proposed was to extend the principle of the Museums Act to the establishment of public libraries also. He was backed by the feeling of many of the towns in the country; and since he had introduced it, he had received communications from several large towns in Scotland and Ireland, which were desirous of having the Bill extended to both of these countries as well as to England. He was

THE PUBLIC LIBRARIES ACT, 1850

fully prepared to adopt any reasonable amendment when the Bill went into Committee.

Colonel C. D. W. Sibthorp (Lincoln) thought this Bill nothing more nor less than an attempt to impose a general increase of taxation on Her Majesty's subjects. He would be happy at any time to contribute his mite towards providing libraries and proper recreations for the humbler classes in large towns, but he thought that however excellent food for the mind might be, food for the body was what was now most wanted by the people. "He did not like reading at all, and he hated it when at Oxford," and apparently he did not see why any one else should want to read. He was on more solid ground, however, when he said that "he could not see how one halfpenny in the pound would be enough to enable Town Councils to carry into effect the immense powers they were to have by this Bill." After being assured by the Home Secretary that there was nothing unconstitutional in a private member introducing a Bill to levy taxes from the Queen's subjects, he moved "that the Bill be read a second time this day six months."

Mr. Brotherton (Salford) expressed much surprise at the opposition offered to the Bill, inasmuch as "the measure was entirely permissive, and the rate was limited to one halfpenny in the pound." The money raised could be applied only to the erection of, or paying rent for, a building for holding a library and a museum. "No power was given to lay out the funds in the purchase of books, specimens, or pictures: all these were left to depend on the voluntary contributions of the inhabitants." The measure, he said, was popular in the large boroughs. "In Salford the Town Council, acting as the representatives of all the ratepayers, had come forward with the greatest alacrity to provide a building, and there had been voluntary contributions made of between 5,000 and 6,000 volumes to the library (which was attended by hundreds every night) in less than six months. He contended that this Bill would provide the cheapest police that could possibly be established; and what was the use of education for the people unless they were enabled to consult valuable works which they could not purchase for themselves?"

Mr. H. Goulbourn (Cambridge University) opposed the Bill on the ground that although providing for a building it did not provide for books, and "he, as an innocent man, certainly had thought that books always formed part of what was necessary for the enjoyment of a library." The halfpenny rate would go a very little way after erecting a building, and instead of providing those valuable books of reference which had been referred to, all that the funds would be able to provide would be the daily and weekly newspapers, and the library would thus become a mere newsroom which only well-to-do leisured persons could run into when the post had just arrived to learn the news. He thought that as all classes would have to pay the rate, whether they derived any benefit from it or

THE PUBLIC LIBRARIES ACT, 1850

not, the Bill was a highly unjust and objectionable measure.

Objections were also raised by several members because power was to be given to Town Councils to levy a rate without consulting the ratepayers, and it was urged that the concurrence of two-thirds of the ratepayers should be obtained by Town Councils before a rate was imposed.

Mr. J. Hume (Montrose), Mr. George A. Hamilton (Dublin University), Lord John Manners (afterwards Duke of Rutland), Mr. Henry Labouchere (Taunton), gave their support to the Bill, as did Mr. John Bright (Manchester), but on the understanding that a clause would be introduced providing for the ratepayers being consulted and giving their consent.

Mr. Spooner (N. Warwickshire) observed that as books which seemed to be not only the best but most necessary furniture for a library were to be left to the chances of voluntary or charitable contributions, the expenses of building and furnishing, for which it was proposed to make a rate, might be supplied from the same source. He objected to the principle of taxing a whole community for objects by which a few would be benefited, and by the institution of lectures hereafter he almost feared that these libraries might be converted into normal schools of agitation. "He anticipated the probability that hereafter there would be a call for increased rates, and that it would be urged that another halfpenny in the pound would not be too much." His anticipations in the latter matter were soon to be fulfilled, and the insufficiency of the additional halfpenny and its crippling effect on public libraries were to be felt for many years to come.

Mr. Roundell Palmer (afterwards Earl of Selborne) dissented from the proposition that they were all agreed as to the principle of the Bill. All would admit that it would be desirable to have good public libraries, but that was not the principle of the Bill. Its principle was objectionable for the reason that it meant taxation without consent of the persons taxed, but also for the reason that the amount to be raised would be totally insufficient for the purposes to which it was to be applied. By passing the Bill they would do no more than enable Town Councils to erect the buildings and to purchase furniture. Why, unless they were possessed of libraries and museums what Town Councils would be justified in erecting buildings in anticipation that charitable persons would afterwards present them with books and curiosities? It was evident that the Bill was intended for ulterior objects, by which powers would be given for the purchase of books, and perhaps also for the fitting up of lecture-rooms. He hoped the House would consider well before they applied to institutions of this nature the principles of public management and compulsory rating instead of the voluntary and self-supporting principle, which he believed to be the life and essence, and the cause of the utility, of

THE PUBLIC LIBRARIES ACT, 1850

such institutions. He intended to take his stand against the substitution of the compulsory for the voluntary principle in all matters of education. Although most truly desirous to see learning extended, and valuing as much as possible good public libraries, he should certainly divide against the Bill.

Mr. J. Heywood (N. Lancashire) and Mr. J. Wyld (Bodmin) spoke in favour of the Bill, considering that it would prove of the greatest utility by the improvement in the morality of the public to which it would lead, thereby diminishing those rates to which the country was subjected on account of crime.

Mr. P. H. Howard (afterwards Baron Howard), M.P. for Carlisle, was opposed to the Bill because it would tend to check the efforts of private enterprise in support of mechanics' institutions and the like. He thought, too, that municipal corporations had usually sufficient work on hand without having this additional duty imposed on them.

Mr. A. Oswald (Ayrshire) would also vote against the Second Reading, believing that it was going to do by Act of Parliament what would be more efficiently done by private enterprise. In Ayr and Kilmarnock and in almost every other burgh in Scotland there were excellent libraries established without any help whatever from that House. He also objected to the Bill because it would increase the rates in Scotland.

Mr. Ewart, in replying, said that they seemed to

THE PUBLIC LIBRARY MOVEMENT

forget that this was merely a permissive Bill. He would not attempt to reply to all the objections which had been urged against it, but would only say that existing libraries had been formed on the Museums Act, on the principle of which he had framed the present Bill. He would carefully consider all those objections. He would pledge himself to introduce in Committee a clause providing for the principle of the ratepayers being consulted before a Town Council imposed a rate.

After several other members had spoken the House divided: Ayes 118, Noes 101; Majority 17.

On April 10th, when the motion for considering the Bill in Committee was made, Mr. Ewart said that he proposed to make two important alterations in it, viz. to limit the operation of the Bill to boroughs whose population exceeded 10,000; and to make it necessary for the Town Council of any borough, before determining to carry the Act into effect, to call a public meeting of ratepayers and to obtain the distinct consent of those present. He begged to state that in Warrington, Liverpool, and other places a movement had already commenced in anticipation of the passing of this Bill to form public libraries freely accessible to all the inhabitants.

Colonel Sibthorp moved, and Mr. Spooner seconded, an amendment that the Bill be committed that day six months. The same speakers who had opposed the Second Reading again raised objections, many of them of a frivolous nature, such as

THE PUBLIC LIBRARIES ACT, 1850

"that the agricultural interest would be injured by the Bill," and "that it would enable the richer and more influential inhabitants of a community to tax the poorer inhabitants for their own special purposes."

Mr. Brotherton spoke strongly in favour of the Bill, urging its permissive nature, its limitation to the provision of buildings only, and the absurdity of objecting to allow a community to tax itself a halfpenny in the pound for a measure which would have the effect of preventing crime, while spending two millions a year for the punishment of crime. In his opinion it was little use to teach people to read unless you afterwards provided them with books to which they might apply the faculty they had so acquired.

Mr. Oswald (Ayrshire) insisted on words being introduced into the Bill to make it clear that it would not apply to Scotland, and Colonel Chatterton (Cork City) wished to know if it was intended to make the Bill extend to Ireland. Mr. Ewart said it was not intended that the Bill should extend to Scotland. With regard to Ireland, if the majority of the Irish members were in favour of the extension he was quite willing to accede to the proposition. He regretted that no less than three of the members for the Universities should have opposed the progress of a measure for the establishment of public libraries. The Bill would not authorize Town Councils to mortgage the general rates for the purposes of the Act, but only to raise money on the security of the special rate for libraries. He denied that it was a measure for the peculiar advantage of the rich. On the contrary, it was far more the poor man's than the rich man's question, in proof of which he referred to the library at Salford, which was found to be frequented by the poor far more than by any other class.

Mr. Bright considered that one-half of the objections against the Bill were not fairly put forward, while the other half did not apply. He believed that in the boroughs generally, not only the Town Councils, but the majority of the ratepayers, were favourable to the measure, which was entirely permissive in its character. He was informed that in the State of New York there were hundreds of such libraries; and if they were desirable there, surely they were equally so here. He gave the Bill his cordial support.

Mr. Roundell Palmer did not understand why, if this Bill were good for England, it was not equally good for Scotland, or why the inhabitants of Dumfries (Mr. Ewart's own constituency) were not to have the opportunity of improving their minds as well as those of Salford.

When the division took place the Ayes numbered 99, the Noes 64; a majority of 35.

In Committee Mr. Ewart moved an alteration in the first clause to provide that the Act should apply only to boroughs of more than 10,000 inhabitants, that the Town Council should convene a meeting of the ratepayers by notices posted on the doors

THE PUBLIC LIBRARIES ACT, 1850

of the town hall and of every church and chapel within the borough, and that two-thirds of the ratepayers present should approve before the Act was adopted.

Sir B. Hall (Marylebone) suggested that instead of a public meeting, a requisition should be issued to be signed by a proper proportion of the ratepayers. He was asked to draw up a clause embodying his proposal for consideration and progress was reported, the Committee to sit again on May 9th.

The Committee sat again on May 16th, when Mr. Ewart again moved his amendment to clause one, with the addition that the notice calling the meeting should be advertised in a local newspaper and should specify a day for holding the meeting not earlier than ten days after the publication of the notices as prescribed, and appointing certain places within the borough where ratepayers could record their votes for or against the adoption of the Act.

Colonel Sibthorp denounced the Bill as absurd in every sense of the word. The people were already sufficiently taxed. He would be happy to subscribe money from his own purse, and not exact money from those who could not afford to pay.

The Bill was reported to be printed as amended, and recommitted for June 13th.

On that date, on the motion for going into Committee, the redoubtable Colonel Sibthorp repeated his objections to the measure. "These were not times for spending money in the way proposed, when it might be much better expended in providing food and employment for the people. Instead of endeavouring to afford them industrious and profitable employment, he supposed they would be thinking of supplying the working-classes with quoits, peg-tops, and football." On this occasion he modified his expression of willingness to give personal monetary assistance, and instead of saying he would be "happy to subscribe," said that "instead of calling upon the unfortunate ratepayers to pay, he would be more disposed to put his hand in his pocket"—perhaps he meant to keep it there, for he made no mention of taking it out again. He moved that the House go into Committee upon this day six months.

Mr. Hume (Montrose) pleaded with Colonel Sibthorp to let them proceed with the details of the measure. He should not be surprised if one of the very first things he (Colonel Sibthorp) would do after the passing of the Bill would be to present his constituents with a handsome sum of money wherewith to purchase a library!

Mr. Wyld (Bodmin) was surprised at the opposition which had been offered to the Bill by the agricultural interest, and could only account for it by supposing that they were alarmed lest it should lead to the diminishing consumption of an article in which they largely dealt (malt); because it appeared from the whole course of evidence on this subject that in proportion as institutions of

THE PUBLIC LIBRARIES ACT, 1850

this kind were established, drunkenness and crime had diminished.

The House divided, and the majority in favour of proceeding with the Bill in Committee was sixty-six, but owing to the evident desire on the part of certain members to waste the time of the House by obstructive tactics, Mr. Brotherton moved that the Chairman report progress, and have leave to sit again on the following Wednesday. This was carried by a majority of thirty-eight against an amendment by Mr. Law (Cambridge University) to sit again that day six months.

The motion for the Third Reading of the Bill came on at the end of a long sitting after midnight, July 29th–30th. Mr. Brotherton made the motion, and the irrepressible Colonel Sibthorp was there to move that it be read a third time that day three months. Even his opposition seemed at last to be weakening, for he was apparently willing to reduce his period of delay by three months. The House divided, and the majority against him was forty-nine.

Colonel Chatterton (Cork City) moved that the Bill do not extend to Ireland. This was supported by Colonel Sibthorp, and a clause to that effect was inserted, and the Bill passed, the House adjourning at a quarter before two o'clock on the morning of July 30th.

The Bill passed the House of Lords without discussion, and received the Royal Assent on August 14th under the title "The Public Libraries Act, 1850."

THE PUBLIC LIBRARY MOVEMENT

The Act as passed enabled Town Councils to establish public libraries and museums, and repealed the Museums Act of 1845. The operation of the Act was confined to boroughs having a population exceeding 10,000 "according to the last count taken thereof by authority of Parliament." The procedure in adopting the Act was as follows: The Mayor, upon the request of the Town Council, was empowered to cause a notice to be fixed on the door of the town hall and on the doors of every church or chapel within the borough, and to be inserted in a local newspaper specifying on what day not earlier than ten days after the affixing and publication of such notice, and at what place or places within the borough the burgesses are required to signify their votes for or against the adoption of the Act. A two-thirds majority of the votes given was necessary to secure adoption. The Act, when adopted, gave power to the Town Council to purchase or rent any lands or buildings for the purpose of forming public libraries or museums of art and science, or both, and to erect, alter, and extend any buildings for such purpose, to maintain them in good repair, to purchase fuel, lighting, fixtures, and furniture, to appoint officers and servants with salaries and remuneration, and to make rules and regulations for their safety and use and for admission of visitors and others, *but they had no power to purchase books or specimens*. They were given power to levy a rate up to one halfpenny in the pound of annual value, and to borrow money

THE PUBLIC LIBRARIES ACT, 1850

on the security of that rate for the above purposes. The buildings so acquired were to be vested in the Town Council, or in any committee appointed by them, to be held in trust for ever. Admission to the libraries to be free of charge. If the adoption of the Act was rejected, no further application for its adoption could be made within the next two years.

Thus after a long struggle, and in the face of opposition hardly credible at the present day, the fight was won, and the first Public Libraries Act became law. This result was achieved through the enthusiasm and perseverance of its chief promoters, William Ewart and Joseph Brotherton, with whom must ever be associated Edward Edwards, whose whole-hearted support is fully disclosed in his evidence, and in the carefully compiled statistics which he had gathered over a number of years, and freely put at the disposal of the Select Committee.

CHAPTER VI

EARLY ADOPTIONS OF THE ACT

Town Councils, however, did not display any undue eagerness to avail themselves of the powers with which the Act entrusted t em. This is not to be wondered at when we consider the meagre financial provision made for carrying it into effect. The produce of a halfpenny rate, in the smaller boroughs at least, must have been demonstrably insufficient to provide even a building, to say nothing of the cost of its administration. Books they were not empowered to buy, but had to beg for.

To the city of Norwich belongs the credit of being the first municipality to adopt the Act. Within little more than a month of its passing, on September 27, 1850, a poll of Norwich burgesses was taken, when 150 voted in favour and only seven against the adoption of the Act. It was not until 1857, however, that a library was opened to the public. Warrington had started a museum and library in 1848 under the Museums Act of 1845, and Salford in 1849 had originated a library and museum through the efforts of the Mayor, E. R. Langworthy, and Mr. Joseph Brotherton, M.P. for the borough. The first part of the library, the reference library, was opened in January 1850, and the lending library in 1854. The Acts were not formally adopted until 1855.

EARLY ADOPTIONS OF THE ACT

In 1850 the town of Brighton purchased the Royal Pavilion estate, and obtained a local Act, known as the Pavilion Act, enabling the town commissioners to levy a rate not exceeding fourpence in the pound to be spent on the upkeep of the estate, "to adapt and preserve the property for the use, profit, enjoyment, and benefit of the town and inhabitants, and also of the visitors thereof and of the public for the purposes of profit, recreation . . . or instruction." Under these wide powers a beginning was made about 1855 with the formation of a library and museum, it having been decided not to adopt the Public Libraries Act. By other local Acts in 1867 and 1876 it was made clear that the establishment of a free library, museum, and picture gallery were purposes within the powers of the Pavilion Act of 1850.

In 1851 Winchester adopted the Act on January 14th, and the library was opened on November 10th.

In 1852 Manchester, Bolton, Ipswich, and Oxford all adopted the Act. In the same year Liverpool obtained a local Act authorizing the levying of a library and museum rate of one penny in the pound. The Manchester library was formally opened on September 2, 1852, in presence of a distinguished company of prominent Members of Parliament and well-known literary men, including Dickens, Bulwer Lytton, and Thackeray, all of whom delivered stirring addresses on the occasion. This was the first public lending and reference library to be opened under the Act of 1850. Bolton's library was opened

THE PUBLIC LIBRARY MOVEMENT

in 1853, and that of Oxford in 1854. Ipswich, which had adopted the Act for the purpose of establishing a museum, did not open its library till 1888. In 1853 there were three adoptions, at Blackburn, Sheffield, and Cambridge. 1854 was a blank as far as adoptions are concerned, but in the following year, in addition to Salford, already mentioned, no fewer than four municipal boroughs were added to the list, viz. Hertford, Kidderminster, Lichfield, and Maidstone. In 1856 Birkenhead came into line, followed in 1857 by the metropolitan borough of Westminster, the first London borough to adopt the Acts, and by the borough of Royal Leamington Spa. In 1858 Canterbury and Sunderland, and, in 1859, Walsall took the necessary steps. Birmingham, Bridgwater, and Northampton were the next to adopt the Acts. Thus ten years after the passing of the first Public Libraries Act of 1850, twenty-five places had decided to provide libraries for themselves either under the Museums Act of 1845, local Acts, or the Acts of 1850 and subsequent Acts. A complete list of all adoptions up to 1926, giving dates of adoption, will be found in the *Report on Public Libraries in England and Wales*, prepared by the Public Libraries Committee of the Board of Education, published in 1927 by H.M. Stationery Office, pp. 235-40.

CHAPTER VII

SUBSEQUENT AMENDING LEGISLATION

The Act of 1850 was extended to Scotland and Ireland in 1853 (16 and 17 Vict. c. 101) enabling municipal boroughs in Ireland, and royal and parliamentary burghs in Scotland to provide library buildings.

The Public Libraries (Scotland) Act, 1854 (17 and 18 Vict. c. 64) repealed the Act of 1853 so far as Scotland was concerned, and allowed the levying of a penny rate, and the purchase of books, maps, and specimens, by the magistrates and council of any burgh adopting the Act. In the same year the Town Improvements Act (Ireland), 1854 (17 and 18 Vict. c. 103) contained a section (par. 99) incorporating the Acts of 1850 and 1853. In the following year Acts were passed for England and Wales and for Ireland. The Public Libraries Act (Ireland) 1855 (18 and 19 Vict. c. 40) consolidated the Acts of 1853 and 1854, and thus became the principal Act for Ireland.

The Public Libraries Act, 1855 (18 and 19 Vict. c. 70) applicable to England only, was entitled "An Act for further promoting the Establishment of Free Public Libraries and Museums in municipal boroughs, and for extending it to towns governed under Local Improvement Acts, and to Parishes." It repealed the Act of 1850 and made the Acts applicable to boroughs, districts, and parishes of over 5,000 population instead of 10,000. The Mayor of a borough, on a request by the Town Council, was obliged to convene a meeting of the burgesses to determine the question of adoption or otherwise, a two-thirds majority of those present and voting being required to secure adoption. District Boards and the Overseers of the Poor in parishes, on the requisition in writing from ten ratepayers, similarly had to convene meetings, the same two-thirds majority being required for adoption. Vestries of two or more neighbouring parishes of an aggregate population of over 5,000 could combine to adopt the Act. The amount to be levied in every case not to exceed one penny in the pound. If adoption was not carried, no further meeting could be called for one year at least. The Lord Mayor of the City of London was required to convene a public meeting on the request of the Corporation. The Act did not extend to Ireland or to Scotland.

It may here be noted that this Act and the consolidating Act for Ireland passed in the same year are the only Acts relating to public libraries in which the word "free" is used in the title of the Act. It is an entire misnomer, and much of the ignorance and misconception with regard to public libraries and their work which prevailed until comparatively recent times, and unfortunately still prevails in certain quarters, may be traced to this misuse of the term "free." Public libraries are free just in the same sense in which the public streets

SUBSEQUENT AMENDING LEGISLATION

and the lamps which light them are free—that is to say, they are maintained out of the rates for the benefit of the community, and no other charge is made for their use. We do not speak of free streets, but of public thoroughfares. Why, then, speak of free libraries? The name has undoubtedly deterred a number of people from supporting the public library movement and from using the libraries from a mistaken idea that they are of the nature of charitable institutions like free breakfasts or free soup kitchens maintained by the wealthier inhabitants for the benefit of their poorer brethren. The public library is emphatically not a philanthropic institution established for the benefit of a class. It is, as Sir John Ballinger has said, "a great co-operative effort of a community." Such an idea may have been in the minds of some of the early promoters of the movement—it certainly was used with telling effect by opponents—yet we have the evidence of Edward Edwards to the contrary. "No fallacy," he said, "can possibly be more obstructive to the efficient and thorough working of the Acts, none more opposed to the views and purposes of those who promoted their enactment. All should feel that they contribute towards the support of the libraries, and that they come to them not in an eleemosynary fashion, but to profit by that which they themselves helped to establish." In his *Memoirs of Libraries* he thus speaks of the principles which guided the promoters of the public library movement in its inception:

THE PUBLIC LIBRARY MOVEMENT

"Two principles to start with seemed plain. The one that the new libraries should be formed in a catholic spirit, the other that they should be freed from all dependence on gifts or on current subscriptions for their permanent support. The first principle involved the corollary that the new institutions and their management should stand entirely aloof from party influences in politics or in religion. The second principle involved the corollary that their maintenance should be by rate, levied on the whole tax-paying community, and administered by its elective and responsible functionaries. Both principles in common involved a third conclusion as obvious and inevitable as the other two: the new libraries must know nothing of classes in the community. Supported alike by the taxation of the wealthiest capitalist and of the humblest householder, they must be so formed, so augmented and so governed as to be alike useful to both. They must in no sense be 'professional libraries,' or 'tradesmen's libraries,' or 'working-men's libraries,' but 'town libraries.' To that end they must contain, in fair proportions, the books that are attractive to the uneducated and the half-educated, as well as those which subserve the studies and assist the pursuits of the clergyman, the merchant, the politician, and the professional scholar. They must be unrestrictedly open to every visitor. They must offer to all men, not only the practical science, the temporary excitements, and the prevalent opinions of the passing day, but the wisdom of preceding

SUBSEQUENT AMENDING LEGISLATION

generations, the treasures of a remote antiquity, the hopes and the evidences of a world to come."

The next Act referring to public libraries and museums was the "Act to consolidate and amend the statute law of England and Ireland relating to malicious injury to property" passed in 1861 (24 and 25 Vict. c. 97), paragraph 39 of which made any person destroying or damaging books, manuscripts, works of art, etc., in any library, museum, or art gallery open to the public, liable to imprisonment for six months with or without hard labour, and, if a male, with or without whipping. The damages to be recovered by action at law.

The Act did not extend to Scotland.

In 1866 an Act to amend the Public Libraries Act was passed on August 10th (29 and 30 Vict. c. 114). Its object was to assimilate the laws relating to public libraries in England and Scotland. The portion of the 1855 Act relating to towns administered under Local Improvement Acts was repealed. The expenses of adoption and carrying into effect of the Act in boroughs might be paid out of the borough rate, or out of a rate to be levied in the same manner as the borough rate, but the amount was not to exceed one penny in the pound of the annual value of property in the borough. The public meeting might be called either by request of the Town Council or by requisition in writing of ten ratepayers. Any parish adjoining a borough, district, or parish (whatever the population of the parish) which had adopted the Act, or was considering its adoption, might, with the consent of more than half of the ratepayers present at the public meeting, unite in adopting the Act. The majority required to adopt this Act and also the Public Libraries (Scotland) Act, 1854, was more than one-half instead of the former two-thirds. The Public Libraries Act, 1855, and the Public Libraries (Scotland) Act, 1854, were made applicable to borough, district, parish, or burgh of whatever population. So much of Section 6 of the Public Libraries (Scotland) Act, 1854, as allowed for the demand of a poll of the ratepayers, and Sections 7 and 8 of that Act were repealed. The time that must elapse before another voting meeting could be called in the event of rejection was limited to one year. If either a library or museum was already established, a museum or library, as the case might be, could be added without further steps being taken to determine its establishment by public meeting.

The above Act and the Scottish Act of 1867 owed their existence to the zeal and persistent efforts of William Ewart.

In 1867 an Act to amend and consolidate the Public Libraries Acts (Scotland) was passed on July 15th (30 and 31 Vict. c. 37). It repealed the Public Libraries (Scotland) Act, 1854, and so much of the Act of 1866 as related to Scotland. It provided for a meeting to adopt the Acts being called on a request by the Town Council, or by ten householders, in any burgh, district, or parish. It em-

SUBSEQUENT AMENDING LEGISLATION

powered the chief magistrate in the case of a burgh, or the sheriff (or sheriff-substitute) in the case of a district or a parish to call such meeting within ten days, to preside at the same, and to certify the adoption or otherwise of the Acts, which could now be adopted by a simple majority of those present. The rate limitation to one penny was continued. The general management of the library was vested in a Committee consisting of not more than twenty members, half of whom were to be members of the Town Council, and the other half ratepayers. The Committee were given power to purchase books, etc., to manage, regulate, and control the libraries and museums, to add a library to a museum or a museum or art gallery to a library if either was already established. The property, however, was not vested in the Committee, but in the Town Council in burghs, or in the Parochial Board in districts and parishes.

In 1871 the 1867 Act was amended by the Public Libraries Act (Scotland 1867) Amendment Act (34 and 35 Vict. c. 59), to give additional facilities to local authorities entrusted with carrying the same into execution. By this Act the borrowing powers of the authorities were limited to an amount not greater than twenty years' purchase of one-fourth of a penny rate. Estimates had to be made up by the Committee in April of each year of the sums required for carrying on the libraries, etc. Accounts were to be audited and published annually. Power was given to make byelaws to be approved by the

THE PUBLIC LIBRARY MOVEMENT

Town Council or Board and confirmed by the Sheriff. Penalties and forfeitures were to be recovered by a small debt action in the name of the clerk to the Committee, an excerpt from the account books certified by the librarian was to be held equivalent to the books themselves. Power was given to lend out books, to make, print, and issue catalogues, and also power to lend books for the use of inmates of industrial schools, training-ships, reformatories, barracks, and similar institutions.

In the same year an Act to amend the Public Libraries Act, 1855, was passed on August 14th, by which local Boards were empowered to put the principal Act (1855) into execution. This Act did not apply to any district the whole or any part of which was within any municipal borough, or within the jurisdiction of commissioners under any Improvement Act.

On June 28, 1877, an Act to amend the Public Libraries (Ireland) Act, 1855, was passed. By this Act (40 and 41 Vict. c. 15) the terms "science and art" and "schools of science and art" were deemed to include "the science and art of music" and "schools of music" respectively. Power was given to pay the salaries of music teachers, and to purchase music and musical instruments for use in the schools. The Committee appointed might now consist in part of persons not members of the Town Council, or Board, or Commissioners. The Committee might borrow money with the approval of the Treasury.

SUBSEQUENT AMENDING LEGISLATION

Later in the same year, on August 14th, an Act to amend the Public Libraries Acts (40 and 41 Vict. c. 54) came into force, altering the law in the United Kingdom in the matter of the method of adoption of the Acts. It stated that whereas a public meeting was in many cases a most incorrect and unsatisfactory mode of determining the adoption, and failed to indicate the general opinion of the ratepayers, it was now competent for the prescribed local authority to ascertain the opinions of the majority of the ratepayers either by the prescribed public meeting or by the issue of a voting paper to each ratepayer, and the subsequent collection and scrutiny thereof. In the process of voting, ratepayers might stipulate for a lower rate being levied than the maximum penny, as well as answering "yes" or "no" for adoption. The term ratepayer was defined as meaning every inhabitant who would have to pay the Free Library Assessment in the event of the Acts being adopted. This Act, framed and introduced by Mr. George Anderson, one of Glasgow's representatives, was the direct result of the rejection of the Acts by a public meeting in Glasgow in 1876.

Another amending Act was passed on July 28, 1884 (47 and 48 Vict. c. 37), enabling library authorities to accept parliamentary grants from any Committee of the Privy Council on Education towards the purchase of a site for and erection of any school for science and art, or school for science, school for art, or teacher's residence under conditions prescribed by such Committee. Power was given under the Act for the erection of buildings for public libraries, public museums, schools for science, art galleries, and schools for art or for any one or more of these objects. Where any one of these had been established any others might be instituted without further proceedings.

In 1887 still another amending Act, the Public Libraries Acts Amendment Act, 1887 (50 and 51 Vict. c. 22), which did not apply to Ireland or to Scotland, was passed. It empowered an English library authority to establish and maintain a lending library without providing any separate building for containing the same, and to place such library under the care and superintendence of a fit person and in a building or room not appropriated for the purposes of the Act.

By this Act the powers and duties of the Treasury under the Public Libraries (England) Acts, 1855 to 1887, were transferred to the Local Government Board. It also enacted that where any parish is partly within and partly without any borough or district which has adopted the Acts, that portion of the parish which is without the borough or district shall be considered a parish within the meaning of the Acts, and the Overseers for the Poor for that parish shall be considered the overseers of the part of the parish situate without the borough or district.

Power was also given under this Act to a District in the metropolis to adopt the Act and to put it into execution, the expenses being paid by the

SUBSEQUENT AMENDING LEGISLATION

District Board, but not to exceed one penny in the pound.

The library legislation relating to Scotland was contained in so many different Acts that it became desirable to have it embodied in a comprehensive consolidating measure. In Glasgow the method of adopting or rejecting the Acts by vote of a public meeting had proved a stumbling-block in the way of adoption. In 1876 a Promotion Committee was formed and a public meeting was held, but it was packed by rowdy opponents, and when a vote was finally taken the motion for adoption was lost by 786 votes. The Act of 1877 provided the alternative of a plebiscite of ratepayers, and this method was taken in 1885, when the rejection was carried by 29,946 to 22,755, a majority of 7,191. A third attempt, in 1888, provided a still more decisive majority against adoption, viz. 9,437. It was not until 1899 that Glasgow obtained powers to levy a penny rate for library purposes under a local Act. In 1901 Mr. Andrew Carnegie gave the munificent sum of £100,000 for the establishment of branch libraries, thus enabling the Corporation to provide the highly efficient system of municipal libraries which it now enjoys.

After the rejection in 1885 the Promotion Committee decided to form a permanent association, under the title of the Glasgow Public Libraries Association, "to secure the adoption by the city of Glasgow of the Public Libraries Acts, and, if necessary or expedient for this end, to originate or

THE PUBLIC LIBRARY MOVEMENT

support any amendment of these Acts which may render them more equitable in their operation." The Association requested their Secretary, Mr. Richard Brown, a member of the Faculty of Procurators of Glasgow, to frame a Bill for the consolidation of the four Library Acts relating to Scotland. The Bill was introduced into Parliament in January 1887, by Mr. James Caldwell, but withdrawn. It was re-introduced by Mr. A. Cameron Corbett (afterwards Lord Rowallan) and Mr. R. B. Cunninghame Graham in February, passed successfully through both Houses of Parliament, and received the Royal Assent on September 16th.

The above-mentioned Act, The Public Libraries Consolidation (Scotland) Act, 1887 (50 and 51 Vict. c. 42), the principal Act for Scotland, repealed the Acts 1867 to 1884 so far as they related to Scotland, with the exception of the Edinburgh Public Library Assessment Act, 1887, which was a separate Act for Edinburgh only, passed in the same year. It provided for the holding of a public meeting to determine the adoption or otherwise of the Acts, on the requisition of the magistrate and council of a burgh, or of ten or more householders in a burgh or parish. The meeting fell to be called by the chief magistrate in the case of a burgh, or by the sheriff of the county in the case of a parish; voting papers to be issued to all householders, to be collected by persons specially appointed and a scrutiny made, a simple majority of votes being sufficient to determine the issue. If the adoption

SUBSEQUENT AMENDING LEGISLATION

was not carried, no similar proceedings could be taken for two years. The expenses of the voting in that case were to be defrayed out of the burgh general assessment. If adoption was carried, the expenses of voting and also of carrying the Act into execution fell to be paid out of the library rate, which was limited to one penny in the pound. Power was given to the library authority to purchase, rent, sell, or exchange lands or buildings for the purposes of the Acts, and all property was vested in the Town Council or the Parochial Board as the case might be. The authority was given power to borrow money, to form a sinking fund, and to accept parliamentary grants under conditions prescribed by the Committee of the Privy Council on Education as in the 1884 Act.

A Committee consisting of not less than ten nor more than twenty members had to be appointed, one-half of them to be members of the Council or Board, and the other half householders not members of those bodies, to manage, regulate, and control all libraries, museums, etc., established under the Acts, and having power to purchase books, works of art and other property, and to sell or exchange duplicates, to establish reading-rooms, to lend out books, to compile and print catalogues, to make byelaws which, when approved by the Council or Board, had to be confirmed by the Sheriff. In short, the Committee had power to do everything necessary to carry on the institutions under their charge, except the borrowing of money. Estimates of the sums required for the ensuing year had to be prepared and submitted to the Council or Board, and the Council or Board were obliged to levy the amount required provided that it did not exceed the produce of a penny rate.

The Act of 1889, applicable to England only (52 Vict. c. 9), amended the 1855 Act in the matter of the method of raising the rate, enacting that the expenses of carrying out the Act shall be paid out of a rate to be raised with and as part of the poor rate. Clause 3 of this Act empowered Commissioners under the Acts 1855 to 1887 for any two or more adjoining parishes, with the consent of the vestries of the parishes, from time to time to agree to share, in such proportion and for such period as may be agreed, the cost of purchase, erection, repair, and maintenance of any library building situated in one of such parishes, and the cost of maintenance of the same as a library.

Another amending Act for England was passed in the following year (53 and 54 Vict. c. 68) determining the qualifications of voters in boroughs and districts, fixing the method of adoption to be by voting papers and not otherwise, and providing for the alteration of the amount of rate to be levied. If the maximum rate to be levied were fixed at one halfpenny it might be raised to three farthings or one penny; if fixed at three farthings, it might be raised to one penny, and the procedure for the purpose was to be the same as that required for the adoption of the Acts, but in no case was more than

SUBSEQUENT AMENDING LEGISLATION

one penny to be levied in any library district except the City of London. Section 3 of the Act of 1889 was extended to enable any library authority, with consent of the voters and of the Charity Commission, to combine with another library authority for the use of a joint library. By this Act any person holding land for ecclesiastical, parochial, or charitable purposes was empowered to grant for the purposes of this Act any quantity of such land not exceeding in any one case one acre. The grant, however, could not be made without the consent of the Ecclesiastical Commissioners, or, if parochial property, without the sanction of the Poor Law Guardians of the parish, or without the consent of the Local Government Board. The vestry of any parish in London and the Board of Works of any district therein were empowered to appropriate lands vested in them for the purposes of the Acts if the Acts were adopted.

The Museums and Gymnasiums Act, 1891 (54 and 55 Vict. c. 22), enabled urban authorities in England and Wales by a resolution passed at a duly advertised meeting of the authority to provide and maintain museums and gymnasiums within their areas. Power was given to acquire local antiquities and all requisite gymnasium apparatus. The museum to be open not less than three days a week without charge, but charges for admission might be made on other days. The Act did not apply to Scotland, or to the administrative county of London.

CHAPTER VIII

FURTHER AMENDING AND CONSOLIDATING LEGISLATION

The Acts relating to public libraries in England and Wales had by now become so numerous and involved that it had for some time been felt that an amending and consolidating Act was highly desirable. The inconsistencies of the law had been frequently discussed by the Library Association, and in 1889 Mr. (afterwards Sir) John Y. W. MacAlister offered a prize of £10 for the best draft of a Public Libraries Bill. Sir James Picton, Sir John Lubbock, and Mr. Richard Copley Christie, Chancellor of the Diocese of Manchester, then President of the Association, were requested to undertake the work of adjudicating on the drafts. Five drafts were submitted, and the prize was awarded to that sent in by Mr. John J. Ogle, Librarian of the Public Library, Bootle, and Mr. H. W. Fovargue, also of Bootle, afterwards Town Clerk of Eastbourne, and for many years Hon. Solicitor to the Association. Mr. Ogle, in his work entitled *The Free Library*, 1897, p. 74, gives particulars of the provisions of their draft Bill. "It would have limited the borrowing powers of library authorities to a sum or sums of money not exceeding the capital sum represented by one-fourth part of the library rate capitalized at the rate of twenty

FURTHER AMENDING LEGISLATION

years' purchase of such sums. This was to be repaid by not more than fifty annual instalments. A special inauguration rate, not exceeding a penny in the pound, for the purchase of books and objects, was to be levied during the first year, in addition to the annual rate; one penny in the pound for a library or museum alone; three half-pence for a library and museum, or in addition to the other objects, not being all the objects authorized; twopence where a library, museum, art gallery, and school of science and art were provided. Exemption of institutions from local rates, and power to demand free copies of Government and local official publications were included, besides proposals to legalize public free lectures, which many thought to be of doubtful legality." The draft Bill was fully discussed at the annual meeting of the Association at Reading in 1890, and the Association afterwards commissioned Mr. Fanshawe, an experienced parliamentary draughtsman, to prepare a consolidating Bill. The prize draft Bill was placed in Mr. Fanshawe's hands in order to facilitate the preparation of a Bill. The new draft Bill was discussed by library authorities all over the country, and by the Library Association, and various amendments were suggested, but on the advice of Sir John Lubbock, who afterwards introduced the Bill into the House of Commons on February 11, 1892, none but the very simplest amendments were inserted. No debate took place in its passage through Parliament, and it received the Royal Assent on June 27, 1892.

THE PUBLIC LIBRARY MOVEMENT

This Act, The Public Libraries Act, 1892 (55–56 Vict. c. 53), is still the principal Act for England and Wales,[1] although small portions of it were repealed by the Act of 1901, and the rate limitation was abolished by the Act of 1919. It provided that every urban district and every parish in England and Wales which is not within an urban district should be a library district. The method of adoption of the Acts was to be by voting papers only, and not by public meeting, a simple majority to decide, and the period before another requisition could be made was limited to one year. In parishes the vestry, on the adoption of the Acts, was required to appoint Commissioners (not fewer than three nor more than nine) as a body corporate to administer the Acts, one-third of the members to retire annually but to be eligible for re-election. Power was given to neighbouring parishes to combine by arrangement for the purposes of the Acts. Library authorities were empowered to provide all or any of the following institutions, viz. public libraries, public museums, schools for science, art galleries, and schools for art. Where any one of these had been provided, no further proceedings were necessary for the establishment of the others. Power was also given to grant land held for charitable purposes to library authorities, except land within the administrative county of London, or land in any urban district of over 20,000 population held in trust as

---

[1] It repealed all previous Library Acts, 1855–90.

FURTHER AMENDING LEGISLATION

an open space.[1] The library authority was empowered to appoint a Committee and to delegate all or any of its powers to the said Committee, which then became the library authority. The persons appointed need not be members of the original authority.

This Act also provided that the city of London should be a library district, and on adoption of the Acts the Common Council became the library authority. The expenses of the Act were to be defrayed out of the consolidated rate or a separate rate raised in the same manner, and the limitation of the rate to one penny in the pound was not to apply to the city of London.

Power was also given under this Act to districts in the metropolis (i.e. all London, except the City) to adopt the Acts upon a requisition by ten voters, and to combine in carrying the Act into execution. Where a parish within a district had adopted the Acts it was to be treated as a parish outside the district.

An Act amending the principal Act of 1892 was passed on June 9, 1893, providing that in an urban district the principal Act may be adopted, and the limitations of the maximum rate to be levied may, within the limits fixed by that Act, be fixed, raised, or removed by a resolution of the urban authority. The consent of the urban authority was substituted

---

[1] The Local Government Act, 1929, provides that parochial property held for charitable purposes may not be granted or conveyed without the consent of the Local Government Board.

THE PUBLIC LIBRARY MOVEMENT

for the consent of the voters. A resolution of the urban authority passed at a meeting of the authority was made sufficient for adoption of the Acts, provided that due notice had been given to every member and published by advertisement in local newspapers; a copy of the resolution to be sent to the Local Government Board. Power was given to two or more library authorities of urban districts to combine for carrying the Acts into execution. A Joint Committee might be formed in such proportions as might be agreed upon for administration, the members of which need not be members of the combining authorities; the Committee to have all the powers of the library authority, except the power of borrowing money.

The next Act passed was an amending Act for Scotland, passed in July 1894 (57 and 58 Vict. c. 20), enabling Town Councils in burghs to adopt the Acts by resolution, instead of obtaining the opinions of the householders. The resolution had to be passed at a special meeting, one month's notice of said meeting having to be given to every member of Council, and, if passed, to be published in the local newspapers and come into force at a fixed date not less than a month after the publication of the advertisement.

Later in the same year, on August 17, 1894, an amending Act for Ireland came into force, giving similar powers to Irish library authorities of adopting the Acts by a resolution, provided that, should the resolution to adopt not be carried,

FURTHER AMENDING LEGISLATION

the voters were to retain the right to have their opinions ascertained in the manner provided by the principal Act. Power was given by this Act to urban authorities to grant the use of a lending library established under the principal Act to persons not inhabitants of their district either gratuitously or for payment. They were empowered to let any building or part thereof not required for the purposes of the Act and to apply the proceeds to the purposes of the Act. Power was given to grant land held for public or charity purposes to the library authority for library purposes, but not without the consent of the Charity Commissioners or the Commissioners of Public Works. Urban authorities of any two or more districts were enabled to combine for the joint use of a library, museum, school for science, art gallery, or school for art. They were given power to accept a parliamentary grant for library purposes upon conditions prescribed by the Science and Art Department. The Local Government Board was authorized to make rules for carrying into effect the objects of this Act.

In 1898 the Libraries Offences Act (61 and 62 Vict. c. 53) provided for the punishment of any person who in a library or reading-room to the annoyance or disturbance of persons using the same:

(1) Behaves in a disorderly manner;
(2) Uses violent, abusive, or obscene language;
(3) Bets or gambles;
(4) Or, who, after proper warning, persists in remaining therein beyond the hours for closing;

THE PUBLIC LIBRARY MOVEMENT

making the offender liable to a penalty on summary conviction not exceeding forty shillings.

The Act applied not only to public libraries but also to any library of a society registered under the Industrial and Provident Societies Act, the Friendly Societies Act, or to the library of a trade union. It did not extend to Scotland or Ireland.

The Public Libraries (Scotland) Act, 1899 (62 Vict. c. 5), provided that where the principal Act of 1887 has been adopted for any two or more neighbouring burghs or parishes, the Magistrates and Council, or the Board, as the case may be, of each such burgh or parish may by agreement combine in carrying the Act into execution, and the expenses shall be defrayed by each in such proportions as may be agreed. The Joint Committee, appointed in such proportions as agreed, shall have all the rights, powers, and duties of the Council or Board or Committee.

In 1901 an Act to amend the Acts relating to public libraries, museums, and gymnasiums (1 Edw. VII, c. 19), provided that the Commissioners appointed for a library district under the principal Act might be either voters in the district or persons who though not voters would, if the district were a rural parish having a Parish Council, be qualified for election as parish councillors. Power was given to the library authority to make byelaws for regulating the use of the library and protecting it from injury; for requiring from users of the library guarantees or security against loss or injury to

FURTHER AMENDING LEGISLATION

books or articles; and for enabling officers and servants of the library authority to exclude or remove therefrom persons committing any offence against the Libraries Offences Act, 1898, or against the byelaws. The Libraries Offences Act was extended to museum, art gallery, or school provided under the Acts. The library authorities of two or more library districts were given power to combine to provide any or all of the institutions which individually they could provide and to share the expenses. On the adoption of the Acts notice was required to be given to the Local Government Board, and notification of all libraries already established must be made to the Board within three months of the passing of the Act. The provisions of the Act enabling authorities to make byelaws were extended to Ireland; and the Museums and Gymnasiums Act, 1891, and the Public Libraries (Amendment) Act, 1893, were extended to the administrative county of London. The Act did not apply to Scotland.

Another Act, for Ireland only, was passed in 1902 (2 Edw. VII, c. 20), which enabled Rural District Councils to adopt the principal Irish Act of 1855. By this Act the Rural District Council was made the library authority for the district to the exclusion of the town commissioners of any town within the district. The money required was to be raised equally over the whole district and to be supplied by the Council of the county comprising the district as part of the expenses of the

THE PUBLIC LIBRARY MOVEMENT

District Council. Any library authority was enabled to make an agreement with the managers of any school for the use of the school as a library. County Councils were empowered to make grants in aid out of the funds for technical education to any library authority for the purchase of books or towards maintenance. The Libraries Offences Act, 1898, was made applicable to Ireland, and power to make byelaws was given.

The above Act was amended in 1911, giving power to library authorities in Ireland to levy a rate up to one penny-halfpenny in the pound, where an art gallery is established in any county borough under the Libraries Acts in addition to a library or museum.

An Act was passed in 1918 which, although not a Libraries Act, properly speaking, makes provision for the supply of books to Scottish libraries in rural areas, viz. the Education (Scotland) Act, 1918. It contains an important section under which the Scottish county library system has been organized. Section 5 of the Act reads as follows:

"5. It shall be lawful for the education authority of a county, as an ancillary means of promoting education, to make such provision of books by purchase or otherwise as they may think desirable, and to make the same available not only to the children and young persons attending schools or continuation classes in the county, but also to the adult population resident therein.

"For the purposes of this section an education authority may enter into arrangements with public libraries, and all expenses incurred by an education authority for those pur-

FURTHER AMENDING LEGISLATION

poses shall be chargeable to the county education fund: provided that where in any burgh or parish as defined by the Public Libraries Consolidation (Scotland) Act, 1887, the library rate by that Act authorized is levied, there shall be raised within such burgh or parish on account of any such expenses such sum as will, with the produce of the said library rate, amount to the sum which would have been raised within such burgh or parish under this section had such library rate not been levied within it."

The above proviso has been repealed in the Local Government (Scotland) Act, 1929, and Section 14, par. 7, of that Act provides as follows:

"In any case where the Public Libraries Acts are in operation within any part of the landward area of a county (i.e. any part of the county other than a burgh), the administrative scheme of the County Council relating to education may provide for the administration of the said Acts throughout the areas within which they are in operation being under the general supervision of the Education Committee; for the appointment as a library committee, for each of the said areas, of the district council of the district or of a committee consisting to the extent of not less than one-third and not more than one-half of persons who, not being members of the Education Committee, are resident within the area; and for the functions of the Committees under the said Acts being exercised by the Education Committee or the library committees as specified in the scheme, and where the scheme makes such provision as aforesaid the provisions of the Public Libraries Acts relating to the appointment of Committees shall not apply."

The proviso in the 1918 Education Act is not very clearly worded, but its intention evidently was to secure that burghs or parishes within a county scheme having a library already established

THE PUBLIC LIBRARY MOVEMENT

and rated for should not be rated by the Education Authority in addition, unless the general rate levied on the county was higher than the rate levied in the burgh or parish with which the Education Authority might enter into an arrangement. Much dissatisfaction has been expressed in various quarters where the Education Committee of the County Council (formerly the Education Authority) has levied an additional rate on burghs and parishes without a definite arrangement having been made as to the library service to be rendered by the Committee to the area so rated, there being no legal obligation on the Committee to give such service in return for the money raised by them.

CHAPTER IX

REMOVAL OF THE RATE LIMITATION

In 1919 was passed "an Act to amend the Public Libraries Acts, 1892 to 1901, and to repeal so much of the Museums and Gymnasiums Act, 1891, as authorizes the provision of museums in England and Wales" (9 and 10 Geo. V, c. 93). This Act is without doubt the most important piece of legislation so far as libraries are concerned that has been carried through since the first Public Libraries Act of 1850 was put upon the statute book. Its most valuable provision was the abolition of the statutory limitation of the rate that may be levied by library authorities for the purposes of the Libraries Acts, a limitation which for three-quarters of a century did more to retard the progress of public libraries than anything else. The measure was not carried without a prolonged struggle. The hampering effect of the penny-rate restriction was early experienced by the authorities to whom was entrusted the administration of the Acts, and many progressive municipalities, by promoting local Acts empowering them to increase the amount of the rate to be levied, or to remove the restriction entirely, had found the means of rendering their libraries more useful to their respective communities. As early as 1865 Oldham had got rid of the restriction altogether, and was followed by St. Helens in 1869; and by

THE PUBLIC LIBRARY MOVEMENT

Huddersfield in 1871. In 1874 Nottingham obtained powers to allow the profits from its gas undertaking to be used for library purposes, and had voted £2,000 per annum to be applied thereto. Preston, in 1880, had the limit raised to a penny-halfpenny in the pound, and three years later the rate limit was abolished so far as Birmingham was concerned. By the beginning of this century some thirty library authorities had in this way obtained relief from the crippling effect of the penny rate, eight towns had increased their library rate to a penny-halfpenny, thirteen to twopence, and two to threepence, which in each case provided for a library, a museum, and an art gallery.

All these authorities had found that under the penny-rate restriction, after providing for the maintenance of their library buildings, lighting, heating, and staffing them, paying sinking-fund charges, insurance, and so forth, very little money was left for the essential purposes of a library, viz. the supply of new books, the replacement of those worn out, and bookbinding. The additional money provided by the extra penny or halfpenny made all the difference between absolute penury and comparative affluence in the matter of book supply. It was felt, however, that the restriction in the matter of rating for libraries, which prevented authorities from spending whatever they considered desirable for the requirements of the public, was an absurd one. Other municipal undertakings were not subject to such restrictions, and it seemed anomalous

REMOVAL OF THE RATE LIMITATION

that libraries should be debarred from performing their proper functions in this invidious manner. The cost, however, of obtaining parliamentary sanction for increased rating powers was prohibitive in all but the largest towns, and it was felt that the permission to increase the rating power which had been granted to certain municipalities should be extended to all, and that the proper procedure was to abolish the rate limit altogether, and allow each community to assess itself to whatever extent it thought necessary for the proper functioning of its library system. This point of view had been forcibly expressed by Mr. W. E. A. Axon, Salford, as early as 1881, in a paper "On Legislation for Public Libraries" read at the London meeting of the Association (*Transactions*, 1881, pp. 31–33), but in the discussion which followed, although the principle was approved, it was held that any proposal to increase the rates would have no chance of passing through Parliament, and no action was taken. At the Buxton meeting in 1896, Mr. Fovargue, Hon. Solicitor, advised the Association not to attempt to interfere with the limit, in the interest of districts which had not yet adopted the Acts.

About the beginning of this century an agitation began with a view to the removal of the rate limitation, and at the Birmingham Conference of the Library Association in 1902, Mr. (now Sir) John Ballinger, then Librarian of the Cardiff Public Libraries, opened a discussion on "The Rate Limit and the Future of Public Libraries." Following on the discussion, a resolution, moved by Councillor Abbott, of Manchester, and seconded by Mr. T. W. Lyster, Librarian of the National Library of Ireland, was passed, instructing the executive of the Association to take immediate steps to secure an amendment of the Public Libraries Acts with a view to the removal of its financial limitations. A special Legislation Committee was appointed with Councillor Abbott as Chairman, and a Bill was drafted by Mr. H. W. Fovargue, Hon. Solicitor to the Association. It was entrusted to Mr. John Burns, M.P., for introduction in the House of Commons, but he having advised that owing to the congestion of parliamentary business it had better be postponed until next session, this course was adopted. The Bill was introduced by Mr. H. J. Tennant, M.P. for Berwickshire, in 1904 and successive years, but never got beyond a first reading, and the Government being unwilling to give facilities for it, it shared in the annual slaughter of the innocents at the end of the session.

In 1913, and again in 1914, the Bill was introduced in an amended form, providing for the extension of the rating power to twopence in the pound, and for empowering County Councils to adopt the Acts and to be the library authorities within their areas. A return from libraries throughout the country was prepared and circulated, showing the urgent necessity for relief from the penny-rate restriction. There were more than a dozen

REMOVAL OF THE RATE LIMITATION

library authorities unable to spend as much as £10 per annum on the purchase of books, thirty-eight were spending under £20, and nearly 100 less than £50. Many Members of Parliament had pledged themselves to support the Bill, but blocking motions by Sir Frederick (now Lord) Banbury and others stopped all discussion, and no progress was made.

Then came the Great War, which put an end for the time being to all attempts to introduce legislation. The financial stringency resulting from war conditions and their aftermath of increased prices became so acute that all library authorities were sore put to it to maintain any sort of library service; several had been compelled to close down their libraries on account of the insufficiency of their rate-income, while many others were contemplating similar action. Some means of relief had to be found, and numerous petitions were presented to the Local Government Board, urging immediate action if the public library service was to be maintained.

At a conference in Manchester called by the North Central Library Association in October, 1918, and at the annual meeting of the Library Association in London which followed immediately thereafter, resolutions were passed urging on the Government the absolute necessity of the removal of any limitation on the library rate, and requesting the Council of the Association to arrange immediately for a deputation to the Local Government Board in order to press for temporary relief pending legislation. It was further agreed to invite the support of all local library authorities in any effort to secure the removal of the rate limitation, and, in particular, to obtain the co-operation of their local Members of Parliament in any legislation that might be introduced into the House.

In January 1919, at the instigation of Mr. G. E. Roebuck, Librarian of Walthamstow, the Walthamstow Library Authority, having in view the financial embarrassment of libraries, decided to call an informal conference of the immediately local authorities to discuss the question and to endeavour to find some means whereby their common difficulty might be overcome. This conference met at Walthamstow Central Library on January 28th under the presidency of Mr. Charles Jesson, M.P. for the borough, and delegates from the Borough Councils of East Ham, Edmonton, Ilford, Leyton, Tottenham, and Walthamstow attended. It was decided that the Councils represented should be requested to approach Parliament with a view to obtaining a grant from Government in aid of rate-supported libraries, or to take the necessary steps to increase the library rate to a sum sufficient to secure efficiency in the public library service.

It was also decided to call a further conference of all library authorities in Greater London, so that conjoint action should be taken, and that Mr. Jesson, who had taken a very keen interest in the matter and had offered to put questions on the situation in the House of Commons, and to intro-

REMOVAL OF THE RATE LIMITATION

duce a deputation to the President of the Local Government Board, might have his hands strengthened when doing so by having a large body of opinion behind him.

This second conference, organized by Mr. Roebuck, was held under the auspices of the Walthamstow Library Authority at the Walthamstow Town Hall on March 13, 1919. Mr. C. Jesson again presided. Sixteen library authorities sent representatives, and after a lengthened discussion as to the best course of action the following resolution was passed unanimously:

"That this conference of delegates representing local authorities of Greater London is of opinion that, in view of the reduced purchasing power of money, it is now impossible to maintain rate-supported public libraries on the pre-war basis of the limited penny rate, and is of opinion that means should be found by the Government for obtaining such sums as are deemed necessary for their maintenance."

This resolution was sent to the Prime Minister and the Ministers for Education and Local Government, and circulated to all library authorities in London. Delegates representing Croydon, Deptford, Hackney, Hampstead, Hornsey, Ilford, and Walthamstow were appointed to meet Mr. Fisher, President of the Board of Education, should he consent to receive a deputation. Mr. Fisher received the deputation on April 10th. It was introduced by Mr. Jesson, who in his remarks stated succinctly the grounds of their appeal. Mr. Fisher asked for a spokesman to be appointed, and the

THE PUBLIC LIBRARY MOVEMENT

deputation requested Mr. W. E. Doubleday, Librarian of Hampstead, to undertake this duty. Mr. Doubleday, who had given much assistance to Mr. Roebuck in organizing the conference of authorities, had been for years an active supporter of the movement for the removal of the rate limitation, and his presentation of the case in its favour proved convincing.

Mr. Fisher assured the deputation that he appreciated the difficulties with which local authorities were faced, and that he was impressed with the facts which had been presented to him. The source of the trouble—the rate limit—could only be removed by special legislation, and any step in that direction must be subsequent to the passage of the Ministry of Health Bill, and the definite allocation of responsibility for public libraries to some Ministry. In the meantime he promised to give the matter his very careful consideration, and expressed a wish to be supplied with figures showing the work done by public libraries.[1]

Mr. Roebuck drew his attention to the statistics in the Report prepared by Professor Adams in 1915 for the Carnegie United Kingdom Trust, and Mr. Fisher intimated that he would be glad to have those figures brought up to date. Mr. Roebuck was requested by the Executive Committee of the Library Association to obtain this information, and he at once set to work and issued a questionnaire to libraries, and within a few days the returns

[1] *Library Association Record*, 1919, p. 85.

REMOVAL OF THE RATE LIMITATION

were tabulated and forwarded to Mr. Fisher. The statistics were published in the *Library Association Record*, 1919, pp. 161–171.

The Scottish Library Association, at a conference in Glasgow on March 27th, following on a paper read by Mr. S. A. Pitt, unanimously passed a resolution expressing the view that the removal of the limitation on the library rate was absolutely necessary if public libraries were to take their proper place in the movement for reconstruction.

In the following May, the Secretary for Scotland, Mr. Robert Munro (now Lord Alness), received a deputation from the Scottish Library Association and a number of representatives from Scottish library authorities, who urged upon him the clamant necessity for the abolition or extension of the limitation on the library rate.

The Secretary for Scotland, in his reply, referred to the long-standing efforts to obtain relief from the penny-rate limit, instancing the representations made to his predecessor in the Scottish Office in 1905 by the Convention of Royal Burghs, urging the increase of the maximum rate to twopence per pound. He was not satisfied that the Convention had altered their view that the maximum rate should be twopence. He referred also to the provision made under the Education Act of 1918 for which he was responsible, whereby under Section 5 power is given to education authorities to purchase books and to enter into arrangements with public libraries for the supply of books at the cost of the

County Education Fund. He pointed out that the matter before him was not purely a Scottish question; it really was a question affecting England, Wales, and Scotland, and that there should be a different law on this matter on the two sides of the Border was unthinkable. He should have, however, to make himself acquainted with the views generally held on the subject among local authorities before coming to any definite decision in the matter.

On May 10th the Carnegie United Kingdom Trust addressed a letter to all local authorities in the United Kingdom possessing rate-supported libraries, and to all members of the House of Commons, pointing out the precarious condition of public libraries under the present financial strain. The Trust had had many applications from local authorities for financial assistance, and this had led them to feel that unless early and effective steps were taken to allow each town to decide for itself what annual sum is necessary to conduct its library efficiently many libraries would have to close their doors or be administered unsatisfactorily. The Trust, therefore, as an impartial body, urged that those addressed should press the Government to give local authorities the right of self-determination in the matter.

In the month of June appeared the Third Interim Report of the Adult Education Committee of the Ministry of Reconstruction dealing with libraries and museums (Cd. 9237). This Report recommended the abolition of the penny-rate limit, the

REMOVAL OF THE RATE LIMITATION

placing of public libraries under education authorities, the union of educational and library administration, the establishment and control of public libraries within their area by County Education Authorities, the provision of technical and commercial libraries, and the presentation of Government publications to public libraries on demand.

As this Report embodied many of the recommendations for which the Library Association had been pressing for some time, it was welcomed; but exception was taken to the suggestion that public libraries and museums should be administered by education authorities. A Memorandum was accordingly prepared for presentation to Mr. Fisher, the President of the Board of Education, embodying the views of the Association on that point.

At the Annual Conference at Southport, at which there was a large attendance of representatives from library authorities, the Memorandum was read and approved. On paragraph 56 of the Report, which lays down the principle that the control of public libraries shall be remitted to special committees of the education authority, the Memorandum stated that to this the Library Association would offer strenuous opposition on the ground that the interest of the general reader is the interest of the library, and that this interest should not be endangered by, or subordinated to, the special interest of education.

The Library Association, as we have seen, had for many years been active in endeavouring to enlist support for its campaign for the removal of

THE PUBLIC LIBRARY MOVEMENT

the rate limit. Its legislation and executive committees had held many meetings, and various expedients had been discussed, none of which seemed to promise much hope of success, although it was understood that Dr. Addison, President of the Local Government Board, was favourably disposed, and recognized the urgent need of legislative action being taken to relieve the situation. One difficulty in the way was that Dr. Addison's hands were full at the time. The powers of the Local Government Board had been transferred to the newly created Ministry of Health, of which he was to be the head, and it had not been definitely decided to what Ministry the control of public libraries should be assigned, if the recommendations of the Report of the Adult Education Committee in this matter were to be carried into force. Dr. Addison was so occupied in organizing the new Ministry that he was unable to devote the necessary time to the consideration of the library question.

At a meeting of the Executive Committee, held in London on November 14, 1919, Mr. John Ballinger, Librarian of the National Library of Wales, who had taken an active part in the campaign since 1902, suggested that he should see Mr. (now Sir) Herbert Lewis, then Parliamentary Secretary to the Board of Education, and endeavour to bring about a meeting with Mr. Fisher and representatives of the Association. Mr. Ballinger's suggestion was cordially agreed to, and it was further decided that an emergency Bill of one

REMOVAL OF THE RATE LIMITATION

clause providing for the removal of the rate limit should be drafted, and that the Committee should adjourn until such time as Mr. Ballinger should be in a position to report the result of his interview with Mr. Lewis.

Meantime the Carnegie United Kingdom Trust had been bringing pressure to bear upon the Board of Education to introduce legislation in a matter which concerned them intimately. Following upon the Report on Library Provision and Policy prepared for them by Professor W. G. S. Adams in 1915, the Trustees had inaugurated an experimental scheme for the gratuitous distribution of books in county areas through the local schools. The experiment was to be tried for a period of five years, at the end of which time the Trustees hoped that each county area in receipt of a library would take over its management and levy a rate for its maintenance. It was then found that although each parish within a county could individually adopt the Libraries Acts and become the library authority for its area, County Councils had no such power, and could not spend a penny on the maintenance of a library system, although County Education Committees were empowered to spend money out of the Education Rate on the provision of books for children and on reference libraries for teachers. The Trustees accordingly made representations to the Board of Education with a view to the introduction of legislation to remedy this defect, since any scheme which they might finance by grant for

THE PUBLIC LIBRARY MOVEMENT

a limited period could not be continued permanently. A deputation from the Trustees was received by Mr. Lewis in March, and it was pointed out that in the absence of enabling legislation their work in the counties would be entirely stopped. Mr. Lewis explained to the deputation the difficulty of carrying any legislation that imposed fresh taxation, however small, and that a Bill to carry out the objects they had in view could easily be stopped by a single objector, unless the Government found the necessary time, which they were not likely to do. He promised, however, to have a Bill drafted and to do his best to carry it through. A Bill was accordingly prepared to enable County Councils to adopt the Libraries Acts, and to become library authorities for the whole or part of their areas. The President of the Board of Education requested Mr. Lewis to take charge of the Bill in the House of Commons.

When Mr. Ballinger met Mr. Lewis he learned that the Board of Education's Bill, though drafted, had not yet been introduced. He informed Mr. Lewis that the Library Association were anxious to have a single-clause Bill introduced abolishing the rate limit, and Mr. Lewis at once took steps to have such a clause added to the Board's Bill.

On November 28th Mr. Lewis introduced the Bill, which was backed by Mr. H. A. L. Fisher, President of the Board of Education, and by Dr. Addison, Minister of Health. In moving its Second

REMOVAL OF THE RATE LIMITATION

Reading, which was carried without dissent on December 2nd, Mr. Lewis said: "I hope the House will allow this Bill to be read a second time. The Board of Education have been receiving most urgent representations by deputation and otherwise from all parts of the country from library authorities who complain that owing to the limitation of the penny rate they are wholly unable to pay any war bonuses to their staffs. There are many of them who are actually unable to buy any new books. There are some who do not know how to meet the expenses of the current year, and I know of cases in which branch libraries have had to be closed. We ask for a second reading of this Bill in order to remove the existing limitation of rate. There is also the further point that the Carnegie Trustees have been establishing libraries in rural areas at their own expense, but they are only able to carry on for a term of years, and their work is brought to a standstill owing to the fact that under the existing law it is doubtful whether any county authority can undertake to carry on the work. We want to make that point perfectly clear."

By diligent watching, Mr. Lewis was able to bring on the Committee stage of the Bill on December 11th, an unexpected gap of two hours of Government time having occurred, which he promptly made use of. Sir F. Banbury (now Lord Banbury), who had taken a prominent part in blocking the various Bills promoted by the Library Association, opposed the Bill clause by clause, and moved that the rate be limited to twopence. He was not successful, and the Bill was read a third time and passed. In the House of Lords certain drafting amendments were made, firstly, making it clear that County Councils as public library authorities shall possess borrowing powers similar to those possessed by all other library authorities; secondly, to put an area which has established a public library under a local Act in substantially the same position as an area which has established a library under the Public Libraries Acts; and, thirdly, to remove all doubt whether the term "borough" includes a metropolitan borough. These amendments were agreed to, and the Act received the Royal Assent on December 23, 1919.

When the adjourned meeting of the Executive Committee of the Library Association took place on December 12th, Mr. Ballinger, who presided on that occasion, was able to inform the members that the Bill had passed its Third Reading on the previous evening.

Thus, after twenty years' agitation, within less than a month from its introduction, there was placed upon the statute book a measure which relieved the library service of England from the crippling restrictions which had hampered its development since its inception and altered the whole outlook of those in whose hands its administration and future progress lie. In addition to removing the rate limit, the Act gave an indemnity as to audit to those progressive municipalities which

REMOVAL OF THE RATE LIMITATION

had been compelled to spend on their libraries more than the proceeds of the rate they were entitled to raise during the current year of the passing of the Act.

In addition to removing the rate limit and empowering County Councils to adopt the Act, the Act of 1919 enabled any library authority, other than the Council of a county borough, to agree to relinquish their powers and duties in favour of the County Council. Local education authorities were enabled to delegate all their powers under the Public Libraries Acts, except the power of raising a rate or borrowing money, to the Education Committee established under the Education Acts, 1870–1918. Museums established under the Museums and Gymnasiums Act of 1891 were transferred to the library authority of the district to be maintained by it.

In 1920 the rate limit for public libraries in Ireland was raised from one penny in the pound to threepence, with a further provision that the said limit of threepence may, with the consent of the Local Government Board, be exceeded to the extent of threepence in the pound, i.e. to the extent of sixpence in all.

In the same year an Act to amend the Public Libraries (Scotland) Act, 1887, raising the rate limit to threepence in the pound was passed. The Bill, backed by the Secretary of State for Scotland, as passed by the House of Commons contained a proviso similar to that embodied in the Irish Act

THE PUBLIC LIBRARY MOVEMENT

enabling the rate to be raised to sixpence with the consent of the Secretary of State for Scotland or of the Scottish Board of Health, but this proviso was deleted by the House of Lords. Why the invidious distinction between Ireland and Scotland in the matter of rating as compared with England should have been made is altogether inexplicable, particularly in view of the pronouncement of the Secretary of State for Scotland to the effect that it was unthinkable that there should be a different law in this matter on the two sides of the Border.

The county library system in Northern Ireland was established under the Public Libraries (Northern Ireland) Act, 1924, wherein County Councils were given power, by resolution specifying the area to which the resolution extends, to adopt the Public Libraries (Ireland) Acts, 1855–1920, for all or any of the rural districts in their county, and to become the library authority therefor. The powers of any Rural District Council to adopt or carry into execution the Public Libraries Acts were withdrawn, and the County Councils were enabled to take over and administer any existing libraries. The County Council were empowered to appoint a County Library Committee which should submit their actions to the County Council for approval. Power was given under this Act to the Council or Commissioners of any urban district or town having adopted the Act to relinquish to the County Council all or any of their powers thereunder, the County Council to take over the administration of the

REMOVAL OF THE RATE LIMITATION

library. The expenses of management incurred by the County Council to be defrayed out of the county funds, the amount required being raised by means of the poor rate equally over so much of the county as comprises the county districts and towns as respects which the County Council is for the time being carrying the Acts into execution. The amount to be raised not to exceed in any one financial year one penny in the pound on the rateable value, provided that in an urban district or town where the County Council are acting as library authority the sum may be raised to twopence in the pound.

In the Irish Free State the county libraries are managed under the Local Government Act, 1925, of the Oireachtas of Seorstát Eireann, Section 65 of which gives power to the Council of any county by resolution to adopt the Public Libraries (Ireland) Act, 1855, for the whole or any specified part of the county, exclusive of any urban district, and to become thereby the library authority for the area covered by the resolution. By the same Act the County Council may arrange with an Urban District Council in its area, or any county borough adjoining, for the use of the library building or library facilities of any public library in such district or borough upon agreed terms. An Urban District Council may relinquish its powers in favour of the County Council. When a County Council is the library authority for two or more separate areas in the county the County Council may, with consent

THE PUBLIC LIBRARY MOVEMENT

of the Ministry of Home Affairs, amalgamate such areas. Power is given to the library authority to incur expenditure out of the library rate on the provision of public lectures and exhibitions (whether free or otherwise) and of libraries in schools.

CHAPTER X

RECENT LEGISLATION

The Public Libraries Act (Northern Ireland), 1924, amending the Public Libraries (Ireland) Acts, 1855–1920, in their application to Northern Ireland, was passed on May 29, 1924, and applies to the six counties Antrim, Armagh, Down, Fermanagh, Londonderry, and Tyrone.

The Act empowers County Councils, by resolution, to become library authorities for their areas, and abolishes the powers of Rural District Councils established by the Act of 1902, and directs that in any rural district where a public library has been established it must be carried on by the County Council. Provision is made for the appointment of county library committees with powers to co-opt, each rural district to have adequate representation. County Councils may borrow for library purposes. Funds for library purposes are to be raised by means of the poor rate, limited to one penny in the pound and spread equally over the rural districts. In an urban district or town where the County Council is acting as library authority the rate may be raised to a limit of threepence in the pound. The Act does not apply to the county boroughs, Belfast and Londonderry. The county library system is now well organized in Northern Ireland.

By the Irish Free State Local Government Act,

1925, Rural District and Urban Councils (except in the County of Dublin) are given authority to relinquish their powers in the matter of libraries to County Councils, who may adopt the Acts of 1855 to 1920.

The Rating and Valuation Act, 1925, Section 2 (6), provides that in England expenses incurred under the Public Libraries Acts, 1892–1919, by the library authority (not being a County Council) of a library district, being a parish, shall, instead of being defrayed out of a rate raised in manner provided by paragraph (c) of subsection (1) of Section 18 of the Public Libraries Act, 1892 (i.e. the poor rate), be levied in each library district by the rating authority together with, and as an additional item of, the general rate.

The passing of the Local Government (Scotland) Act, 1929, has considerably affected Scottish libraries in the matter of rating, as we have seen when dealing with the Education (Scotland) Act, 1918, under which county libraries are administered. Some burghs which have established libraries under the Public Libraries Acts, and are already rated for their upkeep, have also been rated under the county schemes by the education authorities. This has caused a good deal of resentment in the burghs so affected, particularly in certain cases where the burgh authorities consider that they are not receiving an equivalent service in respect of the additional rating. The county education authorities not unnaturally desire to establish schemes

RECENT LEGISLATION

covering their whole area, while the burgh library authorities within the county who have established and maintained their libraries in many cases for a long period are equally desirous of retaining the management of them in their own hands. It is a matter in which it is hoped that co-operation between the authorities concerned will lead to a satisfactory solution of the difficulty.

By Section 41 (1) of the above Act it is provided that the Libraries Acts shall not be adopted in a landward parish or the landward part of a parish except with the sanction of the County Council.

Paragraph (2) of the same section provides that "every estimate of sums required by a Committee under the Public Libraries Acts shall be subject to the approval of the Town Council or County Council, as the case may be."

In the Isle of Man public libraries are administered under the Local Government Consolidation Act, 1916.

The first Act for establishing public libraries was passed by the House of Keys in 1885. It was a measure founded on the model of the English Acts, embodying similar provisions, including the penny-rate limitation, which, unfortunately for the success of the libraries, is still in operation. The Act of 1885 was repealed by the Local Government Act, 1886, which incorporated the provisions of the 1885 Act in paragraphs 220–26. This Act was in turn superseded by the 1916 Act above mentioned.

Control of the libraries is vested in the Town Commissioners, or in a Committee appointed by them, with power to provide all things necessary for the establishment of libraries, including the appointment of salaried officers and servants, the making of rules and regulations, etc.

For the adoption of the Acts the Chairman of Commissioners of any town may, on his own initiative, or on receiving a requisition signed by ten ratepayers, ascertain the opinions of the majority of the ratepayers by issuing a voting paper to each. If consent to adopt the Acts is not accorded, no further proceedings can be taken for a twelvemonth.

CHAPTER XI

PUBLIC LIBRARY PROGRESS AND POLICY

In the foregoing six chapters we have given a chronological account of the legislation concerning public libraries, showing the gradual growth of library law in this country from the meagre and utterly inadequate financial provisions of the Act of 1850 to the more generous recognition of the needs of public libraries accorded by the 1919 Act, which abolished the rate limit, and provided for the establishment of county libraries throughout the land.

Hindrances to Progress

Progress in adopting the Acts was at first very slow. Prior to the passing of the Act of 1855, permitting the levying of a penny rate, only about a dozen localities had ventured to put the Act into operation. The obvious inadequacy of the halfpenny rate to provide even buildings and maintenance—which was all that the Act allowed, as no books could be purchased—must have deterred many municipalities from attempting to establish a library. The policy of relying upon donations for the supply of books was a most mistaken one. No library dependent upon such a haphazard arrangement could ever have functioned properly. It made the public library dependent upon the charity of philan-

THE PUBLIC LIBRARY MOVEMENT

thropic individuals, and so had a tendency to restrict their use to those who were prepared to accept such charity. Under such a plan no continuity of policy in administration was possible.

Although the policy of the halfpenny rate and donations of books was deliberately adopted by the promoters of the Act in order to facilitate its passage through Parliament by the modesty of their requirements, and though they were warranted in thinking that donations in sufficient quantity would be forthcoming to justify a start in establishing the libraries, they evidently did not foresee the great demand for books which followed their establishment, nor did they reckon upon the extraordinary opposition that was encountered when the Bill was before Parliament. This factious opposition came from a quarter where it might least have been expected, from educated persons, representatives of universities, and others who ought to have known better. The idea, however, still prevailed in many minds that to provide education for the working-classes and books for their reading was a risky proceeding, inasmuch as it would tend to give them ideas "above their station in life," and unfit them for their life's work. It was urged, indeed, by more than one objector that if lectures were to be given in connection with the libraries they would become centres of unrest, if not hotbeds of sedition. Opposition came, too, from those who were not readers themselves, and did not see why others should want to read—men like Colonel Sibthorp, who confessed that when a student at the University he had hated reading and could not understand the desire or the need for it.

The cumbrous nature of the machinery for determining adoption or rejection of the Act, a method which was forced upon the promoters of the Acts during their passage through Parliament, proved a considerable stumbling-block to their adoption. It allowed the growth of organized opposition, frequently resulting in the breaking up of the statutory meetings by hooligan mobs, systematic canvassing of voters by parties interested in the rejection of the Acts, who urged the great increase in their rates that would follow adoption, as a reason for rejection, and very often carried the day.

Not every locality that adopted the Acts, however, took the necessary steps to put them into operation. According to the statistics given in the Report of the Public Libraries Committee of 1927, quite a number of places were then in that position—smaller urban districts and parishes for the most part—some of which had made arrangements with other authorities. Whether this was owing to fuller consideration and recognition of the inadequacy of the rating powers it is impossible to say. On the other hand, a number of authorities in large towns, having had this inadequacy demonstrated by experience, took steps to secure by local Acts increased rating powers, and in some cases obtained by this means complete freedom from rate limitation. This form of legislation, however, proved very costly,

THE PUBLIC LIBRARY MOVEMENT

and none but the larger municipalities could afford it.

After the establishment of the earlier libraries, the primitive methods of book service in operation frequently acted adversely on the use made of them by borrowers. The writer remembers at least one library where the issue counter was exactly similar to a railway ticket office at which a borrower handed in a slip with a list of books wanted. With this in hand the assistant went to the shelves, and, if the borrower was lucky, he might be given one or other of the books asked for; if not, his slip was handed back to him with the laconic remark, "All out." After a few experiences of this sort, small wonder that the borrower gave up the attempt to get books at all. These and other crude methods were not uncommon. An improvement came with the invention of the indicator, which certainly was a saver of time over the application slip and ledger charging, but still was a barrier between the reader and his books, which he had no opportunity of examining before borrowing. There were several varieties of these indicators in use in different libraries, an account of which is given in an article by J. D. Brown on library appliances (*Library*, Vol. 3, 1891). The most important advance in library service came with the introduction of the system of "open access" at Clerkenwell Public Library by J. D. Brown in 1894. This system of admitting the borrower to the shelves to choose his own books met with considerable opposition at first, but has now become almost universal, and has proved a very great boon to readers.

The policy of erecting large central buildings which would be an ornament to the town to which they were gifted, but which the income from the penny rate was insufficient to maintain and at the same time provide the books essential for a library, had a disastrous result on the progress of the library service. Even in places where a good stock of books was provided for the library when first started in a central part of the town, the demand for branch libraries in the suburbs led to the erection of buildings for which no capital sum was available. Borrowing had to be resorted to, and provision made for a sinking fund to repay the money borrowed, thus depleting the fund for book purchase and rebinding, which in almost every case was just whatever was left over after providing for the maintenance of buildings, cleaning, lighting, heating, and staffing them.

Mr. Ernest A. Savage, in a memorandum which he prepared for the Departmental Committee on Public Libraries in 1927, and which he has given me permission to use, gave statistics showing the extent to which the provision of branches in a library under his charge had affected adversely the book service by expanding the services beyond the means available for their proper maintenance. For a number of years the library service consisted of one central library only, which during those years had an average annual issue of over 600,000

THE PUBLIC LIBRARY MOVEMENT

volumes. When two branches were added the total issue of central and branches in the first year actually fell by over 58,000, and in the third year was still over 5,000 fewer than before the branches were established. Twenty-five years afterwards, when the central and five branches were in operation, the issue at the central had fallen to 254,000 and the total for the six libraries was 877,000, or only about 68,000 more than the average which the central alone had maintained for years. Obviously the provision of branches in the endeavour to increase the utility of the service had so depleted the book fund that comparatively little advantage had been gained. The additional cost of maintenance and staffing of the additional buildings had acted adversely on the total stock of books available. The library income had grown somewhat with the natural increase in the amount produced by the penny rate owing to the growth of the town, but had not grown in proportion to the additional demands made upon it. The book-stock of the central fell from 56,679 in 1904 to 38,905 in 1923, and the combined stocks of the central and branches fell during the same period by 41,267 volumes. There had been expansion of the area of service beyond the means of supporting it out of a fixed income.

Additional statistics showed that the proportion of the annual incomes of public libraries expended on books and bookbinding ranged from 26 per cent. of the income to less than 7 per cent. The depreciation of stock being calculated at about one-third of income, "any library spending less than this amount on books and bookbinding is inadequately financed, heavily in debt, or too heavily burdened with administrative expenses."

"In the *Departmental Report on the Teaching of English* (1921), p. 330, juvenile libraries are recommended. The Report of the Carnegie U.K. Trustees (1921–23) shows that the provision of juvenile books in public libraries ranges from one book for every eight children in elementary schools to one book for every three children."

It is obvious from these figures that the book supply in most libraries is quite inadequate for the demands made upon it.

The endeavour to maintain issues with an insufficient supply of books has frequently resulted in the books in stock being kept too long in circulation, and so becoming dirty and dilapidated from much handling. The result has been that borrowers who do not care to handle dirty books have been deterred from using the library, and those who are less fastidious, seeing many books in bad condition, have taken little care of them or of those that are new and clean.

The practice of placing expensive books in the Reference Department, not because they really belong to that department on account of their contents, but on the score of price, with the view of preserving them, has had the result not only of restricting their use, but also of locking up capital that might be better employed.

THE PUBLIC LIBRARY MOVEMENT

Another policy which has had a bad effect on the efficiency of the public library as an educational institution is that of buying a number of low-priced books in preference to fewer and better books, with a view to increasing the number of books in stock and enlarging the circulation. The practice, too, of delaying the purchase of books until they are available secondhand is in many cases a questionable economy, since by the time they are to be had in this form the immediate interest in their subject has frequently passed, and they are apt to lie on the shelves unused. These endeavours after economy are the result of insufficient funds. Unfortunately they penalise the readers of good books in the effort to provide something for the many. It has been said that "public libraries too often reflect the low literary standards of the communities in which they are established" (*Report of Committee on the Teaching of English*, 1921, p. 330). The fault of the community is not so much in possessing a low literary standard as in having too low a financial standard of what is required for the maintenance of a properly equipped public library. Until 1919 that standard was the product of a penny rate, resulting not only in stinting the book supply, but in causing the library authority to recruit its library staff with young people having too low a standard of education to be able to assist readers in their choice of books, since the authority could not offer a salary sufficient to attract to the service better educated persons, and were not in a position to insist upon a higher standard of education in those admitted to the service.

The position in this respect has considerably improved of late, particularly in the larger libraries, where a university matriculation standard is now required for appointment on staffs. Under the penny-rate régime the Library Association was obliged to regulate the standard of entrance to its examinations by the standard of education of the only recruits to the library service which library authorities could afford to pay. A vicious circle was thus created which the Association had not felt justified in attempting to break until the rate restriction was removed. The possession of a matriculation standard of education or its equivalent is now a condition precedent of entrance to the examinations of the Association, and a more highly educated personnel of library staffs will gradually come to be universal. Formerly it was the practice of many authorities to pay as high a salary as they could afford to a chief librarian, and to appoint as cheap assistants as they could obtain on the principle of "state salary required." Parsimony of that character could not but result in an inefficient service, harmful alike to the users of the library and to the persons employed in it.

The recently revised syllabus of the examinations of the Library Association (see the *Library Association Year Book*, 1932), which will come into operation in May 1933, is based upon a graduated system of examination, elementary, intermediate,

THE PUBLIC LIBRARY MOVEMENT

and final, which will very materially improve the standard of qualification for the library profession. The Association in 1914 established a Professional Register of qualified librarians, graded as Fellows and Associates, a list of whom will be found in the *Year Book* already referred to. Library authorities should see to it that only persons entered on the Register are appointed to responsible posts in their libraries, and that those appointed to subordinate posts are in membership of the Association, since membership is now an essential qualification for entrance to the examinations, success in which alone qualifies for registration.

A short account of the School of Librarianship at University College, London, will be found in the section dealing with Training for Librarianship. The school is doing good work in training assistants in London and neighbourhood and those who can afford residence and tuition there. The educational work of the Library Association is carried on through the medium of correspondence courses, but something more practical is required. The establishment of a college or school for the higher technical training of librarians in connection with a large library actually serving a particular community is a desideratum. The students of such a college, selected on the results of the Library Association examinations, should be awarded bursaries enabling them to attend the college from any part of the British Isles. Working in an up-to-date library, the students would obtain a thorough training in practical bibliography, business methods, and library economy, such as is only to be acquired in the school of experience. Many of those who pass the written examinations have but an indifferent knowledge of practical bookbinding and the care of books, the preparation of catalogues for the printer, proof-reading, and other technical details of a librarian's work. The college and its library should be thoroughly equipped in all departments, including a business office, a cataloguing room, a bindery, an information file, and a well-stocked library of bibliographical reference.

Mr. Savage concludes his memorandum, which embodies the points we have dealt with above, with a summary of reforms which he deems necessary in the library service in England, with all of which we heartily agree. These are:

(a) Adequate stocks of books, particularly in home reading libraries.
(b) Higher standards in book service; that is, more careful selection of books, based on closer observation of use.
(c) Higher education, and more practical education, for those employed in libraries.
(d) Governing bodies elected and selected especially to manage public libraries; the Scottish constitution of such bodies being taken as a model.

Under the Scottish Acts the membership of the Library Committee must consist of one-half town councillors and one-half householders chosen by the Town Council. Under the English Acts Town

THE PUBLIC LIBRARY MOVEMENT

Councils have power to co-opt householders to the Library Committee, but do not always do so. We regard the power of co-option of persons specially interested in libraries as a very valuable provision. Members of Town Councils, especially in England, are frequently elected on political grounds, and may or may not have special qualifications for service on library committees, but co-opted members are, or should be, selected with such qualifications in view. In Scotland this is invariably the case, and as the co-opted members are frequently reappointed from year to year, a desirable continuity of policy is more readily assured. In addition, in Scotland the Library Committee is an *ad hoc* body[1], and except that its yearly estimates have to be approved by the Town Council, and that it has no power to borrow money, it is practically autonomous, and its proceedings do not require ratification by the Council. Administration is thus more rapid in operation, the decisions of the Committee not being subject to revision or overturn by the larger body of the Council not so well acquainted with library requirements and policy.

Factors making for Progress

We have seen that in the early years of the movement the progress was slow so far as the adoption of the Acts and the putting of them into operation were concerned. After the passing of the Act of

[1] Owing to the additional duties now assigned to Town Councils necessitating delegation of their powers to Committees, these Committees are becoming more and more *ad hoc* bodies.

PUBLIC LIBRARY PROGRESS AND POLICY

1855 the pace of adoption was somewhat accelerated, and by the time when the Library Association was founded in 1877, eighty adoptions had been secured. From that time onward, progress became more rapid and polls of the ratepayers were frequent, resulting in many adoptions, but also in not a few rejections. London, in particular, was slow to adopt the Acts. Lubbock's Act of 1887 gave a decided impetus towards adoption, and many libraries were founded in celebration of Queen Victoria's jubilee. The passing of the Education Act of 1870 was now beginning to have an effect by creating a body of readers with a demand for reading facilities. Prejudice against the library movement was dying out through the spread of education, and the propaganda work of the Library Association was having its effect. But the most important factor in the progress of the movement at this period (1880–1900) was the princely generosity of Mr. Andrew Carnegie and Mr. J. Passmore Edwards in making grants to a great many municipalities for the building and equipment of libraries. Up to 1897 Mr. Carnegie's gifts were confined to Scottish libraries, but later were extended to other parts of the United Kingdom. His crowning benefaction was the creation of the Carnegie United Kingdom Trust, through which libraries have benefited enormously owing to the enlightened policy pursued by the Trustees.

CHAPTER XII

THE LIBRARY ASSOCIATION

The foundation of the Library Association marks an epoch in the history of the public library movement. During the twenty-seven years from the passing of Ewart's Act of 1850 until the formation of the Association there had been about eighty adoptions of that Act. In the next twenty years well over 200 library authorities took steps to provide public libraries. This rapid spread of the movement, which was largely due to the propaganda work of the Association, was greatly accelerated towards the end of the period mentioned by the benefactions of Mr. Andrew Carnegie, Mr. J. Passmore Edwards, and other generous donors of funds for the building of libraries. The Association became the centre of the movement, focussing the efforts of its promoters and giving to their efforts a driving power that was lacking before, inasmuch as it united, as its constitution provides, all persons interested in libraries as well as those actually engaged in library work. In its early days, as will be seen, it attracted to its membership, in addition to the most eminent librarians of the time, many scholars of repute, literary men, local administrators, and book-lovers. For many years a group of the outstanding aldermen and councillors of Manchester, Sheffield, and other cities were prominent in its counsels. Such men as

THE LIBRARY ASSOCIATION

Chancellor Christie, Sir William H. Bailey, Alderman Harry Rawson, Alderman Southern, Alderman Brittain, and Alderman Abbott did much to help forward the library movement by linking up the Association with the Municipal Corporations Association, and other representative bodies, by interviewing M.P.s and other prominent men of affairs, and securing their interest and co-operation.

The Association was inaugurated at the Conference of Librarians held in London in October 1877. In January of that year Mr. Edward B. Nicholson, Librarian of the London Institution, contributed an article to *The Academy* on the Report of the Philadelphia Conference of Librarians, held in October 1876, which resulted in the formation of the American Library Association, urging the advisability of holding a similar meeting in London. On February 16, 1877, he wrote to *The Times*, again advocating an international conference. In the following April he invited the principal metropolitan librarians to meet at the London Library. That meeting unanimously resolved that a conference should be held in the autumn, and appointed an organizing committee, with Mr. Nicholson as Secretary.

Invitations were issued to all libraries in Great Britain and Ireland, as well as to the principal libraries on the Continent and in America. The Conference was held in the London Institution, and was attended by 218 persons, including seventeen representatives from the United States, among whom was Melvil Dewey.[1] Their keen interest, enthusiasm, and assiduous attendance, joined to their newly gained experience of similar gatherings in America, did much to secure the success of the meeting. The French Government deputed a special commission of four members to report on the Conference. The German and Greek Governments were also represented. Of the 139 delegates representing libraries, there came from Belgium, Italy, and Australia, one each; from Denmark, two; from Great Britain and Ireland, 113.

Mr. John Winter Jones, Principal Librarian of the British Museum, presided, and Mr. Nicholson and Mr. Henry R. Tedder, Librarian of the Athenæum Club, London, acted as Joint Secretaries. The Conference sat from October 2nd to the 5th, and at an evening meeting on the last day, presided over by Mr. James T. Clark, Keeper of the Advocates' Library, Edinburgh, Mr. Robert Harrison moved, and Mr. Henry Stevens seconded, and it was unanimously resolved: "That a Library Association of the United Kingdom be founded." A constitution had been drafted, and was submitted to and adopted by the meeting. The constitution provided that the title of the Association should be the "The Library Association of the United Kingdom"; that its main object should be "to unite all persons engaged or interested in library work, for the purpose of promoting the

---

[1] Since this was written Dr. Dewey has passed away at the ripe age of eighty years.

THE LIBRARY ASSOCIATION

best possible administration of existing libraries, and the formation of new ones where desirable. It shall also aim at the encouragement of bibliographical research." Persons engaged in the administration of a library could become members by payment of the annual subscription. Any person not actually engaged in library administration could be elected a subscribing member by a vote of upwards of three-fourths of subscribing members at any monthly meeting after due notice. The number of persons so elected was limited to two-fifths of the whole membership. This limitation was removed in 1889.

It is important to note that from its inception the Association has never been exclusively an association of librarians. It has always been far removed from being a close corporation, or, shall I say, a trade union established for the furtherance solely of the interests of its individual members, although, as we shall see later on, "the promotion of whatever may tend to the improvement of the position and the qualifications of librarians" afterwards became one of the purposes of the incorporated Association. That the Association as founded, and as it remains to the present day, was not a close corporation is borne out by the fact that out of the 218 members of the inaugural Conference no fewer than forty-five were not librarians, but non-professional persons interested in the work of libraries or in bibliographical research. These included such well-known names as William Blades, Professor W.

THE PUBLIC LIBRARY MOVEMENT

Stanley Jevons, Rev. W. D. Macray, Professor Henry Morley, Rev. Mark Pattison, Rev. Charles Rogers, Henry Stevens, and Cornelius Walford, to name but a few.

The subjects dealt with at the inaugural Conference were mainly technical, covering many points in library economy, such as book selection, cataloguing, classification, binding, etc. They were well focussed in the presidential address delivered by Mr. Winter Jones, which forms an admirable summary of the whole duty of a librarian, embodying the result of his wide experience and catholic outlook on library administration. The question of printing the catalogue of the British Museum was fully discussed and advocated. A rather more ambitious project was submitted by Mr. Cornelius Walford, viz. the proposal for the compilation and printing of a general catalogue of English literature, which still remains a counsel of perfection. The question of co-operative cataloguing was introduced by M. Depping, of the Bibliothèque Ste-Geneviève, Paris, with the suggestion that if the system were to be given a trial, a commencement should be made with the cataloguing of the tools of the librarian, "which every library is obliged to possess, because none can do without them, viz. bibliographical works." One of the most important contributions to the Conference was the paper read by Mr. W. H. K. Wright, Librarian of Plymouth, "On the Best Means of Promoting the Free Library Movement in Small Towns and Villages." He sug-

THE LIBRARY ASSOCIATION

gested the union of small towns around a central one within a radius of, say, twenty miles for mutual help. His second suggestion was to utilize schools as branch or general libraries, and a third was that an effort should be made to secure State aid in the formation and support of free libraries and museums. He prophesied that "with such State aid, ere another generation shall have passed away, the free library movement will have spread like a great tidal-wave over the whole country, every town, village, and hamlet participating in its advantages." His prophecy took more than one generation to reach its fulfilment, however, perhaps because the State aid was not forthcoming. In discussing the paper, Professor Leone Levi remarked that the term "free" applied to libraries established under the Acts furnished unwilling ratepayers with the objection that others had to pay for those who used them. Mr. Yates, of Leeds, also thought the term "free library" unfortunate. He believed that it deterred some people from using such libraries, conveying an impression that they were intended for the sole use of the working-man. He preferred the American term, "public library."

At the final sitting of the Conference, after the adoption of the constitution of the Association, Mr. John Winter Jones was elected President; Mr. J. T. Clark, Rev. H. O. Coxe, Bodley's Librarian, and Rev. Dr. J. A. Malet, Librarian of Trinity College, Dublin, were elected Vice-Presidents; Mr. Robert Harrison, Librarian of the

THE PUBLIC LIBRARY MOVEMENT

London Library, was chosen as Treasurer; and Mr. Nicholson and Mr. Tedder, the Conference Secretaries, became the Joint Secretaries of the Association. In addition to these office-bearers, the first council consisted of the following:

W. E. A. Axon, Secretary of the Manchester Literary Club.
Francis T. Barrett, Mitchell Library, Glasgow.
George Bullen, Keeper of the Printed Books, British Museum.
Peter Cowell, Public Library, Liverpool.
Andrea Crestadoro, Public Library, Manchester.
Richard Garnett, Superintendent of the Reading Room, British Museum.
J. D. Mullins, Public Libraries, Birmingham.
W. H. Overall, Corporation Library, London.
J. Small, University Library, Edinburgh.
W. S. W. Vaux, Royal Asiatic Society, London.
Benjamin R. Wheatley, Royal Medical and Chirurgical Society, London.
James Yates, Public Libraries, Leeds.

No council more thoroughly representative of the élite of the British librarianship of that day could have been appointed.

It was decided that the first annual meeting of the Association should be held at Oxford.

THE OFFICIAL JOURNAL

It was further resolved that the *American Library Journal* be adopted as the official journal of the Association, conjointly with the American Library Association, the title being changed to *The Library*

THE LIBRARY ASSOCIATION

Journal. This joint arrangement lasted for a few years, but it was soon found to be inconvenient that all accounts of the proceedings of the Library Association should reach members only from America, and in 1880 a separate monthly report, to include announcements, etc., and to act as a medium of communication between members was established, entitled *Monthly Notes*, under the editorship of Mr. William Brace and Mr. Ernest C. Thomas. *The Library Journal*, nevertheless, remained the official journal until 1882. *Monthly Notes* was succeeded in 1884 by *The Library Chronicle*, which, edited by Mr. Thomas, continued until 1888. In 1889 *The Library*, founded, owned, and edited by Mr. (afterwards Sir) John Y. W. MacAlister, was adopted as the official organ of the Association, and continued as such until December 1898. A section of it was entitled "The Library Chronicle." Mr. MacAlister was appointed Joint Secretary along with Mr. Thomas at the Glasgow meeting in 1888. He at once threw himself with characteristic energy and enthusiasm into his secretarial duties. Mr. Thomas acted along with him until 1890, when he resigned. Mr. MacAlister held the post of Hon. Secretary until the end of 1898, and it was due to his untiring efforts that in that year the Association was granted a Royal Charter of Incorporation. It was then felt that the newly incorporated Association should possess an official organ of its own. An endeavour was made to come to an arrangement with Mr. MacAlister for the transfer of his property in *The Library* to the Association, but this failed. The *Library Association Record* was then founded in January 1899, under the editorship of Mr. Henry Guppy, Librarian (then Joint-Librarian) of the John Rylands Library, Manchester. Mr. MacAlister's *Library* was revived in a second series in December 1899, as a more purely bibliographical magazine, and since 1920 has been amalgamated with the *Transactions* of the Bibliographical Society. Mr. Guppy edited the *Library Association Record* with much acceptance until April 1903, when, owing to the pressure of other duties, he was obliged to tender his resignation, receiving the heartiest thanks of the Association for his able and self-sacrificing labours. After Mr. Guppy's resignation the Council decided that the *Record* should be edited by the Publications Committee, the conduct of the various departments being allotted to sectional editors who had agreed to undertake the work. This arrangement continued until 1923, when the *Record* ceased to be a monthly publication, and was issued quarterly under the editorship of Mr. Arundell Esdaile, Secretary of the British Museum, its present editor. Monthly publication was resumed in January 1931.

ANNUAL MEETINGS

The first annual meeting of the newly formed Association was held at Oxford on the first three days of October 1878. Mr. Winter Jones was unable, owing to ill-health, to occupy the presi-

THE LIBRARY ASSOCIATION

dential chair, and his place was taken by the Rev. H. O. Coxe, Bodley's Librarian, one of the Vice-Presidents. The Council submitted a Report on its work during the year, showing how interest in the objects of the Association had been maintained by the holding of monthly meetings in London, at which papers and suggestions on all subjects relating to the aims of the Association were considered, and library appliances and designs were examined. The inaugural Conference of 1877 had appointed several committees to examine and report upon various projects, and reports from these committees were submitted and discussed.

The Report submitted by the Metropolitan Free Libraries Committee detailed the endeavours that had been made to secure the adoption of the Acts in London. The Committee had appealed to seven Vestries, but were unable to report any success, although they had been untiring in their efforts. In the cases where Vestries had ascertained the opinion of the ratepayers the result was a decided rejection.

The Committee on a General Catalogue of English Literature presented a preliminary report, embodying a digest of the evidence given before the Society of Arts in March 1878 on the subject of a Universal Catalogue of Printed Books. The report indicated the lines on which such a catalogue of English literature should, in their opinion, be constructed, but regretted that the authorities of the British Museum could not at present see their way to take part in the preparation of the proposed

THE PUBLIC LIBRARY MOVEMENT

catalogue. Without their co-operation the difficulties of the task would be infinitely increased.

The Report of the Committee on Poole's Index to Periodical Literature showed that twenty members had undertaken to index twenty-four English periodicals which the Committee considered it desirable to include in the Index.

In addition to a number of papers on technical subjects, such as indicators, stock-books, accessions-catalogues, book-scales and size-notation, bindings and their preservation, etc., contributions on topics of more general interest were read and discussed. These included the working of subscription libraries in connection with public libraries, cathedral libraries, local collections in provincial libraries, old parochial libraries in England and Wales, the signification of libraries by Professor Leopold Seligman, and the Universal Postal Union and International Copyright by Henry Stevens, of Vermont. All these papers were printed *in extenso* with the discussions thereon in the handsome volume of *Transactions and Proceedings*, edited by the Secretaries, Mr. Tedder and Mr. Thomas, and published for the Association at the Chiswick Press.

We have given this somewhat lengthy account of the proceedings to show the wide range of subjects that came under review at the first annual meeting, and to indicate how well the Association in its infant days endeavoured to fulfil the objects for which it had been founded.

These objects have been steadily kept in view at

THE LIBRARY ASSOCIATION

all subsequent annual meetings of the Association. Space cannot be given to a detailed account of these meetings to date, but some reference may be made to a few of the earlier meetings to show how enlightened a policy animated those who conducted the affairs of the Association in its earlier years.

At the second meeting, held in Manchester in 1879, Mr. E. B. Nicholson, who has the best claim to be considered the founder of the Association, read a well thought-out paper on the consolidation and amendment of the Public Libraries Acts for England. He pointed out how the very multiplicity of the Acts hindered their adoption, inasmuch as anyone who might wish to move in the matter must make himself acquainted with four separate Acts, a principal Act, and three amending Acts. Among the matters requiring amendment he suggested that power should be given to a municipality to levy an additional voluntary rate, and that Town Councils, Vestries, and Boards of Guardians should be given power to adopt the Acts. London should have special legislation and be treated as a unit, and the suggestion was made that the Metropolitan Board of Works should be authorized to levy a library rate. He was in favour of the inspection of public libraries, the inspectors to report yearly to Parliament.

Following on Mr. Nicholson's paper, it was resolved to endeavour to influence Parliament in favour of such an amendment of the law as would remedy the defects which had been pointed out at

THE PUBLIC LIBRARY MOVEMENT

the meeting, and to cause a Bill to be introduced for that purpose.

The Metropolitan Free Libraries Committee reported through the Council that they had merged the Committee in the Metropolitan Free Libraries Association, an association embracing all persons willing to pay a minimum yearly subscription of five shillings, with the Bishop of London as its President, and a long list of distinguished men on its Council. Its object was to obtain the consolidation and amendment of the Public Library Acts for England. Mr. Tedder and Mr. Nicholson had been appointed Treasurer and Secretary respectively. In 1880 the Council decided to join action with the Metropolitan Association in their efforts to get the Bill, which had been drafted by Messrs. Tedder and Nicholson, introduced into Parliament. The Bill was introduced by Sir John Lubbock (afterwards Lord Avebury) in January 1881, but was withdrawn owing to objections to certain of its proposals raised by the Birmingham and Manchester Library Authorities. It was again introduced in 1882 and 1883, but never reached a second reading, being either talked out or blocked.

The third annual meeting was held in Edinburgh in October 1880. At this meeting Mr. J. T. Clark, Keeper of the Advocates' Library, maintained the bibliographical traditions of the Association by contributing "Notes on Early Printing in Scotland, 1507–1600." Mr. Thomas Mason, then Assistant-Librarian at the Mitchell Library, Glasgow, gave an

THE LIBRARY ASSOCIATION

historical account, along with a statistical table, of the free libraries of Scotland. Mr. John Maclauchlan, Librarian and Curator of Dundee Library and Museum, read a paper on "How the Free Library System may be extended to Counties," a question which had been dealt with by Mr. Wright, of Plymouth, at the inaugural Conference in 1877, though on somewhat different lines. He outlined a scheme, the details of which were followed in almost every particular many years later when the county library system was inaugurated. His plan was to make a County Government Board the authority for adoption instead of individual parishes. A Library Board for the whole county would be elected either by the ratepayers or by a general local government board. A central office or depot for books should be acquired which would be a store-room and office only, not a library, thus saving the expense of extravagant buildings which had so frequently hampered the after-operations of many libraries. A twopenny rate would be required. He gave a detailed estimate of how a rate of twopence might be expended in the counties of Perthshire and Stirlingshire.

On the technical side of librarianship Mr. J. D. Mullins, Librarian of the Birmingham Public Libraries, contributed a paper on "The Librarian and His Work," in the course of which he dealt with the training of assistants. In the discussion which followed the reading of Mr. Mullins's paper, Mr. Harrison, Treasurer of the Association, pro-

THE PUBLIC LIBRARY MOVEMENT

posed a resolution standing in the name of Mr. Tedder, who was unable to be present: "That it is desirable that the Council of this Association should consider how library assistants may best be aided in their training in the general principles of their profession." The resolution was carried unanimously and led ultimately to the present successful scheme of examinations, and the granting of diplomas and certificates.

At the fourth meeting, held in London in September 1881, an important paper was contributed by Mr. W. E. A. Axon, Manchester, on "Legislation for Free Public Libraries." He claimed that the assumption that public libraries owe their right to exist to the passage of Ewart's Act of 1850 and subsequent Acts is a wrong one. Ewart's Act did not *create* the right, it *limited* it, while providing the machinery by which a town could make known its desire that such an institution should be established at the public cost. His contention was that if the existing Acts were expunged from the statute book, these institutions would still have the right to continue, and communities would still have the right to call new ones into existence. English town libraries existed centuries before there was any legislation on the subject. He instanced the Guildhall Library, the Norwich and Bristol Libraries, etc. No proposal, he maintained, for remodelling the Libraries Acts could be wholly satisfactory that did not restore to local representative bodies the right to establish libraries for the public good, and that

THE LIBRARY ASSOCIATION

did not allow each community to decide for itself the amount of money it was prepared to set apart for that higher education of the citizens, which can best be performed by the agency of large and well-managed public libraries.

At the fifth annual meeting held at Cambridge in 1882, from September 5th to the 8th, a number of historico-bibliographical papers were read. Dr. Richard Garnett gave a detailed account of the methods employed in the printing of the British Museum Catalogue and of the progress made in that great undertaking. Henry Bradshaw's presidential address dealt with the formation of libraries, giving a succinct account of Cambridge libraries and their founders. He also dealt with the primary duties of a librarian as one who saves the time of those who frequent his library by enlightened guidance. Mr. Henry R. Tedder contributed a paper on "Librarianship as a Profession," pointing out the essential qualifications required; the need of proper training for librarians like the members of other liberal professions, the duties of a librarian, his remuneration, and the employment of women as librarians, which last he heartily supported. On the subject of training he endeavoured to show that it is impossible to maintain a proper professional spirit without some sort of organized training, supported by a recognized system of preliminary examination.

Since 1882 the Association has continued to hold an Annual Conference at different towns in the

United Kingdom, with the exception of 1914, 1916, and 1918 during the Great War, when only the annual business meeting required under the constitution was held.

In 1892 the experiment was tried of holding a Conference abroad, and a visit was paid to Paris, which was greatly enjoyed. That meeting is of importance as having led to an important step in the direction of the training of library assistants through the reading of two papers by Miss M. S. R. James and Mr. John J. Ogle on the subject. The papers were again read at a meeting in Liverpool later in the year, and gave rise to a very full discussion, resulting in the appointment of a Committee to report on the matter, an account of which will be found under the section dealing with Training for Librarianship.

At the annual meeting in Belfast in September 1894, Mr. Charles Welch, Librarian of the Guildhall Library, London, contributed a paper on "The Public Library Movement in London; a Review of its Progress, and Suggestions for its Consolidation and Extension."[1] His paper was again read and discussed at a meeting at the Mansion House in London on October 18th.

In the course of his address, Mr. Welch drew attention to the slow progress of the movement in the Metropolis, pointing out that after the joint adoption of the Act in 1857 by the parishes of St. Margaret and St. John, Westminster, twenty-two

[1] *The Library*, 1895, pp. 97–109.

THE LIBRARY ASSOCIATION

years elapsed before another metropolitan library was started in the suburban parish of Richmond in 1879. Queen Victoria's jubilee in 1887 provided a stimulus to the movement for the adoption of the Acts, but whilst the movement spread rapidly in the rest of the country the Metropolis remained largely indifferent or hostile. Mr. Welch endeavoured to account for this attitude partly by the unwillingness of the sorely taxed ratepayers to agree to an increase of taxation for any purpose whatever. He went on to allege that there existed "a deep-seated objection held very widely among men of culture and lovers of good literature and loyal promoters of education, men whom it is of the highest importance to gain over to the support of the free library." He held that their opposition was based not upon the principle underlying library legislation, but upon its developments as seen in the present condition and management of the public libraries throughout the country. The gist of his argument, in support of which he quoted extracts from the speeches delivered in Parliament when the Ewart Act of 1850 was before the House of Commons, was to the effect that it was the intention of the promoters of the movement to provide for the education and intellectual advancement of the people, and only in a subsidiary degree for their "innocent recreation." He contended that the London libraries were not carrying out the clear intentions of the legislature, inasmuch as from statistics which he quoted it was shown that the issue of fiction, as compared with other classes of literature, reached a general average of 75 per cent., and in several districts of over 80 per cent. of the total issues. He held that the student had been ousted from his rightful place by the inordinate favour afforded to the demands of the general reader and the devourer of fiction.

Mr. Welch's strictures called forth a vigorous reply from Mr. Edward Foskett in a paper on "The Educational Value of the Public Library Movement,"[1] in which the writer showed that although the percentage of fiction borrowed was high as compared with the issues in other classes, it must not be assumed that the percentage of fiction in stock bore the same relation to the entire stock of the library. So far from the student being ousted by inordinate favour being shown to the devourer of fiction, the proportion of fiction in most libraries was not more than 30 per cent. of the total stock.

The fiction bogey which for years was paraded by detractors of the public library died hard. It had to be pointed out time after time that the large issue of fiction as compared with other classes of literature was easily explained by the fact that novels are quickly read and returned to be borrowed again by others, while with regard to non-fictional literature a borrower will retain a book for the full period of its loan.

[1] *The Library*, 1895, pp. 110–19.

THE LIBRARY ASSOCIATION

SECOND INTERNATIONAL CONFERENCE, 1897

At the Aberdeen annual meeting of the Association in 1893 the question of holding a joint meeting in this country with the American Library Association was mooted, and much friendly correspondence on the matter took place between the two associations during the next three years. At the 1896 Conference at Buxton congratulatory telegrams were exchanged, and it was finally arranged that a large number of American librarians and their friends would come to London in 1897. The idea of a joint meeting of the two associations developed into the larger scheme of an International Conference which it was considered would appropriately mark a date just twenty years after the first International Conference of Librarians in 1877.[1]

A representative Organizing Committee was formed, and invitations were issued to the Ministers of Public Instruction in Europe, and to all the great libraries of the world to send delegates. The Conference was held from July 13th to the 16th in the Council Chamber of the Corporation of the City of London at the Guildhall.

Delegates were present from nearly every civilized nation in the world, to the number of 641. The papers and discussions thereon were published in a handsome volume of *Transactions*. The presidential chair was occupied by Sir John Lubbock

[1] *Transactions and Proceedings of the Second International Library Conference*, 1897, Preface.

THE PUBLIC LIBRARY MOVEMENT

(Lord Avebury); Alderman Harry Rawson, of Manchester, acted as Chairman of the Organizing Committee, and Mr. H. R. Tedder and Mr. J. Y. W. MacAlister held the offices of Treasurer and General Secretary respectively.

Sir John Lubbock's introductory address dealt with the progress of the public library movement all over the world, with special reference to the United Kingdom. He showed that 350 places had adopted the Libraries Acts between 1850 and 1896. The libraries contained over 5,000,000 volumes, and their annual issues amounted to over twenty-seven millions. The programme of the Conference was a very full one, almost every aspect of library work being covered. An exhibition of library appliances formed an important feature of the Conference.

At the annual meeting of the Association held later in the year, the President, Mr. H. R. Tedder, in his inaugural address dealt with the history of the Association from 1877 to 1897. He claimed that the Association had promoted the growth of a common brotherhood among librarians of all degrees. Its influence had been great in bringing out a general recognition that librarianship is a profession, and not a mere employment which any more or less educated person may follow. The Association was peculiar in having so many non-librarian members—that is, men and women who either as members of library committees, as owners of libraries, or as bibliographers take a special

THE LIBRARY ASSOCIATION

interest in the work of libraries. The Association's influence in aiding the public library movement, in collecting and distributing information, in guiding public opinion, in giving library committees a higher standard of proficiency in the choice of librarians through the work of its Education Committee had been potent. Its efforts in the matter of the improvement of public library legislation had been of public importance. At the conclusion of his address, Mr. Tedder enumerated the qualifications which every librarian ought to possess. A good general education and a knowledge of languages is an essential preliminary qualification; next comes professional training, kept up by converse with fellow-workers. The study of bibliography is of paramount importance, nothing being more absurd than to think that it can only concern rare, old, and curious books. Love of books and reading is essential. The librarian must thoroughly know his own books so as to be able to help his readers, and must keep himself in touch with the progress of modern thought, so as to guide his committee in the selection of books.

CHARTER OF INCORPORATION

At a meeting of the Council of the Association held on Friday, March 29, 1895, Mr. MacAlister, the Hon. Secretary, proposed that steps should be taken to secure for the Association a Royal Charter of Incorporation.[1] He pointed out the advantages

[1] *The Library*, Vol. 7, 1895, p. 166.

THE PUBLIC LIBRARY MOVEMENT

to be derived from the possession of such a Charter. It would greatly enhance the prestige of the Association, and would enable it to hold property and to take legal proceedings, which it could not do as matters stood, unless upon the individual responsibility of its officers or other members. Lord Dufferin, the President, and Sir John Lubbock, a life-long friend of libraries and of the Association, had both kindly promised to aid in obtaining a Charter.

The Council approved the proposal and instructed Mr. MacAlister to ascertain the probable cost, and to report. He at once communicated with the Privy Council and the Home Office and ascertained that the cost in fees, etc., would amount to about £100. He obtained the promise of a number of subscriptions to an Incorporation fund, and was instructed to call a special meeting to decide the question as soon as the amount required was subscribed. Several meetings of the Association were held to consider the draft of a revised constitution which had been prepared by the Council. This was finally approved at a special general meeting on January 30, 1896. The draft constitution was submitted to the Privy Council and a somewhat lengthy correspondence followed. An official announcement appeared in *The London Gazette* of August 4th to the effect that the petition for the grant of a Charter had been presented to Her Majesty Queen Victoria on August 1st, and referred to a Committee of the Privy Council, with whom any objections had to be lodged by September 12th. Considerable delay

THE LIBRARY ASSOCIATION

occurred owing to some alterations having been suggested by the Privy Council, and the Charter was re-drafted by the Hon. Solicitor and the Hon. Secretary embodying the changes suggested, and sent to the Secretary of the Privy Council in 1897. It was not until May 9, 1898, that Mr. MacAlister was able to present to the first statutory general meeting of the Incorporated Association Her Majesty's Letters Patent under the Great Seal setting forth the Royal Charter of Incorporation which he had received from the Home Secretary. It was then moved and carried by acclamation:

"That the Fellows and Members of the Library Association gratefully accept the Royal Charter of Incorporation which Her Majesty the Queen has most graciously conferred upon them, and regard it as at once a gracious recognition of the work accomplished by the Association, and an incentive to still greater efforts in the future for the promotion of its objects."

The following resolution was then passed unanimously:

"That the heartiest thanks of the Association be given to Mr. MacAlister for his great services to the Association; first, in proposing that a Charter should be petitioned for, and, secondly, for his unflagging efforts in the face of great difficulties until the incorporation of the Association has crowned his efforts with success."

By the granting of this Charter the Library Association became the responsible representative body of the profession.

THE PUBLIC LIBRARY MOVEMENT

The objects of the Association, as set forth in the Charter, are:

(1) To unite all persons engaged or interested in Library work by holding Conferences and Meetings for the discussion of bibliographical questions and matters affecting Libraries or their regulation or management or otherwise.
(2) To promote the better administration of Libraries.
(3) To promote whatever may tend to the improvement of the position and the qualifications of Librarians.
(4) To promote the Adoption of the Public Libraries Acts.
(5) To promote the establishment of Reference and Lending Libraries for use by the public.
(6) To watch legislation affecting Public Libraries, and to assist in the promotion of such further legislation as may be considered necessary for the regulation and management or extension of Public Libraries.
(7) To promote and encourage bibliographical research.
(8) To form, collect, collate, and publish (in the form of Transactions, Journals, or otherwise), information of service or interest to the Fellows and Members of the Association, or for the promotion of the objects of the Corporation.
(9) To collect and maintain a Library and Museum.
(10) To hold examinations in Librarianship and to issue Certificates of efficiency.
(11) To do all such lawful things as are incidental or conducive to the attainment of the above objects.

Cataloguing Rules

Ever since its formation the Library Association has been much occupied with the question of cataloguing and the best methods of making known to the public the contents of libraries. A Committee was appointed in 1878 to consider and report upon

THE LIBRARY ASSOCIATION

the subject. The Committee adopted as a basis the condensed rules for cataloguing (based on C. A. Cutter's "Rules for a Printed Dictionary Catalogue") issued by the American Library Association, and published in the *Library Journal* for March 1878. These rules were very carefully considered by the Committee, and they then drew up a set of rules which they recommended for adoption at the Manchester meeting in 1879. The rules were further considered and revised at the Edinburgh and London meetings in 1880 and 1881, again revised at Liverpool in 1883, and remained in force for a number of years.

Mr. L. Stanley Jast contributed a series of articles to the *Library World* during 1899 and 1900 "On Classified and Annotated Cataloguing; Suggestions and Rules." In 1902 he read a paper "On the Library Association Cataloguing Rules,"[1] at the Manchester meeting, which resulted in the appointment of a Committee to take up the question of the revision of the rules which had been out of print for a number of years. The Committee consisted of Messrs. Francis T. Barrett (Glasgow), J. D. Brown, W. E. Doubleday, Henry Guppy, E. W. Hulme, L. Stanley Jast, T. W. Lyster, G. T. Shaw, and H. R. Tedder, with power to add to their number. Messrs. Franklin T. Barrett (Fulham), G. K. Fortescue, L. Inkster, C. W. Sutton, and the present writer were afterwards added to the Committee.

[1] *Library Association Record*, Vol. 4, pp. 579–582.

THE PUBLIC LIBRARY MOVEMENT

The Committee having obtained from Mr. Herbert Putnam, Librarian of Congress, a number of copies of the American Association Rules drafted by a revising committee of the A.L.A., at once set to work on the revision. Messrs. Jast, Barrett (Fulham), E. W. Hulme, and the present writer in turn acted as Hon. Secretary to the Committee, and Mr. H. R. Tedder presided over their deliberations. Some twenty-five meetings were held.

Not long after the formation of the Committee a letter was received from Mr. Melvil Dewey suggesting the issue of a combined joint code. The proposal was cordially adopted at the Newcastle meeting in 1904, and lengthy negotiations involving much correspondence with the A.L.A. Committee followed. Miss Alice B. Kroeger, Hon. Secretary, and Mr. J. C. M. Hanson, Chairman of the A.L.A. Committee, helped matters forward materially by attending meetings and giving us the benefit of their views when on separate visits to this country.

The difficulty of arriving at definite rules on several points was enhanced by the difference in the prevailing methods of cataloguing in the two countries. The American Committee were legislating for librarians who used the card catalogue almost exclusively, while the British Committee had in view the production of printed catalogues, according to the then prevailing practice in this country in most libraries. An entry once made in a printed catalogue cannot be changed, whereas with a card catalogue changes can readily be made by

THE LIBRARY ASSOCIATION

the simple expedient of lifting the cards bodily from one heading to another. There were eight rules upon which the two Committees were unable to come to an agreement, and it was ultimately decided to print the two forms, American and British, side by side. A statement of these will be found in an article which the present writer contributed to the *Library Association Record*, Vol. 11, 1909, pp. 289 et seq. The work of preparing examples to the rules, of supplying information as to Library of Congress practice, and of editing the whole for press was admirably done by Mr. Hanson.

REGISTRATION OF LIBRARIANS

The question of establishing a Register of qualified librarians was raised by Mr. W. R. B. Prideaux in an article in the *Library Association Record* for January 1906, entitled "Professional Education and Registration." The Library Assistants' Association (now the Association of Assistant Librarians, and since 1930 a constituent part of the Library Association) had been considering the question for some time, and a joint meeting of the Library Association and the Library Assistants' Association was held at the London School of Economics in January 1908, in order to endeavour to come to an agreement as to the establishment of a Register and the best method of doing so. It was contended by some that a separate body of professional librarians only should be formed, whose members should constitute the Register. Those in favour of this plan held that inasmuch as the Library Association had a large number of non-professional members it was not the proper body to control a Register of professional librarians, whilst the Library Association representatives felt that, as their Association was the only chartered body enjoying the right to hold examinations in librarianship and to issue certificates of proficiency, it was their province to institute the Register. At the joint meeting above referred to, a paper was read, prepared by Mr. L. Stanley Jast and Mr. W. C. Berwick Sayers, the respective Hon. Secretaries of the two Associations, and after a lengthy discussion the meeting decided to record its conviction that the only proper body to hold a professional Register was the Library Association, and requested the Council of the Association to consider and publish a report on the whole question in time for it to be considered at the annual meeting in 1908. This was accordingly done, and at the said meeting a resolution, proposed by Mr. John Ballinger, was carried by a large majority, to the effect that the scheme of registration should take the form of a classification of the membership of the Library Association, which would distinguish between professional and non-professional members, and that the Council should prepare a scheme in accordance with the Report submitted. The scheme was prepared and submitted to the annual meeting at Sheffield in 1909, and carried almost unanimously, only seven voting

THE LIBRARY ASSOCIATION

against it. Amended byelaws in accordance with the scheme were afterwards approved by the Privy Council. Under these byelaws it was provided that the Association should consist of Fellows, Honorary Fellows, Members, Associate Members, and Student Members.[1]

The byelaws were amended in 1911 to provide for the certification of branches of the Association, and again in 1913 to provide for the election as Associate Fellows of Chairmen or Vice-Chairmen of library committees, or other non-professional persons, whose election would be advantageous to the interests or objects of the Association.

In 1928 a complete revision of the byelaws was undertaken and approved by the Privy Council, by which it was provided that the Association should consist of Honorary Fellows, Members, Institutions, and Corresponding Members.

Honorary Fellows.—Persons who have rendered distinguished service in promoting the objects of the Association.

Members.—Librarians, bibliographers, members of library committees, and other persons connected with the administration of libraries, or interested in the objects of the Association.

Institutions.—Libraries or other institutions entitled to nominate a delegate who shall be a member of the governing body of the institution.

Corresponding Members.—Persons living outside the British Isles, and foreign institutions.

---

[1] *Library Association Record*, Vol. 11, 1909, pp. 558-60.

THE PUBLIC LIBRARY MOVEMENT

The revised byelaws provide that the Council shall maintain a Register of librarians, who being members of the Association shall be classified as Fellows and Associates. Any librarian who is a member of the Association may apply to be entered upon the Register in one or other of the following classes:

(1) *Fellows*.—All Members engaged in library or bibliographical service who are Fellows at the date of the new byelaws may be entered on the Register as Fellows. The following may be elected Fellows: (*a*) Holders of the L.A. Diploma, or the Diploma of a recognized School of Librarianship, or of the complete certificate issued by the Library Association prior to 1901; (*b*) University Graduates holding certificates in Bibliography, Library Organization, Cataloguing, and Classification issued by the Library Association or by a recognized School of Librarianship, and who have had three years' full-time library service approved by the Library Association; (*c*) Any person distinguished in librarianship or scholarship, provided that the election to Fellowship shall be agreed to by a two-thirds majority of the Council present.

(2) *Associates*.—All persons engaged in library or bibliographical service classified as Members at the date of the new byelaws may be entered on the Register as Associates. The following may be elected Associates: (*a*) Librarians holding four certificates of the Library Association or of a recognized School of Librarianship, and with three years' full-time library service; (*b*) University Graduates having three years' full-time library service, and holding an official position in a library approved by the Library Association.

Fellows and Associates have the right to use the letters F.L.A. and A.L.A. respectively after their names, as long as they remain on the Register.

THE LIBRARY ASSOCIATION

THE DEPARTMENTAL COMMITTEE'S REPORT ON PUBLIC LIBRARIES

The holding of the Jubilee Conference of the Library Association in Edinburgh in 1927, and the presentation thereat of the influential Report on Public Libraries in England and Wales, issued earlier in that year by the Departmental Committee of the Board of Education, may be said to have inaugurated a new era in the history of the public library movement in this country.

The Committee was appointed by Mr. C. P. Trevelyan, then President of the Board of Education, in 1924. It met on thirty-nine days, issued a questionnaire to all public library authorities, and took oral evidence from fifty-two witnesses representing all aspects of library work, library and education authorities, and teachers. Its terms of reference were:

"To enquire into the adequacy of the library provision already made under the Public Libraries Acts, and the means of extending and completing such provision throughout England and Wales, regard being had to the relation of the libraries conducted under these Acts to other public libraries and to the general system of national education."

The personnel of the Committee was as follows:

Sir Frederic G. Kenyon, Principal Librarian of the British Museum (Chairman).
Mr. (now Sir) John Ballinger, Librarian of the National Library of Wales.
Mr. W. R. Barker, Legal Adviser to the Board of Education.

THE PUBLIC LIBRARY MOVEMENT

Mr. E. Salter Davies, Director of Education for the County of Kent.

Dr. Albert Mansbridge, Chairman of the British Institute of Adult Education.

Lieut.-Colonel J. M. Mitchell, Secretary to the Carnegie United Kingdom Trustees.

Mr. J. Owen, H.M.I.

Mr. Frank Pacy, Hon. Secretary of the Library Association.

Mr. S. A. Pitt, City Librarian, Glasgow.

The Lady Mabel Smith.

Mr. A. E. Twentyman, Librarian to the Board of Education.

Mr. C. O. G. Douie acted as Secretary to the Committee.

A special session of the Conference was set apart for the consideration of the Report. The Earl of Elgin, President of the Association, occupied the chair, and Sir Frederic Kenyon, the Chairman of the Committee, gave an admirable résumé of the principal features and recommendations of the Report. He said they were there to hear what the librarians of the United Kingdom and the guests from overseas had to say about the Report—whether they agreed with its main conclusions, and whether they wished to put the weight of the Library Association behind it. The Report was afterwards discussed by a number of speakers, chapter by chapter, and generally approved, the principal discussion taking place upon the question of the establishment of a central cataloguing agency, a large majority being in favour.

The main recommendations of the Report were as follows:

That County Councils which have not adopted

THE LIBRARY ASSOCIATION

the Acts, or which in adopting the Acts have excluded part of their areas, should be constituted library authorities by statute for that part of their area which still remains without statutory provision (par. 68).

The Committee regarded it as essential that library authorities with a population under 20,000 should enter into arrangements for co-operation with larger units, either boroughs or counties (par. 81). Co-operation was also desirable throughout the library service and was a vital necessity to small towns and villages. A scheme of co-operation with the Central Library for Students (now the National Central Library) was proposed (par. 82). This scheme is now in operation and a system of "outlier" libraries has been established, over 100 such libraries having agreed to co-operate.

The Committee noted that progress in the provision of library facilities had been very marked since 1921. The population in urban areas had grown from 23,987,903 in 1921 to 24,168,702 in 1924, and during that period the number of volumes in stock had increased by two millions, an increase from 48·4 per cent. to 52·3 per cent. in relation to population. The total issues grew from about 54½ millions to over 73½ millions. The number of borrowers increased from 1,986,123 to 2,500,961, being from 9·3 per cent. of the population to 11 per cent. The increase in expenditure over all was £59,000, representing a cost per head of population of 1s. (pars. 85–86).

THE PUBLIC LIBRARY MOVEMENT

The suggested transfer of public libraries in boroughs to the control of Education Committees (except with the goodwill of all concerned) would, in the opinion of the Committee, involve more loss than gain. The co-ordination of public libraries with the educational system of the country was to be sought along the lines of co-operation rather than subordination. That libraries and organized education in schools and universities are closely interrelated is unquestionable; if libraries were to claim their autonomy they must offer the fullest and most friendly co-operation to the education authorities (pars. 103–104).

The responsibility for the provision of school libraries should rest with the Education Committees which should supply the funds, and in respect thereof should receive a grant from the Board of Education. The Education Committee, however, "would be wise in all cases to seek the co-operation of the Library Committee and the expert advice of the librarian" (par. 111).

The appointment of co-opted members on Public Library Committees was of considerable advantage, but care should be taken that the number co-opted should never be so great as to weaken the influence of the Library Committee on the Council. The majority of the Committee and the Chairman should, as a general rule, be members of the Council. It was desirable that the Education Committee and the Library Committee should have a certain number of members in common (pars. 127–128).

THE LIBRARY ASSOCIATION

"A public library authority should be empowered (i) to become a member and to pay the membership fee of associations existing for the study of library problems; (ii) to pay the expense of sending a limited number of members or officials to conferences held for the purpose of discussing library problems; and (iii) to contribute towards the expenses of such conferences" (par. 132).

"Exemption from income tax should be extended to all premises held for the purposes of the Public Libraries Acts irrespective of the question whether they satisfy the conditions at present contained in the Income Tax Act, 1921. Such an amendment of the Act would involve no appreciable loss to the Revenue" (par. 146).

As to the stocks of libraries, "no library should be satisfied with a stock of books which represents less than thirty volumes per 100 of the population" (par. 199).

"Public library authorities should be authorized by legislation to provide lectures and to pay lecturers" (par. 216).

"The two main requirements for a librarian are a liberal education and technical training. In a certain limited sense the latter is the more indispensable, since no one can conduct the business of a library without some acquaintance with the technique of classification, cataloguing, the care of books, and other library routine. But in a wider sense it is the other qualification that is the more essential. For the welfare of the library service it is essential to recognize that librarianship is a learned profession" (par. 234).

The qualification required for admission to the courses of the School of Librarianship and the Library Association examinations is the University matriculation standard or its equivalent. The Committee considered that this should be the minimum, in fact, they would like to see it raised, placing, as they did, a very high value on the possession by librarians of a wide general culture in the higher stages of the profession. They considered that the library service should aim at attracting a large proportion of graduates to its higher grades (par. 258).

The Committee considered it essential that the School of Librarianship at the University of London should be maintained (par. 261). They recommended that scholarships tenable at the School should be offered by local authorities. Any doubt which exists as to the power of public library authorities to make grants in aid of the fees and travelling expenses of their staff attending the School of Librarianship, summer schools, and other courses for the training of librarians should be removed by legislation (pars. 247 and 262).

To sum up, the Committee considered "that the training of librarians, as it at present exists, is on the right lines, and that the main needs of the future are (1) to educate public opinion to demand that trained librarians should be the rule and not the exception; (ii) to enforce on library authorities

THE LIBRARY ASSOCIATION

their responsibility for giving due weight to training in their selection of candidates, and for giving facilities to their staff to continue their training, both technical and educational, while in their service; and (iii) so to improve the conditions of library service, especially in respect of work and remuneration, as to attract a good type of candidate, with wide interests and a sound general education" (par. 268).

"The trained librarian should be paid no less than the trained teacher, and the one profession should be not less attractive than the other. Just as in the Universities much has been done to raise the status of librarians to a level comparable with that of the teaching staff, so, the Committee considered, it should be in the local government service" (par. 276).

The Third International and Jubilee Conference, 1927

It was a fortunate circumstance that the issue of this valuable Report coincided in point of time with the Jubilee Conference of the Library Association, which was a thoroughly international gathering. There were present 117 overseas librarian delegates and their friends, including eighty-two from the United States, a large number of whom took part in a pre-conference tour through the United Kingdom, jointly provided by the Carnegie United Kingdom Trustees and the Library Association, and personally conducted by Lieut.-Colonel

THE PUBLIC LIBRARY MOVEMENT

Mitchell, Secretary to the Trustees, and other members of the Association. An opportunity was thus afforded them of seeing something of our larger cities and rural districts, visits being paid to many of the more important libraries in the course of the journey.

At the Conference important papers were read and discussed on county libraries and their place in a national educational scheme, on high-school libraries, small libraries, library planning, the work of American libraries, the future of the Central Library for Students, etc. The establishment of an International Library and Bibliographical Committee was arranged, and its constitution drafted, providing for the holding of conferences at least once in every five years. The Committee held its first Conference at Rome in 1929.

The presidential address of Lord Elgin to the Edinburgh Conference was entitled "A Jubilee; a Centre and a Free Swing," and brought out the salient points of the Departmental Committee's Report. The essence of the Report was the emphasis which it laid upon the necessity for the building up of a truly National Library Service by the co-ordination of all the agencies engaged in the provision of reading matter for the public. A National Library Service did not mean a service controlled by a Government Department, but a service which forms part of the national life; in other words, a service which touches every individual citizen and is appreciated and valued by all.

THE LIBRARY ASSOCIATION

Lord Elgin laid much stress upon the value of Freedom in the service—"freedom of the locality to develop its resources without dictation; freedom of the library in its construction and accessibility, and freedom of the individual to seek for what he desires." He paid tribute to the value of allowing each would-be borrower freedom to browse among the shelves before making his choice, but the reader should be aided by the sound advice of the librarian as to the choice of book which would best enable him to learn his subject thoroughly and to avoid mistakes. There was required a fuller appreciation by every citizen of the value of books and reading in developing his own character instead of accepting a mould of character and ideals shaped for him by others. There was need of a larger effort on the part of municipal and other authorities to place reading facilities within the reach of all, and a more generous recognition of those who labour in the service as librarians as being members of a learned profession, and in return for this recognition an even greater effort on the part of the profession to qualify themselves for their responsible task and to form by loyal co-operation a strong brotherhood welcoming everyone who is interested in the furtherance of their ideal, the building of good citizenship.

The centre of the National Service was the Central Library for Students which was established in 1914, mainly by the Workers' Educational Association, in conjunction with Toynbee Hall, to supply books to members of their tutorial classes.

THE PUBLIC LIBRARY MOVEMENT

In founding the Central Library, Dr. Mansbridge and his associates had shown courage and foresight. How to link up the Central Library with other libraries under a scheme of "Outliers" had had the careful consideration of the Carnegie Trustees. The ambition of the Trustees had been to build up a scheme whereby any individual reader or circle of readers wherever stationed could obtain on loan works in which they were interested. He was glad that the Report of the Committee had endorsed the views of the Trustees, and had even gone farther by recommending that the Central Library should receive national recognition, not as a departmentally controlled institution, but as a free agency closely allied to and linked with the British Museum. As an aid to carrying out this scheme it was necessary that the different branches of the library profession should be united in one strong body to lend weight to their demand for a truly national service.

The recommendation that the Central Library for Students should receive national recognition has been given effect to by a grant from the Treasury towards its maintenance, the changing of its title to the National Central Library, and the grant of a Royal Charter.

The Carnegie United Kingdom Trustees have acquired from the University College authorities a large vacant property in the Bloomsbury district, which they have handed over to the National Central Library as its headquarters. Part of the property has been gifted to the Library Association

THE LIBRARY ASSOCIATION

for its headquarters. Although forming part of the same building, this portion will be entirely self-contained and will solve the problem of accommodation for the office work, Council and Committee meetings, the Library of the Association, etc., which has been exercising the minds of the Council for very many years.

AMALGAMATION OF LIBRARY ASSOCIATIONS

The Council of the Library Association had for several years prior to the Jubilee Conference been endeavouring to carry out the policy of increasing its membership and bringing into one comprehensive association all the different local and special associations which had been formed since its establishment.

In 1924, when it was learned that a Special Libraries Association to include commercial, scientific, and other special libraries was about to be formed, strong efforts were made by the Council to induce the promoters to amalgamate with the Library Association, but without success. Many of those in favour of a separate association felt that their interests were so special and distinct from those of public libraries that they would be lost sight of in the larger association, and so the Association of Special Libraries and Information Bureaux (ASLIB) came to be formed.

The recommendation of the Jubilee Conference in favour of having one strong body gave a valuable fillip to the efforts of the L.A. Council in that direction. It was decided to institute a forward policy, and to this end to obtain the services of a full-time paid secretary, to secure premises for headquarters which should be the property of the Association, and generally to embark on a policy which would involve a larger expenditure than the funds available from their limited membership would be able to meet. The Executive Committee was accordingly instructed to approach the Carnegie United Kingdom Trust with a view to obtaining a grant in support of the extended policy.

The Trustees expressed cordial sympathy with the decision come to, and agreed to offer to the Association a grant of £1,000 for the year 1928, £900 for 1929, £800 for 1930, plus a further sum in each year, up to a maximum of £200, on a pound for pound basis in respect of revenue from subscriptions of new members in each of those three years. The Trustees further indicated that they would be willing to consider an application for diminishing grants for 1931 and 1932, if the conditions attached to the earlier grants were complied with, and a satisfactory increase of membership obtained.

The main conditions attached to the offer were that the Association agree to carry into effect as soon as possible the relevant recommendations contained in the Report approved at the Edinburgh Conference; that the post of secretary be advertised, and that it be made clear that both library and administrative experience would be taken into account in making the appointment; that the Association undertake to make an effort to induce the other library groups and associations to come within a single unit; that a detailed annual report and financial statement be made to the Trustees; and that the Association endeavour to set aside a reserve fund.

The effect of the generous offer of the Trustees, which was gratefully accepted, was to still further stimulate the activities of the Council. They secured the services of a full-time paid secretary, Mr. Guy W. Keeling, who had filled a similar post with ASLIB, and who threw himself with such energy and enthusiasm into his duties that he was threatened with a serious breakdown, and had to be given leave of absence for a lengthened period. An Assistant Secretary, Mr. P. S. J. Welsford, was appointed, who carried on the secretarial duties in his absence. Mr. Keeling's health, never robust, failed to stand the strain of office work, and in 1931 he was obliged to resign his appointment.

In their endeavour to secure the amalgamation of the separate library groups and associations into one association, and thus fulfil one important condition of the Carnegie grant, the Council were highly successful. Negotiations were entered into with the Association of Assistant Librarians, with the North Midland Library Association, and with the Scottish Library Association, and those three bodies ultimately agreed to join hands with the main Library Association. Articles of agreement with the first two Associations were signed at the Brighton Conference in 1929, and with the Scottish Association at the Cambridge Conference in 1930. The credit for the successful outcome of the negotiations is very largely due to the untiring efforts of the Hon. Secretary, Mr. Ernest A. Savage, whose advocacy of the amalgamation was whole-hearted, and who spared neither time nor trouble to bring about this happy result.

The membership of the Association in 1931 reached a total of 3,843, but there are still quite a number actively engaged in the library service who have not enrolled. The Council will not be satisfied until practically every member of a library staff is in membership of the Association, and every library authority has taken up institutional membership. In this direction there is still a good deal to be accomplished.

OFFICERS OF THE ASSOCIATION

Honorary Secretaries

1877–78. E. W. B. Nicholson and H. R. Tedder. Nicholson resigned, May 1878.
1879–80. H. R. Tedder and E. C. Thomas. Tedder resigned, July 1880.
1880–82. E. C. Thomas and C. Welch. Welch resigned, September 1882.
1883–86. E. C. Thomas.
1887–89. E. C. Thomas and J. Y. W. MacAlister. Thomas resigned, October 1889.
1890–92. J. Y. W. MacAlister and Thomas Mason.
1893–98. J. Y. W. MacAlister.

THE LIBRARY ASSOCIATION

1898–1901	Frank Pacy. Resigned, August 1901, but carried on to December.
1902.	Basil Soulsby, January 1st to February 10th.
1902–6	Lawrence Inkster (February 28, 1902–September 1906).
1906–15.	L. Stanley Jast. Resigned, October 14, 1915.
1915–28	Frank Pacy. Died, June 24, 1928.
1928–	E. A. Savage, appointed September 27, 1928.

Secretaries

1901–10	Mrs. Kate Reilly, Assistant Secretary (November 1, 1901–September 8, 1910).
1919–22	Captain Ernest C. Kyte, appointed, June 13, 1919. Resigned, 1922.
1928–31	Guy W. Keeling, appointed, January 20, 1928. Resigned, June 1931.
1931–	P. S. J. Welsford, Assistant Secretary, 1929–31, appointed Acting Secretary, November 6, 1931.

Honorary Treasurers

1877–89.	Robert Harrison. Resigned, January 1889.
1889–1924.	Henry R. Tedder. Died, August 1, 1924.
1925–28.	Bernard Kettle. Resigned, September 24, 1928.
1928–29.	John Henry Quinn. Appointed, September 24, 1928. Resigned, December 1929.
1929–	H. Tapley Soper. Appointed (interim), December 1929. Elected, August 1, 1930.

Honorary Legal Advisers

1894–1927.	Henry West Fovargue, Town Clerk of Eastbourne. Resigned, September 30, 1927.
1928–30.	Rt. Hon. Hugh Pattison Macmillan, K.C. (now Baron Macmillan of Aberfeldy). Appointed, January 20, 1928.
1930–	Alderman J. S. Pritchett, B.C.L., Recorder of Lincoln.

CHAPTER XIII

TRAINING FOR LIBRARIANSHIP

"The object of the educational work of the Association, which is entrusted to its Education Committee, is twofold: (*a*) to improve the efficiency of library assistants, to increase their interest in their work, and ultimately to improve their status and ability to earn a livelihood; (*b*) to further the development of librarianship in theory and practice, and to subserve the efficient working of libraries."[1]

The knowledge which an assistant acquires in the course of his daily duties is necessarily of an empiric character. His superiors have not the time to devote to his tuition in anything other than routine work. No instruction in the theory of library economy is possible, nor can the aims and objects of library policy be discussed. It is the function of the educational scheme of the Association to provide not only technical training in methods of routine work, but also instruction in the principles involved in the classification and cataloguing of books, bibliography, and the organization of libraries as centres of adult education, as aids to scientific study, i.e. intellectual pursuits and recreations.[2]

The time has long since gone by, it is to be hoped, when it was considered that anyone with a

[1] *Library Association Year Book for 1914*, p. 55. [2] Ibid.

TRAINING FOR LIBRARIANSHIP

love of books and reading was fit to be a librarian, though such an idea seems to die hard, if one may judge from the appointments of untrained persons to responsible positions in libraries which from time to time are still occasionally made.

That training in librarianship is being more and more recognized by library authorities as essential is evidenced by the fact that many authorities now make it a condition of promotion in the library service that assistants shall obtain this training, and as an inducement thereto have instituted schemes whereby the possession of certificates carries with it the right to increases of salary. Since 1914 admission to the Fellowship of the Association has been granted only to those who have obtained the Diploma, the holding of certificates in four of the main subjects of the examination scheme entitling to Associateship only.

The history of the various schemes for the training of library assistants and others desirous of entering the library service may be briefly recounted as follows:

EXAMINATION

At the Edinburgh meeting of the Association in 1880 Mr. Robert Harrison moved a resolution standing in Mr. H. R. Tedder's name, he being unable to be present. The resolution was to the effect that it was desirable that the Council should consider how library assistants might best be aided in their training. The resolution was carried unani-

THE PUBLIC LIBRARY MOVEMENT

mously, and a Committee was afterwards appointed by the Council to consider and report. The Committee consisted of Dr. Richard Garnett (Chairman), Messrs. Robert Harrison, Edward B. Nicholson, Henry R. Tedder, and the Secretaries, Messrs. Edward C. Thomas and Charles Welch. They presented their Report to the Council in June 1881, outlining a scheme of examinations embodying:

A. A preliminary examination before appointment in the following subjects: (1) Arithmetic. (2) English Grammar and Composition. (3) English History. (4) Geography. (5) English Literature.

B. An examination after appointment on (1) English Literature, especially of the last hundred years. (2) Some one other European Literature. (3) Principles of the Classification of the Sciences. (4) Elements of Bibliography, including Cataloguing. (5) Library Management and Administration. A cataloguing knowledge of at least two languages besides English to be necessary for a Second-Class Certificate. A First-Class Certificate to be given, after a satisfactory examination, to a librarian or assistant of at least two years' experience for an advanced knowledge of the five subjects last mentioned, with the addition of a sixth subject, General Literary History. A cataloguing knowledge of at last three languages to be necessary for the higher Certificate.

Persons not engaged as library assistants might be admitted to the examinations on obtaining a permit from the Council.

The Committee's Report was presented to the annual meeting in London in 1881, and was received, but not adopted, the Committee being thanked for their services.

At a monthly meeting of the Association in 1881

TRAINING FOR LIBRARIANSHIP

another Committee, consisting of Messrs. Henry Bradshaw (President), Peter Cowell, John D. Mullins, and William H. Overall, was appointed, and the Report was again presented at the Cambridge meeting in 1882, following on Mr. Tedder's paper on "Librarianship as a Profession." After a lengthy discussion it was adopted, and remitted to the Council to put into operation.

It was not, however, until July 1885 that the first examination under the above scheme was held at two centres, viz. London and Nottingham. As a result of this examination, second-class certificates were granted to Mr. Albert Butcher, of Welling, Kent, and Mr. J. J. Ogle, then assistant at the Public Library, Nottingham.

Examinations continued to be held at irregular intervals at a number of centres throughout the country until 1891, when a new scheme of examination was adopted at the annual meeting at Nottingham, following upon the Report of a special Committee, consisting of Messrs. Peter Cowell, W. May, J. D. Mullins, J. J. Ogle, and C. W. Sutton, which had been appointed to consider the regulations. The new Syllabus retained the Preliminary Examination, adding Cataloguing as a sixth subject. The six subjects were retained in the ordinary, or professional, examination, but candidates for a full Certificate had to show a knowledge of more advanced text-books than those prescribed for a pass Certificate. A Board of twelve Examiners was appointed, and it was decided that examinations

THE PUBLIC LIBRARY MOVEMENT

should be held in June and December each year. Candidates were required to pass the Elementary Examination or some other public examination in general knowledge of equal value, before entering for the professional examination. Certificates were to be granted *pro tanto*, to be exchanged for a full Certificate when all six subjects were passed. No fees were charged for the examinations.

In 1894 the Syllabus of Examinations was again revised. The Preliminary Examination was discontinued, and future examinations were restricted to professional subjects only, viz.:

1. Bibliography and Literary History.
2. Cataloguing, Classification, and Shelf Arrangement.
3. Library Management.

Each section might be taken separately and Certificates *pro tanto* granted as formerly. An entrance fee of 10s. was charged for the professional examination.

Up to this time it will be noted that no instruction in the subjects of the Syllabus had been provided by the Association. In 1895 Mr. John J. Ogle, Librarian of Bootle, endeavoured to supply this want in some measure by opening a "Library Assistants' Corner" (afterwards entitled "Our Junior Colleagues' Corner") in the pages of *The Library*, in which he dealt with notes and queries on subjects of practical librarianship, giving a series of questions to be answered by assistants. Mr. MacAlister offered a monthly prize for the best

TRAINING FOR LIBRARIANSHIP

answers to the questions. At the end of 1899, Mr. Ogle, having resigned the librarianship of Bootle on his appointment as Director of Technical Instruction there, was obliged to give up the conduct of the "Corner," and Mr. Henry Guppy, as editor of *The Library Association Record*, carried it on until 1901.

The Examinations continued to be held under the 1894 Syllabus until 1904, when the scheme was rearranged to embrace:

(*a*) Study in various prescribed subjects, namely:
  1. Literary History.
  2. Elements of Practical Bibliography.
  3. Classification.
  4. Cataloguing.
  5. Library History and Organization.
  6. Practical Library Administration.

(*b*) Examinations in each subject, and the writing of a satisfactory essay upon some aspect of each subject.

(*c*) Practical experience of not less than twenty-four hours a week for at least three years as a member of the administrative staff of one or more libraries approved by the Council of the Library Association.

Each subject might be taken separately and Certificates granted *pro tanto*. Qualification (*c*) did not apply to candidates for Certificates in the separate sections, but, in order to obtain the full Certificate or Diploma, candidates had to pass in the six subjects, write the prescribed essays, and have the practical experience. No examination fee was charged, and the Preliminary Examination was discontinued.

THE PUBLIC LIBRARY MOVEMENT

A further revision of the Syllabus was made in 1907. A fee of 2s. 6d. was charged for each examination, candidates being allowed to take as many subjects as they liked without extra fee. Certificates were granted in three grades, Honours, Merit, and Pass. Candidates for the full Certificate or Diploma were required to submit—

1. A thesis showing original thought or research on some subject within the scope of the Syllabus, approved by the Council.
2. Certificates in all six sections.
3. A Certificate of their practical experience.
4. A Certificate, approved by the Council, showing that the candidate possessed an elementary knowledge of Latin, and of one modern foreign language.

Owing to the evident deficiency in the elementary education of many candidates it was decided to restore the preliminary test in general knowledge for those intending to enter for the May examinations in 1916. The need for this was shown, when out of ninety candidates at the test examination in January of that year only thirty passed. This preliminary test was discontinued after 1924, and candidates for the professional examinations were in future required to produce certificates of University matriculation standard before entering. For a list of Certificates accepted as equivalent to matriculation standard, see the current Syllabus in the *Library Association Year Book*.

Further revisions of the Syllabus have modified the scheme in various details. The possession of an elementary knowledge of Latin is not now compulsory but optional, its place being taken by a second modern language; the writing of an essay in each of the sections of the examination is not required; nor is the writing of a thesis on some subject within the scope of the Syllabus essential to the granting of the ordinary Diploma. It is still, however, demanded of those who wish to obtain a Diploma with Honours.

The latest complete recasting of the Syllabus, which will come into operation in May 1933, provides for a graduated system of examinations, including:

1. The Elementary Examination.
2. The Intermediate Examination.
3. The Final Examination, Parts I, II and III.

The Elementary Examination will include (1) Elementary English Literary History, (2) Elementary Classification, Elementary Cataloguing and Accession Methods, (3) Elementary Library Administration. All three divisions must be passed at one examination.

The Intermediate Examination will include (1) Library Classification, (2) Library Cataloguing. Candidates to pass in both subjects at one examination.

The Final Examination will include:

Part I. (a) English Literary History, or (b) the Literary History of Science, or (c) the Literary History of Economics and Commerce.

Any candidate who has graduated at an approved University in (a) English, or (b) Science, or (c) Economics, may apply for exemption from Part I of the Final Examination.

THE PUBLIC LIBRARY MOVEMENT

Part II. Bibliography and Book Selection.
> Paper 1. General Bibliography and Book Selection.
> Paper 2. Historical Bibliography,
> *or* Palæography and Archives,
> *or* Indexing and Abstracting.

Part III. Advanced Library Administration.

This part of the Final Examination covers the whole field of the subject and a high standard of work at the examination will be expected.

Up to the present, candidates have been permitted to take the six subjects of the scheme in any order of preference, but when the 1933 Syllabus comes into force new candidates must take the course in the prescribed order of elementary, intermediate, and final. It will be noted that certain options have been introduced into Parts I and II of the Final Examination in order to meet the requirements of students who desire to qualify for service in scientific, commercial, or technical libraries, or libraries of historical research.

Summer Schools

At a meeting of the Association at Liverpool in December 1892, two important papers were read, viz.: (1) "A Plan for Providing Technical Instruction for Library Assistants," by Miss M. S. R. James, Librarian of the People's Palace, London (*The Library*, Vol. 4, p. 313); and (2) "A Summer School of Library Science," by Mr. J. J. Ogle (*The Library*, Vol. 4, p. 319). These two papers elicited

TRAINING FOR LIBRARIANSHIP

a very full discussion (*The Library*, Vol. 5, p. 161), and a Committee, consisting of Miss James, Mr. MacAlister, Mr. Ogle, and Mr. H. R. Tedder, was appointed to consider and report upon the question of holding a Summer School at which library assistants and students of librarianship might have an opportunity of visiting representative libraries and of hearing demonstrations of the various practical methods and details of a librarian's work.

The Committee reported favourably, and the first Summer School was held in London for three days in July 1893, when visits were paid to the British Museum and other London libraries, to typefoundries, printing, and bookbinding establishments. Mr. MacAlister generously offered a prize of three pounds for the best report of the proceedings. Forty-five students from various parts of the country attended, and the success of the School was such that it was decided to hold a second School in the following year, Mr. MacAlister again offering prizes.

The Summer Schools were continued in 1895 and the two following years, under the superintendence of a Summer Schools Committee, of which Mr. Charles Welch was Chairman. These were well attended. Mr. Ogle acted as Hon. Secretary for the School in 1894 and 1895, and Mr. W. E. Doubleday in 1896. Mr. Doubleday's other duties prevented him from continuing, and in September 1896, Mr. Henry D. Roberts took over the work. These Schools were not designed specifically as

THE PUBLIC LIBRARY MOVEMENT

training for the examinations of the Association, but the Committee in charge of the Schools decided to systematize the work so as to assist those who desired to study for the examinations by the delivery of lectures on the technical subjects of librarianship, and this was carried out at the 1896 and 1897 Schools.

After the 1897 School, which was the most successful of the series, having been attended by seventy-four students, technical classes were started at the London School of Economics, and the North-Western Branch of the Association instituted a Summer School of technical classes at Manchester in 1897. The Council, considering that the ground was well covered by these two agencies, decided to suspend the London School in 1898 and 1899. In response to several requests, a series of visits to libraries in the London district was organized in 1900, but the response was so poor that the Council on the recommendation of the Summer School Committee discontinued the School.

As already mentioned, the North-Western Branch's Summer Schools were originated in 1897, and continued with conspicuous success until 1913, holding meetings at Manchester, Liverpool, Wigan, St. Helen's, Preston, Blackburn, and Southport. After the war the School was resumed in 1920 and 1921, but was then discontinued, the Branch's Education Committee concentrating upon the lectures and classes provided in Manchester under the auspices of the Extra-Mural Department of the University.

TRAINING FOR LIBRARIANSHIP

ABERYSTWYTH SUMMER SCHOOL

A highly successful series of Summer Schools of Library Service was held at Aberystwyth during the years 1917 to 1928. Sir William Osler, Bart., Professor of Medicine, Oxford University, at one of the meetings of the Royal Commission on University Education in Wales, raised the question of establishing a school for library training in connection with the further development of University Education in Wales, and expressed his opinion that Aberystwyth with the University College and the National Library offered exceptional facilities for such a school.[1]

The governing bodies of the College and the Library took the matter up, and in conjunction with the Library Association's Education Committee, a scheme of lectures was drawn up based upon the Syllabus of the Association, with the addition of the subjects of Archives and Bookbinding.

Sir William Osler delivered an inaugural address on "The Library School in the College,"[2] and (Sir) John Ballinger, whose whole-hearted enthusiasm and fostering care as a director of the School were responsible for the great success of this and the following Schools, gave an address on the plans of the National Library.

The President of the Library Association, (Sir) John Y. W. MacAlister, offered three prizes for

[1] *Library Association Record*, 1917, p. 347.
[2] Ibid., 1917, pp. 287–308.

THE PUBLIC LIBRARY MOVEMENT

class work, and fifty-eight students were enrolled from all parts of the United Kingdom.

Lecturers and students resided together at the Alexandra Hall, the women's hostel of the College, an admirable arrangement which provided opportunities for teacher and taught to discuss subjects to their mutual advantage.

The subjects dealt with by different lecturers at the various Schools comprised:

Bibliography and Book Selection (H. Thomas, A. J. K. Esdaile, James Hutt, E. A. Savage).

Bookbinding (C. Hanson, bookbinder, National Library of Wales).

Books of Reference (S. A. Pitt, Walter Powell, J. H. Quinn, John Minto).

Cataloguing (Henry Guppy, Miss Ethel S. Fegan, James Hutt, J. H. Quinn).

Classification (A. J. Hawkes, L. Stanley Jast, E. A. Savage, W. Williams).

Commercial and Technical Libraries (S. A. Pitt, C. R. Sanderson).

Rural (County) Library Organization (W. Williams and D. G. Griffiths).

Indexing (Walter Powell).

Library History and Library Organization (James Hutt, C. Riddle, C. R. Sanderson).

Library Planning and Fittings (John Ballinger).

Library Routine (Practical Library Administration) (L. Stanley Jast).

Library Work with Children (John Ballinger, Harry Farr).

Literary History (Professor J. W. H. Atkins, Miss Gwendolen Murphy).

Palæography and Archives (Hubert Hall, Charles Johnson).

Printing (George Jones, *Cambrian News*).

Welsh Literature (Professor Henry Lewis, Swansea).

TRAINING FOR LIBRARIANSHIP

Introductory lectures were also delivered at several of the Schools by Frank Pacy, Hon. Secretary of the Library Association, and evening talks in the Hall of Residence on the care of books and on the ethics of librarianship, by Mr. John Ballinger, and on collections of illustrations in libraries, by J. H. Quinn. Ten Schools in all were held from 1917 to 1922 and from 1925 to 1928. The Schools unfortunately were not self-supporting and were discontinued after 1928.

Birmingham Summer School

Many students having expressed regret at the discontinuance of the Aberystwyth Schools, the Library Association arranged to hold a Summer School at Birmingham in co-operation with the University, from August 25 to September 6, 1930. The students resided at Chancellor's Hall (the University Hall of Residence), Augustus Road, Edgbaston, Birmingham. Seventy-seven students from all parts of the country attended, the School being open to non-members of the Association at an increased fee.

Public lectures were given by Mr. Hilary Jenkinson, of the Public Record Office, on "Business Handwriting from the Twelfth to the Nineteenth Century," and by Mr. Arundell Esdaile, Secretary of the British Museum, on "Dr. Johnson"; and single School lectures by Dr. W. Bonser on "University Libraries"; Mr. T. Duckworth (an inaugural address); Mr. L. Stanley Jast on "The Outstanding

THE PUBLIC LIBRARY MOVEMENT

Developments in Public Library Methods since about 1900"; Mr. J. H. Pafford on "Continental Libraries"; Mr. A. F. Ridley on "Special Libraries and Information Bureaux: their place in the library world"; and Mr. H. Woodbine on "Modern Fine Printing."

Regular courses of lectures were given on "Palæography and Archive Science," by Mr. Hilary Jenkinson; "Dr. Johnson and His Circle"—the special period of English Literary History prescribed for examinations—by Mr. T. C. Kemp; "Bibliography," by Mr. H. Woodbine; "Classification," by Mr. G. L. Burton; "Cataloguing," by Mr. Leonard Chubb; "Library Organization," by Mr. C. Jackson; and "Library Routine," by Mr. Leonard Chubb.

Visits were paid to the Birmingham and Coventry Public Library systems, to the Birmingham University Library, to the Rendel Harris Library at Woodbrooke, to the Worcester Cathedral Library, and to the Works Library of the Dunlop Rubber Company, as well as to local printing and other works.[1]

Mr. F. J. Thacker and Mr. Leonard Chubb, and their colleagues of the Birmingham Library Staff, made admirable arrangements for the conduct of the School.

A second School was organized in August 1931, when ninety-six students were registered, including representatives from Denmark, Germany, and Hol-

[1] *Library Association Record*, 1930, pp. 285–86.

TRAINING FOR LIBRARIANSHIP

land. The same regular courses of lectures were conducted by the lecturers of the previous year, and public lectures were given by Colonel Luxmoore Newcombe, of the National Central Library, on "Regional Co-operation"; by Mr. L. R. McColvin on "Those who do not use Libraries"; and by Mr. G. E. Flack, Nottingham University College Librarian, on "University Libraries."

Organized visits were again paid to libraries in the neighbourhood and to printing and bookbinding establishments, and excursions were made to Lichfield, Worcester, and Stratford-on-Avon.

Mr. H. M. Cashmore and Messrs. Chubb and Thacker at the close of the School were specially thanked for their services in its organization. The great success of these Schools it is to be hoped will ensure their continuance.

THE EDUCATION COMMITTEE

At a monthly meeting of the Association in December 1896, Mr. Henry D. Roberts, then Librarian of St. Saviour's Public Library, Southwark, contributed a paper entitled "Some Remarks on the Education of the Library Assistant: a Plea."[1] In his paper, Mr. Roberts emphasized the lack of facilities for the technical education of library assistants, and, at the conclusion of it, moved a resolution, which, after discussion, was carried unanimously, asking the Council to arrange for courses of lectures on library management

[1] *The Library*, 1897, pp. 103–112.

during the winter. The Summer School Committee, to whom the matter was referred, reported in favour of the project. They submitted a scheme for classes on Cataloguing, Elementary Bibliography, and Historical Printing. Their Report was adopted, a small grant of money was made, and the Committee, with increased powers, and under the new title of "The Education Committee," were requested to undertake the management of the classes.

Dr. Garnett was the first Chairman of the Committee, and he was succeeded in 1902 by Mr. H. R. Tedder, who held that office until shortly before his death in 1924. Ever since the foundation of the Association Mr. Tedder had strongly advocated the training of assistants, and it was as a result of his paper on "Librarianship as a Profession"[1] that the first scheme of examinations was instituted. Mr. James Hutt, who has done yeoman service for the Association in the educational field, served as Chairman until 1929, when he was succeeded by the present writer.

Mr. Roberts, who had acted as Hon. Secretary of the Summer School since 1896, was appointed Hon. Secretary of the Education Committee, a position which he continued to occupy with great zeal and ability for ten years. He was succeeded by Dr. E. A. Baker, who filled the office with much acceptance until his appointment as Director of the School of Librarianship in 1919. Since then the secretarial work of the Committee has been carried

[1] *Transactions of the Fifth Annual Meeting*, 1882, p. 163.

TRAINING FOR LIBRARIANSHIP

out by the Secretary of the Association and his staff.

The classes organized by the Education Committee commenced in March 1898, and in the course of five years the whole of the examination syllabus of the Association was gone through. The lecturers were Messrs. Franklin T. Barrett, F. J. Burgoyne, Douglas Cockerell, Cecil Davis, W. E. Doubleday, Henry Guppy, J. Macfarlane, J. H. Quinn, H. D. Roberts, John Southward, and Miss Hentsch.

LONDON SCHOOL OF ECONOMICS

In 1902, on the recommendation of the Education Committee, the Council arranged with the London School of Economics to co-operate in conducting courses of instruction in the subjects of the examination syllabus on the following conditions, viz. that the Council of the Association should nominate the lecturers; that the classes should be open to all comers; that the Association continue to hold the professional examinations and to grant certificates; and that the Council should have equal representation with the Governors of the School of Economics on the Committee managing the classes.[1]

These lecture courses were carried on very successfully until 1917, when they were discontinued, and owing to the establishment of the University of London School of Librarianship they have not been resumed.

---

[1] "The Education of the Librarian," by H. D. Roberts (*Library Association Record*, 1906, p. 556 et seq.).

THE PUBLIC LIBRARY MOVEMENT

UNIVERSITY OF LONDON SCHOOL OF
   LIBRARIANSHIP

In a Report by the Education Committee on training in Librarianship, adopted by the Council in March 1919, a general scheme was set forth for a School at University College, as formulated by a Joint Sub-Committee of the Association and the College authorities. The scheme was submitted to the Carnegie United Kingdom Trustees with an application for a sufficient endowment for the School.

The Trustees considered the application very sympathetically and made a grant of £7,500 payable in five yearly instalments of £1,500, and the School was duly established in the month of October under the management of a Joint Committee, the Library Association members of which were the President (Sir J. Y. W. MacAlister), the Hon. Treasurer, and Chairman of the Education Committee (H. R. Tedder), the Hon. Secretary of the Association (F. Pacy), with Messrs. Quinn, Sayers, and Twentyman.

Dr. Ernest A. Baker was appointed Director of the School, and the lecturers were A. J. K. Esdaile (Bibliography), W. R. B. Prideaux (Cataloguing and Library Routine), W. C. Berwick Sayers (Classification); B. M. Headicar (Library Organization), H. West Fovargue (Library Law), R. W. Chambers (Literary History), E. A. Baker (Literary History and Book Selection), Hilary Jenkinson (Palæography and Archives).

TRAINING FOR LIBRARIANSHIP

From the start the success of the School has been marked. Ninety-eight students were enrolled in the opening year, and the average yearly attendance is over 100.

The course of training for the Diploma in Librarianship is open:

(a) To matriculated students.
(b) To non-matriculated students whose preliminary education appears to the School of Librarianship Committee to be sufficient to enable them to take advantage of the course of training.

The course normally extends over two academic years for day students, and over not less than three years nor more than five years for evening students, and includes approved instruction in all subjects to be taken at the examination. Full-time paid service for twelve months in an approved library in addition to attendance at lectures and passing examinations is a condition precedent of obtaining the Diploma. Such library service may be made either before entering or after completing the School course.

Exemption from attendance at courses in which a student has received approved training may be granted to University graduates or to students who, while satisfying the requirements for admission, have already held salaried posts in recognized libraries for not less than five years, provided that before being admitted to the examination for the Diploma every day student shall pursue an approved course in London University extending over not

THE PUBLIC LIBRARY MOVEMENT

less than one year, and every evening student a course extending over not less than two years.

The subjects of the ordinary course and examination are as follows:

(i) English Composition: one paper.
(ii) Latin *or* Greek *or* Sanskrit *or* Classical Arabic: one paper.
(iii) An approved modern European language *or* an approved modern Oriental language: one paper.
(iv) Bibliography: two papers.
(v) Cataloguing and Indexing: two papers.
(vi) Literary History and Book Selection: two papers, together with a practical examination in Book Selection.
(vii) Classification: two papers.
(viii) Palæography and Archives: two papers.
(ix) Library Organization (including Public Library Law): two papers.
(x) Library Routine: two papers.

A graduate of the University or of another approved University in a Faculty other than the Faculty of Arts may take an alternative course and examination for the Diploma in the following subjects:

(i) (as above).
(ii) and (iii) Two approved languages other than English: one paper in each.
(iv–vii) (as above).
(viii) *Either* (*a*) Palæography and Archives (as above) *or* (*b*) History of Science: two papers.
(xi) Library Economy (i.e. Library Organization and Routine, so far as it is not peculiar to Public Library Administration): two papers.
(xii) Special Library Services: two papers.

TRAINING FOR LIBRARIANSHIP

For other information, apply to the Director of the School, University College, Gower Street.

A feature of the School has been the delivery of free public lectures on library and bibliographical topics during each session.

The holding of Easter and Summer Vacation Schools in different towns in England and on the Continent has been another successful feature. Such Schools have been held at Brussels, Paris, Florence, Heidelberg, Rome, and Geneva, and have proved very popular and instructive.

The School is performing a valuable service in the matter of training for librarianship that is calculated to raise the status of the profession throughout the country. Similar Schools might with advantage be established as part of the curriculum at other Universities.

OTHER SCHOOLS AND CLASSES

Successful Schools have also been held, and continue to be held, under the auspices of the North Midland Branch of the Association, of the Scottish Library Association (at Edinburgh and Glasgow in alternate years), and of University College, Dublin.

The Midland Division of the Association of Assistant Librarians organized classes open to the Division only, lectures being given gratuitously by members of the Birmingham staff. These classes were afterwards merged in the scheme of correspondence classes for the whole kingdom instituted by the above Association.

Classes are conducted at Glasgow under the auspices of the Scottish Library Association, lectures and practical work in class being given at Glasgow High School as continuation classes of the Glasgow Education Authority.

At Liverpool classes have been held under the auspices of the Liverpool Technical Education Committee, with the co-operation of the Liverpool Public Libraries Committee; and at Manchester similar classes have been conducted at the Municipal School of Technology.

Thus facilities for training have been provided at many of the principal towns in the United Kingdom and have been fully taken advantage of by many assistants anxious to qualify themselves for their life-work. One looks forward to the time when, at no very distant date it is to be hoped, there will be established at the larger municipal libraries permanent library schools where systematic practical training in librarianship will be available for all already in the service and for those who aspire to take up librarianship as a profession.

CORRESPONDENCE COURSES

Correspondence courses were inaugurated in the session 1904–5, and their conduct was entrusted to Messrs. J. D. Brown and J. H. Quinn, who were lecturers at the London School of Economics on the subjects of Library History and Organization, Practical Library Administration, and Cataloguing. The courses consisted of ten lessons in each subject.

TRAINING FOR LIBRARIANSHIP

A selection of technical literature was prescribed for reading, questions thereon were set, and various exercises on the principal subjects of the courses were given. The teacher corrected and commented upon the papers.

In 1908 the scheme was enlarged to include lectures on Literary History at King's College, London, by Mr. A. C. L. Guthkelch, Miss Belgrave, and Professor Gollancz, at the London School of Economics; on Bibliography by Mr. A. W. Pollard and Mr. H. D. Roberts, and on Library History and Library Routine, by Mr. J. D. Brown. Other lecturers in later years were L. Stanley Jast, H. W. Fovargue, Dr. E. A. Baker, J. H. Quinn, W. C. Berwick Sayers, and W. R. B. Prideaux. The correspondence courses on Cataloguing, Library History, and Library Routine were conducted by Messrs. W. R. B. Prideaux, E. A. Savage, and W. S. C. Rae, respectively, twelve lessons being given in each subject. The subjects of Classification by Mr. W. C. Berwick Sayers; of Literary History by Mr. W. E. Stebbing, B.A.; of Practical Bibliography by Mr. T. E. Turnbull and Mr. R. A. Peddie; and of Book Selection by Mr. J. D. Stewart, were added later. Other conductors of courses were Mr. G. E. Roebuck on Library History, Mr. J. D. Young on Book Selection, Miss Ethel S. Fegan on Cataloguing and Library History.

These courses have been carried on to date, their administration having been taken over by the Association of Assistant Librarians Section in 1930.

Although these correspondence classes are not of equal value with oral tuition as a means of training, they have enabled many assistants residing at a distance from centres where oral tuition is obtainable to prepare for and to pass the examinations with credit.

In addition to the official training schemes recorded above, several librarians established classes for their staffs in their own libraries. Mr. Jones, at Kensington Public Libraries, formed the staff into a society under the name of "The Kensington Book-fellows," he himself acting as president. Papers were read on literary and technical subjects, and a reading class in connection with the Summer School was formed. Social meetings also were held.

At Cardiff, Mr. Ballinger also formed the library staff into an association for the study and discussion of questions relating to practical librarianship, regular classes for instruction being held at stated intervals. Lectures were delivered by himself or by his deputy, and questions were set on the subjects of the lectures.

At Newcastle, too, classes for courses of study were instituted and carried on by two of the senior assistants, one of whom was Mr. H. D. Roberts, for the junior members of the staff. These classes were not technical but educational, three of the principal subjects being Latin, French, and Shorthand. Application was afterwards made to the Durham College of Science, and the Rutherford College, Newcastle, for permission being granted

TRAINING FOR LIBRARIANSHIP

to members of the library staff to attend classes at the Colleges free. This was readily granted, and they were also permitted to attend the Science and Art classes at several of the Board Schools in the evenings.

CHAPTER XIV

BRANCH AND DISTRICT ASSOCIATIONS AND SECTIONS

In various districts of the United Kingdom branches of the Association have been formed which have done much to spread the library movement, to form a rallying-ground for members whereby they may maintain contact with each other by frequent meetings to read and discuss papers on library matters, and to enjoy social intercourse. Much successful missionary work has in this way been carried out in districts which were dilatory in adopting the Public Libraries Acts, and information has been supplied to those interested in the spread of libraries and in the movement for adult education.

The first of these local associations to be formed was the *Librarians of the Mersey District*. Meetings began to be held in 1887, the Secretary and moving spirit being the late Charles Madeley, Librarian of Warrington, which borough was the first to establish a museum and library under the Museums Act. Quarterly meetings were held and were open to all librarians and assistants in Lancashire and Cheshire. The holding of meetings was discontinued on the reorganization of the North-Western Branch in May 1905.

The North Midland Library Association was formed

BRANCH AND DISTRICT ASSOCIATIONS

in March 1890. The district embraced the counties of Nottingham, Derby, Leicester, Northampton, and Lincoln. The reading of papers and discussions on them, and the making of visits to libraries in the district, printing, and bookbinding and other establishments, were features of this and other similar associations. Mr. John Potter Briscoe, Librarian of Nottingham Public Library, was elected the first President, and Mr. John T. Radford, Librarian of the Nottingham Mechanics' Institute, the first Hon. Secretary. Each of them held office for the first three years to 1892–93. It was then decided that the succeeding Presidents should serve for one year only at a time, so that the honour should go round. Mr. William Crowther, of Derby, held office as President on six separate occasions, Mr. Radford on three occasions, and the librarians of the principal towns in the area also served a year of office in turn. An innovation was made in 1920–21 and the three following years, when the Chairmen of the Committees of Nottingham, Leicester, Derby, and Newark held the office.

In 1929 the Association became a Branch of the Library Association, and the first meeting of the Branch was held at Leicester in January 1930. It was then decided that the office of President should be held for two consecutive years instead of one only, Mr. Walter A. Briscoe, Librarian of Nottingham, being the first President for 1930 and 1931.

When Mr. John Potter Briscoe demitted the office of President in 1893–94 he was elected Hon.

Secretary, and held that office until 1907–8, being re-elected in 1909–10 and 1910–11. Mr. Arthur Lineker served in 1908–9, and again in 1911–12 and 1912–13, when he gave place to Mr. Walter A. Briscoe, who held office until appointed President in 1917–18. Mr. W. P. Woolston, Nottingham, was Hon. Secretary in 1917–18, and President in 1919–20. Mr. Reginald W. Brown, Northampton, was Hon. Secretary from 1918 till 1920, being succeeded in that year by Miss Kate E. Pierce, Librarian of Kettering, the present holder of the office.

The Association of Assistant Librarians, originally known as the Library Assistants' Association, was formed at a meeting of students of the Library Association Summer School held at the Library Bureau on July 3, 1895. Mr. R. A. Peddie was called to the chair, and on the motion of Mr. W. W. Fortune, then Sub-Librarian of the Lewisham Public Libraries, it was resolved that an Association of Library Assistants should be formed. It was understood that the Association would be entirely distinct from the Library Association, its purpose being declared to be "to unite all persons engaged in library administration other than chief librarians."

The first meeting was held at 20, Hanover Square, Mr. R. A. Peddie being elected the first President. Mr. Fortune, who had agreed to act as interim Secretary, found himself unable to continue his services in that capacity, and Mr. F. Meaden Roberts, St. George's, Hanover Square Library,

BRANCH AND DISTRICT ASSOCIATIONS

was appointed. The newly-formed Association had the warm support of Mr. MacAlister and Mr. L. Inkster, both of whom kindly placed rooms at its disposal for meetings.

From its start the Association showed great activity. At first, fortnightly meetings were held, but afterwards once a month. At one of the early gatherings Miss M. S. R. James, who took a keen interest in the affairs of the Association, suggested the formation of a library of technical literature for the use of members. She secured a donation of two guineas from a friend, and herself gave a set of bound volumes of *The Library* to date. The library grew rapidly, many donations were received, and the text-books recommended by the Summer School Committee were purchased. The library is housed at the Public Library, Islington, and books are loaned to members residing at a distance on payment of postage.

In January 1898 *The Library Assistant*, the official organ of the Association, was founded, and has maintained a vigorous existence until the present day. It is distributed free of charge to members, and may be purchased by non-members. Its objects are to provide a record of the meetings of the Association, summaries of papers and discussions, the printing in full of important contributions, with notices of appointments vacant, and notes and news of interest to the members. While excluding chief librarians from membership, the Association is in the fullest sympathy with the objects of the Library Association, and seeks to aid it in its endeavours to provide the adequate professional education of assistants. Lists of books of the month and short reviews of technical books are given. The editor is Mr. T. E. Callander, Fulham Public Library. Various Branches, now termed Divisions, of the Association have been formed throughout Great Britain and Ireland. The first Branch to be established was the North-Western, and there are other active Branches (Divisions), viz. the Midland, North-Eastern, Eastern Counties, South Coast (now divided into the South-Eastern and South-Western Sections of the South Coast Division), South Wales, and Yorkshire. There is also an Irish Branch, the Association of Assistant Librarians of Ireland, with Belfast as headquarters.

The Association has always taken a keen interest in the education of its members. Study circles for technical education were early established, and for the past two years the entire charge of the correspondence courses of the Library Association, of which it now forms a very numerous and important section, has been handed over to it.

The Society of Public Librarians was founded in 1895, and was the outcome of a desire for an association, the membership of which should be restricted to librarians of public libraries, where matters affecting the interests of workers in public libraries could be discussed without the intervention of non-members of the profession. While not

BRANCH AND DISTRICT ASSOCIATIONS

antagonistic to the Library Association, some librarians felt that that body was too heterogeneous in composition to allow of free discussion on many such matters. The movement was initiated by the late Mr. Edward Foskett (Camberwell), Mr. C. W. F. Goss (then of Lewisham), and the late Mr. John Frowde (Bermondsey). Its objects were declared to be "To promote the interests of rate-supported libraries in London and vicinity by consultation and co-operation; to promote professional friendship and good feeling by affording opportunities for mutual social intercourse; to improve the professional status of its members by free discussion on library management and equipment, and questions of public library and literary interest."

The inaugural meeting was held at the Library Bureau, Bloomsbury, on December 4, 1895. Mr. Frowde was elected first President, and occupied that office until 1899, Mr. Goss undertaking the duties of Hon. Secretary. Subsequent Presidents were Messrs. Z. Moon (Leyton), W. C. Plant (Shoreditch), Frank E. Chennell (Willesden), W. Bridle (East Ham), C. W. F. Goss (Bishopsgate Institute), C. Whitwell (West Ham), S. Hatcher (Canning Town), H. J. Hewitt (Chiswick), B. J. Frost (East Ham), D. McDougall (Plaistow), and W. Hynes (Kensal Rise).

Mr. Goss continued to act as Hon. Secretary until 1907, when he became President, and Mr. H. Smith (Bishopsgate Institute) became Hon. Secretary until 1930; Mr. C. Godding holding office in 1931.

THE PUBLIC LIBRARY MOVEMENT

Monthly meetings during the winter months were held continuously from 1895 to 1930 for the discussion of papers by members on matters of professional interest. The social side was not neglected, and annual summer visits to places of historic and literary interest were a feature. The work of the Society is now largely covered by the London and Home Counties Branch of the Library Association, and meetings of the Society have been suspended, though it has not disbanded and meetings will be called as occasion arises.

The Birmingham and District Library Association was established on October 4, 1895, on the initiative of the late R. K. Dent, Librarian of Aston Manor Public Library. Its objects were declared to be the providing of opportunites for interchange of thoughts and opinions on library work, the visiting of libraries in the vicinity of the place of meeting, and the promotion of good-fellowship among all who take part in library work, whether as librarians, members of staffs, or members of library committees.

Meetings have been held in Birmingham, Wolverhampton, Worcester, Shrewsbury, Warwick, Leamington, Coventry, Stratford-on-Avon, Wednesbury, Walsall, West Bromwich, Oldbury, Dudley, Aston Manor, Handsworth, etc. Mr. Dent was appointed the first Hon. Secretary, and held that office for the long period of eighteen years, until he was elected President in 1913–14. Mr. G. Beetlestone, Librarian, Aston Branch Library, Birmingham, succeeded as

BRANCH AND DISTRICT ASSOCIATIONS

Hon. Secretary, and served until 1919–20; Mr. Julius T. Lakin held the office for three years, from 1920–21 to 1922–23, after which he was succeeded by Mr. Francis J. Thacker, Public Reference Library, Birmingham, the present holder of the office.

The Association, which became the Birmingham and District Branch of the Library Association in 1929, has had a long list of Presidents who have worthily maintained the dignity of the chair, and shown a keen and active interest in the affairs of the Association, which throughout its long career has been one of the most enterprising of these local associations. The Presidents have served for one year only at a time, the chief librarians of Birmingham, and their deputies, and the librarians of the principal towns in the area have each held the office in turn. Mr. Dent, who was the father and founder of the Association, served during the war years from 1913–14 to 1918–19. The Chairman and other members of various library committees in towns where the meetings have been held have occupied the presidential chair on no fewer than eleven separate occasions, thus showing their keen appreciation of the good work done by the Association.

The area covered by the Branch includes the counties of Warwick, Worcester, Stafford (South), Shropshire, Hereford, Gloucester, and Oxford, with an aggregate population of four and a half millions.

The following are some of the more important events in the history of the Branch:

THE PUBLIC LIBRARY MOVEMENT

In 1901, and again in 1907, a three days' Summer School for library assistants was held in Birmingham.

Between 1911 and 1914 courses of preparatory lectures for the L.A. Examinations were delivered in Birmingham, but were discontinued during the war.

At the request of the Library Association, a Conference was held in Birmingham on May 2, 1919, at which papers were read and discussions held on the following subjects: "Libraries and Reconstruction: the Financial Position" (Walter Powell); "The Functions of Technical Libraries" (Ernest A. Savage); "The Commercial Library" (S. A. Pitt); "Library Work with Children" (Sydney E. Harrison and Miss Annie J. Dawes). Resolutions were passed in favour of every effort being made to secure the removal of the rate limitation; of the establishment of technical and commercial libraries under the control of municipal authorities, supported by a Government grant; and of the establishment of children's libraries and reading-rooms as part of the municipal library system, and of the circulation of lending books in schools being undertaken by the education authority in co-operation with the library authority.

From 1923 the Association became an institutional member of the Library Association.

In 1928 a scholarship of £15 was founded through the generosity of a Past-President and the Vice-President, with the aid of a grant from the

BRANCH AND DISTRICT ASSOCIATIONS

Association. The scholarship has been awarded in 1928, 1929, and 1931 for the best essay on a prescribed subject dealing with library management.

As from April 1, 1929, the Association became the Birmingham and District Branch of the Library Association.

In 1930 a Joint Committee of the Branch and the Midland Division of the Association of Assistant Librarians' Section was appointed to co-ordinate the professional and educational work of the area. This Committee successfully organized the Library Association Summer Schools held in Birmingham at Chancellor's Hall, Edgbaston, in 1930 and 1931. The membership of the Branch in 1931 reached a total of 370.

The North-Western Branch was formed at a meeting held in the Public Library, Manchester, on July 15, 1896. It was the first Branch to be established under the policy inaugurated by the Association for forming local branches of the Association, with corresponding secretaries, in districts where at least six fellows or members are located. The N.W. Branch included all members of the parent Association in Lancashire and Cheshire, with such other members as might signify their desire to be included. The Branch has always been a very active one. In the second year of its existence it founded a Summer School limited to those actually engaged in library work, and prizes for proficiency were given. The late Mr. Charles Madeley, Warrington, was the first Hon. Secretary of the Branch, and Mr. G. T. Shaw, then Librarian of the Athenæum, Liverpool, took up the duties of Secretary of the Summer School, which was very successfully carried on for many years. Mr. Edward McKnight, Librarian of Chorley, succeeded Mr. Madeley as Secretary in 1906. Mr. James Hutt, then Librarian of the Liverpool (Lyceum) Library, became Secretary in 1911, and held that office until his appointment to Portsmouth in 1917, when he was succeeded by Mr. J. W. Singleton, Librarian of Accrington, the present Secretary (1931).

The Northern Counties Library Association was founded in 1901 on the initiative of Mr. Basil Anderton, Chief Librarian, Newcastle-upon-Tyne. At the inaugural meeting Mr. Anderton was elected President, and Mr. J. W. C. Purves, Librarian of Workington, Hon. Secretary. The membership was at first drawn from an area embracing the counties of Northumberland, Durham, Westmorland, Cumberland, and Yorkshire, as far south as Leeds, but Yorkshire was afterwards excluded. Meetings were held at stated intervals in various towns within the area, and were well attended. Mr. Purves was succeeded as Hon. Secretary in 1904 by Mr. H. E. Johnston, Gateshead, who died in 1914. Mr. B. R. Hill, Sunderland, acted as Hon. Secretary for a period during the illness of Mr. Johnston; and Mr. William Wilson, Darlington, took over the duties of Hon. Secretary and Treasurer in 1914.

After January 1, 1915, the membership was reduced from ninety-six to sixty-three, owing to

BRANCH AND DISTRICT ASSOCIATIONS

the operation of the new byelaw of the Library Association concerning Branches which excluded from Branch membership those professional members who were not in membership of the parent body. The result was that no meetings of the Branch were held after August 1915 until May 21, 1919, when they were resumed for a short period, Mr. W. E. Hurford, Newcastle, acting as Hon. Secretary. Since 1921 the Branch has ceased to function.

The Presidents of the Branch served for two years in succession. The office has been filled successively by Messrs. Anderton, T. W. Hand (Leeds), Butler Wood (Bradford), Baker Hudson (Middlesbrough), G. W. Byers (Harrogate), A. H. Furnish (York), Alderman D. S. Ward (Harrogate), Ernest Bailey (South Shields), and J. W. C. Purves (Workington).

Annual Joint Conferences of the North Central, North-Western, and North Midland Branches have been held in various centres since 1921. The Birmingham and District Association (afterwards Branch) has joined in these Conferences since 1927. The Conferences are held in the different Branch areas in rotation. Meetings have been held in Norwich, Ilkley, Chester, Harrogate, Nottingham, Lytham St. Anne's, Matlock, Leamington Spa, Leicester, Morecambe, and Hereford. The importance of these Joint Conferences was emphasized at the Hereford meeting by Mr. Jast and Lieut.-Colonel Mitchell. In addition to bringing together a large number of members for discussions and social intercourse, they serve to relieve to some extent the congestion of the Annual Conferences of the Association. It was suggested that some of the more purely professional matters on the programmes of Annual Conferences might with advantage be delegated to the Branches and Sections, which would leave the larger Conference freer for attention to matters concerning the general affairs of the Association and to questions of interest to the public.

Bristol and Western District Branch had its origin in a meeting convened by Mr. E. R. Norris Mathews, City Librarian, Bristol, in May 1903. It was resolved to form a Branch of the L.A. as a means of intercommunication for members in that area and for the holding of meetings for the discussion of all matters relating to librarianship and bibliography.

At the Leeds Conference in the following September a constitution and byelaws were adopted and a Council appointed. Alderman John Walls, Chairman of the Bristol Public Libraries Committee, was elected President, Mr. Mathews, Hon. Treasurer, and Mr. L. Acland Taylor, then Deputy Librarian, Bristol, Hon. Secretary.

The Branch, unfortunately, had but a short career. In January 1910, in consequence of a communication from the Hon. Secretary of the Library Association drawing attention to the byelaw as to membership of Branches being confined to members of the Association, it was decided to

BRANCH AND DISTRICT ASSOCIATIONS

dissolve the Branch, since the result of the application of this byelaw would so reduce the membership of the Branch as to make it too small to continue.

The Scottish Library Association had its origin in a meeting of Scottish librarians, presided over by Dr. F. T. Barrett, held on the occasion of the Glasgow meeting of the Library Association in 1907. The question of forming a Branch of that Association or of establishing a separate association was discussed, and it was decided that as Scottish libraries are administered under separate Acts of Parliament and have problems of their own, the better plan would be to have a separate Association for Scotland, but affiliated to the Library Association.

The inaugural meeting at which the Association was constituted was held in Edinburgh in October 1908, and the first annual meeting took place in Edinburgh on May 12, 1909. Annual meetings have since been held in different Scottish towns, being confined at first to one-day meetings, but latterly extending over two days.

The following have held the office of President for the periods indicated: Francis Thornton Barrett, LL.D., City Librarian, Glasgow (1908–1911); Alexander Hastie Millar, Chief Librarian, Dundee (1911–1915); Hew Morrison, LL.D., Principal Librarian, Edinburgh (1915–1919); George Milne Fraser, Chief Librarian, Aberdeen (1919–1921); John Minto, M.A., Librarian, Signet Library, Edinburgh (1921–1925); Ryrie Orr, M.A.

THE PUBLIC LIBRARY MOVEMENT

F.E.I.S., Chairman, Greenock Public Library Committee (1925–1927); Septimus A. Pitt, City Librarian, Glasgow (1927–1928); Frank Carr Nicholson, M.A., Librarian, Edinburgh University (1928–1929); Ernest A. Savage, Principal Librarian, Edinburgh (1929–1931); Septimus A. Pitt, City Librarian, Glasgow (1931–1932).

The office of Hon. Secretary has been filled successively by James Craigie, Sandeman Public Library, Perth (1908–11); W. Munro Mackenzie, Dunfermline Public Library (1911–1915); Edgar H. Parsons, Stirling's Library, Glasgow (1915 to date).

David Duff, Librarian, Ayr (1908–11); James Craigie, Perth (1911–16); W. Storrie Beveridge, Public Library, Edinburgh (1916–30); James H. Stewart, Public Library, Edinburgh (1930 to date), have in turn served as Treasurer.

The Association offers annually a scholarship of the value of £15 for the most meritorious essay on a prescribed subject.

A short-term school of training for assistants, of one week's duration, was founded in 1922, and successive schools have been held in Glasgow or Edinburgh in 1923, 1925, 1926, 1928, and 1930. The syllabus covers lectures and demonstrations on the subjects embraced in the Library Association professional examinations. The lecturers have been drawn from the membership of the Association, and their services have been given gratuitously.

Local District meetings for the discussion of

BRANCH AND DISTRICT ASSOCIATIONS

topics of professional, bibliographical, and literary interest are held in Edinburgh and Glasgow during the winter months, and visits are paid to printing offices, bookbinding, leathermaking, papermaking, and other establishments of interest to the members.

The Council have under consideration the drafting of a consolidating and amending Bill for Scottish public libraries.

In January 1931 the Scottish Library Association entered into union, as a Branch, with the Library Association. The membership totals 423.

An important Conference was held at Dunblane on March 6–8, 1931, under the auspices of the Carnegie United Kingdom Trust and the Scottish Library Association. The object of the Conference was twofold: (1) to discuss the library policy of the Trustees for the quinquennium 1931–35, and (2) to examine the relation between county and municipal authorities under the library clauses of the Local Government (Scotland) Act, 1929.

At the Conference resolutions were passed in favour of inter-loans of books between libraries, and the establishment of a National Central Library for Scotland. In the matter of co-operation between county and burgh authorities, after prolonged discussion it was resolved that, pending future legislation, where money is raised as part of the education rate by the county authority for library purposes, some reasonable return should be given to the burgh authority, such return to be determined after consultation with the burgh authority.

THE PUBLIC LIBRARY MOVEMENT

The North Central Branch had its origin in a meeting held at Leeds on June 29, 1916. At this preliminary meeting it was decided to form a Library Association covering the West Riding of Yorkshire and all that part of Lancashire and Cheshire which lies to the east of a north-and-south line drawn to the west of Greater Manchester, including such places as Eccles, Altringham, and Accrington, which are near to or on such a line.

Considerable opposition was shown to the proposal from members of the North-Western Branch and of the Northern Counties Library Association, both of which were affected thereby. The L.A. Council, however, issued a Branch certificate in favour of the new Association, and it was duly constituted. The successive Presidents were Messrs. Henry Guppy, L. Stanley Jast, Councillor F. Bentley, Chairman of the Leeds Libraries Committee, and Mr. T. W. Hand, Librarian of Leeds Libraries. Mr. Jast was the first Hon. Secretary, and he was succeeded by Mr. Edward Green, Librarian of Halifax Public Library, who held office until 1928.

In 1918, when the Council of the Library Association decided not to hold the Annual Conference that year, the North Central Branch called a two-days Conference in Manchester in October, which was attended by members from all over the kingdom, many representatives of technical institutions and societies being present and taking part in

BRANCH AND DISTRICT ASSOCIATIONS

the discussions. The subjects discussed were Commercial and Technical Libraries, the Libraries of Business Firms, Work with Children, and the Financial Position of Libraries.

After the discussion on Mr. Pitt's paper on "The Commercial Library," Mr. Jast moved "That this meeting urges upon the Council of the Library Association the formation of a special Technical and Commercial Section of the Association," which was declared carried.

Following on Mr. Jast's paper on "Library Work with Children," it was moved and carried unanimously that the provision of children's libraries and reading-rooms adequately equipped and suitably staffed is an urgent national need ... that the reading-rooms should remain, as now, part of the municipal library system, and that the circulation of lending books in the schools should be undertaken by the education authority in co-operation with the library authority.

Mr. Alderman Abbott, Manchester, who had for years taken an enthusiastic interest in the campaign for the abolition of the penny rate for public libraries, contributed a paper on "The Financial Position of Public Libraries," and after discussion it was moved and carried "That this meeting of library authorities and librarians, representing all parts of the country, urges on the Government the absolute necessity of the removal of any limitation on the library rate." It was further moved and carried "That the Council of the Library Association

THE PUBLIC LIBRARY MOVEMENT

be requested to arrange immediately for a deputation to the Local Government Board in order to press for temporary relief pending legislation."

In thus strengthening the hands of the Council of the Association the Branch played an important part. In its earlier years the meetings were well attended, and much useful work was done, but later the interest flagged and the attendance dwindled, and in July 1928 it was decided to discontinue the Branch.

Library Association of Ireland.—At an Irish Library Conference held at University College, Dublin, on June 26–29, 1923, organized by Mr. Lennox Robinson, Secretary to the Carnegie Trust in Ireland, it was decided, on the motion of Mr. J. J. O'Neill, to form an Irish Library Association, and a Committee was appointed to make the necessary arrangements. The Association was duly formed, and has established an official Journal, with the title *An Leabharlann* (*The Library*). A library of professional literature, reports, plans, etc., is being formed for the information and use of the members.

An earlier *Irish Library Association* was founded in June 1904 and flourished for several years with a membership of over 130. Its Journal, *An Leabharlann*, contained articles on Irish history and literature, as well as on library history and administration.

Northern Ireland Library Association.—At a meeting of representative municipal and county libra-

BRANCH AND DISTRICT ASSOCIATIONS

rians held at Belfast on June 23, 1928, it was decided to form an association with the above title, to unite all persons engaged in, or interested in, library work in Northern Ireland. In the following year the Association became a Branch of the Library Association. Mr. J. B. Goldsbrough, Chief Librarian, Belfast, was elected Chairman; Mr. A. Stewart Roy, County Antrim, Hon. Secretary; Mr. D. J. H. Simpson, Belfast, Hon. Treasurer.

A successful Conference representing the library authorities of Ulster was convened by the Belfast Libraries, Museum, and Art Committee, with the support of the Carnegie Trustees, on March 24, 1927. It was decided to appoint a representative committee of librarians to draw up a scheme of co-operation between the various counties in Northern Ireland in the matter of book distribution. In this matter of co-operation Mr. Thomas Gorrie, Chairman of the Standing Library Committee, Carnegie U.K. Trust, stated on behalf of the Trust, that it was their considered policy to help in setting up a system of co-operation by which the smaller libraries might under proper conditions borrow from the stronger libraries.

The London and Home Counties Branch was formed at a meeting held at the Public Library, Buckingham Palace Road, on May 1, 1923, under the chairmanship of Mr. Herbert Jones, Librarian of Kensington. A Council was appointed consisting of six representatives for London, and six for the remaining counties, viz. Essex, Herts, Middlesex,

THE PUBLIC LIBRARY MOVEMENT

Bucks, Berks, Kent, Surrey, and Sussex. Members of the Library Association and professional librarians nominated as delegates by library authorities are eligible for election to the Branch. No provision was made for the election of non-professional members in the rules and regulations then drawn up. Mr. W. Benson Thorne, Bromley Public Library, was elected Hon. Secretary and Treasurer. Mr. H. Rowlatt, Borough Librarian of Poplar, Chairman of the Branch, presided at the first meeting held at the St. Bride Institute. Forty-seven members and twenty-three visitors, mainly younger members of library staffs, were present. Monthly meetings are held regularly at various centres in London and district from October to May, at which papers are read and discussed. Annual meetings have been held at Worthing, Hampstead, Richmond, Croydon, Southend, Watford, Colchester, and Twickenham. Joint meetings have taken place with ASLIB and with the Association of Assistant Librarians. The Branch adopted in 1928 a Code of Public Library Rules and Byelaws with a view to their use in different libraries. Mr. J. H. Quinn succeeded Mr. Rowlatt as Chairman of the Branch and served for two years. He in turn was followed by Colonel L. Newcombe for 1927–28. Mr. Thorne, the present Chairman, who had filled the office of Secretary so well from its start, was elected in 1929.

The Association of Special Libraries and Information Bureaux (ASLIB) was formed at a Conference

BRANCH AND DISTRICT ASSOCIATIONS

held at High Leigh, Hoddesdon, Hertfordshire, in September 1924, of those interested in special libraries and agencies for the collection, treatment, and distribution of information. The Carnegie United Kingdom Trust gave a grant in aid, and the first Conference Proceedings were published in 1925. Annual Conferences have since been held at Balliol College, Oxford, 1925, 1926; Trinity College, Cambridge, 1927; New College, Oxford, 1928; Trinity College, Cambridge, 1929; New College, Oxford, 1930; Lady Margaret Hall, Oxford, 1931. Reports of the Proceedings of these Conferences are published by the Association.

The objects of the Association are: To examine, foster, and co-ordinate the activities of special libraries, information bureaux, and similar services; to act as a clearing house for these services; to develop the usefulness and efficiency of special libraries and information bureaux, under whatever titles they may function; and generally to promote, whether by conferences, meetings, or other means, the wider dissemination and the systematic use of published information. The Association aims at assisting members who desire information of any kind to get into touch with the appropriate library or other body specializing on the subject; it does not itself attempt to build up any centralized organization to provide the detailed information direct.

In 1928 the Association published the *ASLIB Directory*, edited by Mr. G. F. Barwick, late Keeper of Printed Books, British Museum.

THE PUBLIC LIBRARY MOVEMENT

The Association also publishes a quarterly bulletin for members, entitled *ASLIB Information*, as a means of regular communication between officers of the Association and members.

A panel of about 200 expert translators covering forty-one languages has been formed for those who require such service.

The Association has adopted the Decimal Classification of the Institut International de Bibliographie as the system best adapted for making available the rapidly increasing mass of recorded information to workers in every intellectual field.

The Union Catalogue of London Libraries, the compilation of which is being carried out at the National Central Library, owes its origin to a large extent to ASLIB, at whose Conferences the value of such a catalogue was emphasized and its compilation was strongly advocated.

The Association has worked in conjunction with the Library Association in the production of the Report of the Durability of Paper Committee of that Association, which has demonstrated that durable papers can be produced and sold at commercial prices. The use of such papers is essential in the printing of all records of permanent value.

The Association has done good work from the librarian's point of view in regard to securing uniformity of page size in journals, with the consequent standardization of advertisement net space page size for all trade and technical journals. Communications have also been made with the Pub-

BRANCH AND DISTRICT ASSOCIATIONS

lishers' Association with the view of securing more adequate bibliographical information in publishers' catalogues, and uniformity in the use of trade terms, e.g. impression, edition, re-issue, etc.

The Association's offices are at 16, Russell Square; General Secretary, S. S. Bullock.

The University and Research Section of the Association was formed at the Blackpool Conference in 1928. It had been felt that the preponderance in numbers of municipal librarians in the Association had tended to push into the background matters and interests more immediately concerning members representing national, university, university college, and research libraries, and that this had led to many of the latter holding aloof from membership. The proposed section, it was urged, could assume responsibility for sectional meetings at Annual Conferences, and could in various ways ensure adequate attention to the important functions of university and research libraries, and would, it was hoped, lead to an increased membership of the Association.

At the inaugural meeting at Blackpool, a Committee was formed with Mr. Arundell Esdaile, Secretary of the British Museum, as Chairman, and Mr. R. H. Hill, Bodleian Library, Oxford, as Hon. Secretary. This Committee met in London in January 1929, drafted rules, and issued a circular inviting membership.

Meetings have since been held at the Association Headquarters in London in the beginning of

THE PUBLIC LIBRARY MOVEMENT

January to coincide with meetings of the University Libraries Joint Standing Committee, and at the Annual Conferences at Brighton, Cambridge, and Cheltenham, when papers on subjects of special interest to the section have been read and discussed. The members of the section hold an annual dinner at Conference time.

A Welsh Branch of the Association was formed at an inaugural meeting in Cardiff on September 23, 1931. Mr. Harry Farr, Librarian of Cardiff, was elected Chairman, and Mr. W. Ll. Davies, Librarian of the National Library of Wales, Aberystwyth, Hon. Secretary. A provisional agreement has been arrived at for the establishment of a regional scheme for Wales and Monmouth, with headquarters at Aberystwyth, with a subsidiary scheme for Glamorgan and Monmouth, with headquarters at Cardiff.

CHAPTER XV

OTHER LIBRARY ASSOCIATION ACTIVITIES

In addition to the successful efforts of the Association in promoting the adoption of the Public Libraries Acts, in securing better legislation for libraries, and in the training of library assistants, the Association has done much good work in other directions, all tending towards rendering the public library of more value to its users.

Exhibitions

At the International Conferences of 1877, 1897, and 1927, exhibitions of library appliances illustrating the working arrangements of libraries in all their departments were held. Similar exhibitions were also held at different annual meetings of the Association, e.g. at Liverpool in 1883, and at Reading in 1890. At these exhibitions there were shown plans and designs of buildings, book-cases, shelving, etc. In recent years, books, new and second-hand, book-bindings, and leathers for binding have formed a very important feature of the annual exhibitions, in addition to library appliances of all sorts. Most of the prominent bookselling and bookbinding firms are annual exhibitors, and the exhibition is formally declared open by the President of the Association.

THE PUBLIC LIBRARY MOVEMENT

PUBLICATIONS

Many of the publications of the Association are of purely professional interest, but certain others of general interest to users of public libraries may be mentioned.

The chief publications will be found listed in chronological order in the Annals of the Association, compiled by the Hon. Secretary, Mr. E. A. Savage, published in the 1932 issue of the Association's *Year Book*.

From 1903 to 1908 a series of classified lists of Best Books on all subjects were issued. The best books of the years 1902 to 1904 were printed in the *Library Association Record, 1903–1906*. Those for 1905–6, 1906–7, and 1907–8 were published separately and met with a ready sale, but, unfortunately, this most useful publication, a labour of love by Mr. H. V. Hopwood, of the Patent Office, had to be discontinued owing to his serious breakdown in health through overwork.

A Sound Leather Committee of experts was appointed by the Association to investigate the quality of bookbinding leathers. Many of those then in use deteriorated quickly, but as a result of the recommendations made by the Committee in their Report entitled *Leather for Libraries* (1905) a great improvement in the quality of leathers put upon the market was effected with great advantage to the public.

The Code of Cataloguing Rules issued con-

OTHER LIBRARY ASSOCIATION ACTIVITIES

jointly with the American Library Association in 1908 did much to improve and standardize the cataloguing practice in public libraries. A pamphlet on machine book sewing, with remarks on publishers' bindings, in the same year led to an improvement in this class of work.

An Interim Report by the Book Production Committee published in 1913 was instrumental in improving the general get-up of books. A revised edition of this pamphlet, which had been long out of print, was issued in 1931 by the Durability of Paper Committee, and embodied the recommendations contained in their Report on that important subject. The result of their labours has been the placing on the market standard papers which should be used for the printing of all books likely to be of permanent value.

The Subject Index to Periodicals which began in 1915 has been of great service to readers and researchers by making available the most up-to-date information on all sorts of subjects published in the principal magazines and journals of this country and in a selection of foreign periodicals.

During the Great War the lack of libraries to supply information to our manufacturers and commercial men was acutely felt. The Association appointed a special Technical and Commercial Libraries Committee which did much valuable work in co-operation with scientific and technical associations and institutions in securing the establishment of such libraries in most of the larger industrial centres throughout the country. These proved of the utmost value in the sphere of reconstruction after the war.

The publication of a guide to Reference Books in 1929, with its supplement in 1931, has proved of value in reference library work.

In 1930 the Association published a classified and annotated guide to young readers entitled *Books to Read* (Supplement, 1931), which has been widely distributed by the Carnegie United Kingdom Trust, and many copies have been sold. The publishers of the books listed in these volumes very generously presented a copy of each work for exhibition, and the collection is housed at the headquarters of the Association in London.

LIBRARY PUBLICITY

In 1921 two important papers were published in the *Library Association Record* on the question of "Library Publicity," by Mr. Lionel R. McColvin and Mr. Walter A. Briscoe. Both writers urged the need for bringing before the public the services which the public library is capable of rendering to every citizen. They held that it was the duty of the Library Association to endeavour by every possible means to influence public opinion to the realization of the fact that public libraries can be helpful to every trade, every science, every art, and almost every recreation. It was shown by the comparatively small proportion of citizens using the public libraries that their value was not fully appreciated,

OTHER LIBRARY ASSOCIATION ACTIVITIES

and to remedy this state of matters publicity was essential. Mr. Briscoe's article was expanded and published as *Library Advertising: Publicity Methods for Public Libraries.*

At the annual meeting of the Association in Manchester in 1921, Mr. Briscoe moved: "That a Library Publicity Committee be formed for national propaganda purposes." The motion was carried, and a Committee consisting of Messrs. Briscoe, Jast, G. P. Jones, Sayers, Singleton, and Stephen, with Mr. Jast as Chairman, and Mr. Briscoe as Hon. Secretary. A section of the *Record* was devoted to the monthly publication of Publicity Notes, a Press campaign was instituted directing attention to the educational importance of public libraries and decrying the idea of any further economy being practised at their expense. A number of London and provincial newspapers joined in the campaign. A pamphlet entitled *Education and Public Libraries*, embodying the views of leading educationists and public men, was widely distributed and was favourably received and commented upon in most papers. Messrs. Grafton & Co. "released" a library film showing different libraries at work, which could be hired for exhibition at local cinemas at a small fee. A second pamphlet was issued in 1922, entitled *Public Libraries and the People*, and again many libraries purchased copies and distributed them. Broadcasting was next resorted to, Mr. Jast speaking of children's libraries at Manchester, Mr. G. T. Shaw at Liverpool, and Mr.

THE PUBLIC LIBRARY MOVEMENT

Roebuck at Walthamstow, bringing the public library before the public through wireless talks. Publicity posters were issued by various public libraries, and were a useful feature of the campaign.

In 1929 Mr. L. R. McColvin published his useful work on *Library Extension Work and Publicity*, containing a mass of valuable information on almost every aspect of public library development.

The publicity campaign was highly successful, and might with advantage be repeated from time to time.

THE NET-BOOK AGREEMENT

Up to about thirty years ago the practice had prevailed of booksellers giving discounts on books to purchasers. The discount so given varied, but gradually became stabilized at 25 per cent. off published prices. Undercutting was rife, and the book trade, so far at least as the bookseller was concerned, had become very unremunerative. Most booksellers were obliged to resort to stocking sidelines in fancy goods of all sorts in order to make ends meet. Bookselling pure and simple did not pay.

In order to remedy this state of matters an agreement was made between publishers and booksellers which came into force in January 1900, that books published at net prices were to be sold by booksellers at the full published price, no discount being allowed on any book marked "net." At first, comparatively few books were so marked, fiction

OTHER LIBRARY ASSOCIATION ACTIVITIES

and school books in particular not being so treated. But the number of books published "net" quickly grew, until practically every book published was a net book. Many readers will recall the Book War which The Times Book Club waged against the system, particularly against a later agreement which provided that no book might be sold as second-hand at less than the published price until the expiry of six months after publication. In the end, the book trade won the battle for the net-book system.

Public libraries felt that they, as large purchasers of books, were entitled to better terms than the casual purchaser of a single book. It was contended that not only were the public libraries large purchasers, many of the larger libraries buying many copies of a particular book, but also that their orders gave less trouble to the bookseller, as they provided him with exact particulars of the books ordered, publisher, price, date, etc., their accounts were paid regularly, and no bad debts were incurred. It was further claimed that but for the orders from public libraries many important and costly books could never be published at all. The trade, however, both publishers and booksellers, strongly resisted the giving of any discount to libraries, contending that to do so would break down the net-book system which had proved of so great value to the booksellers.

At a monthly meeting of the Library Association in March 1902 the question of "net books" was raised by Mr. W. E. Doubleday, Librarian, Hamp-

THE PUBLIC LIBRARY MOVEMENT

stead Public Libraries, who read a paper on the subject, and moved the following resolutions which were carried and afterwards approved by the annual meeting of the Association at Birmingham in September, viz.:

1. That this meeting of the Library Association—whilst heartily wishing the bookselling trade every success—regrets that, under existing trade arrangements, booksellers are prohibited from allowing libraries any discount from the published price of net books.

2. That having regard to the fact that libraries are extensive purchasers of new books, the Council be and are hereby requested to approach the Publishers' Association, or to take such other steps as may be deemed expedient, with a view to obtaining such freedom of action for the booksellers as they may desire in respect of the terms of discount to be allowed to libraries.

In accordance with the foregoing resolutions, the Council of the Library Association requested the Publishers' Association to receive a deputation on the question. The Publishers replied that as they had established the system at the request of the retail trade they were not prepared to reopen the question.

A similar reply was received from the Associated Booksellers, declining to receive a deputation, in May 1904.

In October 1906 the Council appointed a Committee to consider and draft a further letter to the Associated Booksellers, but the reply was both unsympathetic and unsatisfactory.

The Publishers' Association were again approached. It was pointed out to them that many

OTHER LIBRARY ASSOCIATION ACTIVITIES

booksellers were willing to supply net books to libraries on discount terms, and the publishers were asked to permit them such freedom of action with respect to public libraries.

In February 1907 an important Conference convened by the Library Association Council was held at 20, Hanover Square, when sixty representatives of library authorities were present, and fifteen others had written expressing sympathy with the objects of the Conference. In all, over 150 delegates and members attended. Mr. H. R. Tedder presided, and gave a succinct account of the history of the movement. He stated that the Conference had been called to consider what steps should be taken to secure preferential terms for public libraries.

Mr. W. W. Topley, a member of the Croydon Public Libraries Committee, moved the following resolutions:

1. That this Conference representing various public and non-commercial libraries of the country is of opinion that the present system of net-book supply presses most unfairly upon these institutions which exist for the public benefit, and urges upon the Publishers' Association the desirability of allowing special terms to be conceded to this class of buyers, the justice of the demand having been already recognized by the publishers of the United States.

2. That a Committee of the Conference be appointed to bring the foregoing resolution before the Publishers' Association.

3. That in the event of the reply of the Publishers' Association being unsatisfactory, the Committee is instructed to prepare and submit some scheme of co-operation among public libraries.

THE PUBLIC LIBRARY MOVEMENT

Alderman Abbott (Manchester), Mr. John Ballinger (Cardiff), Councillor H. Plummer (Chairman of the Manchester Public Libraries Committee), and others supported the motion. Alderman H. W. Keay (Eastbourne, President of the Associated Booksellers) presented the case for the booksellers, arguing that in many cases where public libraries had been established they had caused a loss to booksellers, and were generally detrimental to the book trade. The booksellers could not make exceptions in their favour, but must charge net prices all round to maintain the net-book system.

The resolutions were carried and an influential Committee, including the President and officers of the Association, the speakers at the Conference, and others, was appointed.

A small deputation from the Committee waited upon a Committee of the Publishers' Association on May 9th, and were most courteously received. The Publishers' representatives seemed favourably disposed, but said they must report to their Association and communicate with the Associated Booksellers. The Hon. Secretary of the Library Association afterwards received a letter from the President of the Publishers' Association stating that they had referred the matter to the Booksellers, who had discussed it at their annual meeting in June and decided that it would be most undesirable to make any exception to the net-book rule. In view of this attitude of the Booksellers, the Council of the Publishers' Association expressed regret that

OTHER LIBRARY ASSOCIATION ACTIVITIES

they were unable to meet the wishes of the Library Association.

At the annual meeting of the Library Association at Glasgow in September 1907, Councillor Abbott and Mr. W. E. Doubleday opened a discussion on the question, and it seemed to be the opinion of the meeting that the solution of the matter was to be found in the co-operation of the various library authorities in the establishment of a book-purchasing bureau. Mr. Doubleday, in a note in the *Library Association Record* in November 1908, expressed doubts as to whether such an agency could be formed, and if formed, whether the publishers would supply books to it on trade terms.

For many years the *non possumus* attitude of the Publishers' and Booksellers' Associations put an end to negotiations between them and the Library Association, but in 1925 the question was re-opened. A special Net-Books Committee was appointed by the Library Association Council, and a Conference between representatives of the two Associations and the Committee was held on July 9th at Stationers' Hall. The question was fully discussed, but the result was as before. The Publishers wrote intimating inability to allow net books to be supplied at less than the full net prices.

Meanwhile, certain booksellers, anxious to do business with public libraries, were supplying books to libraries at less than full net prices in defiance of the agreement; others were getting behind the agreement by supplying books labelled, catalogued, and made ready for issue to the public in lieu of or in addition to discount. These practices the two Associations were anxious to prevent, but found it difficult to accomplish without the co-operation of the Library Association, and so they were willing to look more favourably on the suggestion that it would be desirable to come to an arrangement whereby any discounts that might be given would be made legitimate.

About this time (Autumn 1928) a Joint Committee of the Publishers' and Booksellers' Associations was reporting upon the organization of the book trade, and the opportunity was taken to get this committee to examine the situation. It reported in favour of a compromise, and after much negotiation, Mr. Doubleday, as Chairman of the Net Book Committee, was able to state to the Council in 1929 that an agreement had been reached and was ready for ratification.

The agreement provided that public rate-supported libraries and other libraries in institutional membership of the Library Association on condition of giving access to the public during their official hours of opening, are to be recognized by the trade as Book Agents entitled to a commission on their book purchases. The net-book system is thus preserved in its integrity.

Under the scheme, which came into operation in 1929, libraries expending £500 or more in a year upon the purchase of new books became entitled to a rebate of 10 per cent.; those spending between

OTHER LIBRARY ASSOCIATION ACTIVITIES

£100 and £500 to 5 per cent., and the amount of this commission had to be taken out in books at full published prices. These terms applied only to books issued in Great Britain and Ireland. Licences necessary to obtain this rebate are issued, to libraries complying with the conditions of the scheme, upon the recommendation of the Joint Advisory Committee—a standing Committee of the Publishers' and Booksellers' Associations to which two members of the Library Association are added for library business only. In 1931 the scheme was modified to allow the amount of the commission to be taken either in cash or kind at the option of the licensee, and by a further amendment in the following year the commission was increased to 10 per cent. for all licensed libraries purchasing new books to the value of £100 and upwards *per annum*.

The agreement remedies a grievance which had been strongly felt by library authorities ever since the establishment of the net-book system. The libraries are able to obtain more books for the same expenditure of public money, and the turnover of the bookseller is not diminished. In the attainment of this satisfactory result Mr. Stanley Unwin, representing the Publishers' Association, and Mr. W. E. Doubleday, on behalf of the Library Association, worked long and unselfishly to achieve an agreement acceptable to libraries, publishers and booksellers alike. To these two gentlemen and to the members of the Joint Advisory Committee, the gratitude of all concerned has been cordially expressed.

CHAPTER XVI

COUNTY LIBRARIES

In the first chapter of this work we have mentioned some of the various schemes for the supply of books to readers in rural districts. In England there were the libraries founded by Dr. Thomas Bray and his "Associates," and similar libraries founded by philanthropic persons, mainly for the use of the poorer clergy, though usually open to others on the production of good credentials. Most of these foundations, however, in spite of legislative enactments designed to secure their continuance, fell into decay and disuse through the apathy of those whose business it was to foster them, and by the lack of financial support.

In Scotland there were the parochial, presbyterial, and synodical libraries established by the General Assembly of the Church of Scotland in the early years of the eighteenth century, which became dormant partly on account of dissensions in the Church itself and partly through want of funds for their support. Towards the end of the second decade of the nineteenth century the system of itinerating libraries founded by Provost Brown, of Haddington, for the county of East Lothian, proved very successful for a number of years, but not long after his guiding hand and financial support were removed by death, those who were left to administer

COUNTY LIBRARIES

them were unable to find voluntary local librarians sufficiently enthusiastic to carry on the work. In the early years of this century Mr. James Coats, of Ferguslie, Paisley, presented 336 libraries to various outlying districts throughout Scotland, but mainly in the Highlands and Islands. These libraries consisted of well-selected collections of from 300 to 700 volumes each, and were gratefully received and much appreciated and much used by those who were the recipients of them. They were housed for the most part in schools, a condition of the presentation being that they should be housed free of cost and that no charge should be made for their use. In the course of a few years, however, owing to the absence of any provision for rebinding or renewal of the books or for additions to the stocks, they gradually became derelict.

All these schemes died of inanition in much the same way. They became less efficient and gradually fell into disuse when their philanthropic founders were no longer there to guide and foster them and to inspire others with their own enthusiasm.

Several schemes for the establishment of village libraries in different counties of England have to be recorded. In 1856 there was founded, under the auspices of the Yorkshire Union of Mechanics' Institutes, the Yorkshire Village Library, designed to afford to rural readers the same facilities for reading as were given to town dwellers through the Mechanics' Institutes. The headquarters of the Library was in Leeds, from which boxes of books were distributed to various centres throughout the county at an annual charge of a guinea per box. The scheme was in operation with varying success until the establishment of the county library system with which it became amalgamated.

Sir Henry Peto established a Book Lending Association at Dorchester for the county of Dorset about 1907. Boxes of thirty books were distributed three times a year to schools and village institutes in return for an annual charge of £1, one-quarter of the cost being met by the local education authority. On the formation of the Dorset County Library the scheme was handed over to it.

In 1905 Mr. Andrew Carnegie gave a grant of £1,600 towards the formation of a system of circulating libraries by Dr. Percival, Bishop of Hereford, with headquarters in Hereford. Boxes of fifty books, exchanged three times a year, were distributed to villages in the county at a charge of £1 per annum.

Similar schemes have been in operation in Buckinghamshire and in the Isle of Wight, where the Seely Library, established in 1904, was amalgamated with the County Library in 1924.

In 1913 Mr. Andrew Carnegie vested in the Carnegie United Kingdom Trust a sum of over two million pounds, the income of which he directed should be applied "for the improvement of the well-being of the masses of the people of Great Britain and Ireland. In the trust deed he made reference to public libraries as desirable objects of

COUNTY LIBRARIES

benefactions, as he considered them "entitled to a first place as instruments for the elevation of the masses of the people."

Having decided to give a foremost place to libraries in their scheme of benefactions, the Trustees invited Professor W. G. S. Adams to prepare a "Report on Library Provision and Policy," which they published in 1915. "From that Report the Trustees learned that, though there were many directions in which money could usefully be employed for the development of library provision, the great gap in that provision was to be found in the rural and the small urban areas, and that the main cause of the gap was that the financial resources of these areas were not sufficient to enable them to provide libraries for themselves. The line of policy which appeared to be indicated was the establishment of a unit of library provision larger than the parish; and the only available unit was the county."[1] The selection of the county as the unit was influenced by the knowledge that the corporate action of a larger area would enable the same sum of money to produce a greater result.

The Trustees began their scheme of establishing rural libraries by aiding with grants of money the schemes which we have referred to above as being already in operation. Grants were then offered to two counties, Staffordshire and Oxfordshire, of a sum to cover an experimental period of five years' work on the basis of the capital cost, including

[1] *Public Libraries Committee Report*, 1927, par. 292.

THE PUBLIC LIBRARY MOVEMENT

premises, books, and equipment, and the cost of maintenance for that period. The grant made to Staffordshire, which was the first county to accept the offer of the Trustees, was £5,000, afterwards increased to £7,500. This grant and subsequent grants were made on the understanding that at the end of the experimental period the accepting county would undertake to administer the library out of county funds. It was then discovered that although each individual parish within a county could adopt the Public Libraries Acts and so become the library authority for its area, no such power was vested in the larger area itself. The Carnegie Trustees at once took steps to have this anomaly remedied. They made representations to the Board of Education, pointing out that as their grants to county areas were limited in operation to a period of five years, at the end of that period the county authorities would be unable to take over the administration of the libraries which the Trustees had founded, unless legislation were introduced to enable counties to adopt the Acts and become library authorities for their areas. This action on the part of the Trustees, combined with the pressure brought to bear by the Library Association and various municipal authorities, led to the introduction into Parliament of a Bill by the Board of Education, which became the Public Libraries Act, 1919. Under this Act County Councils were empowered to adopt the Acts and to establish libraries within their areas, but must delegate their administration to Education Committees.

COUNTY LIBRARIES

Since the passing of the Act of 1919 County Councils throughout England (with the exception of three small counties), aided by the Carnegie Trustees, have adopted the Acts for the whole or parts of their areas, and have established libraries the success of which has demonstrated the urgent need there was for their creation.

The basis of the county library system is the formation of a central collection of books, the distribution of a selection from the collection to centres throughout the area and the loan of those books to the inhabitants through the medium of a local library. Where no such library exists, the school is the most readily available centre for the distribution of books, with the schoolmaster acting as voluntary librarian. The original capital cost of libraries and book-boxes was provided by the Carnegie Trustees. The system of lending by means of boxes of books has been added to, or is being superseded in many counties by a travelling library van or vans containing a large collection of books from which readers themselves select the books they wish to borrow.

The expenditure met by the counties in the year 1925 was at the rate of three-farthings per head of population served in county libraries (excluding those in their first year). For the year 1930–31 the cost of maintenance in three of the largest counties was approximately equal to the produce of a penny rate. The cost per head in these counties is between 3d. and 5d. This cost is likely to be considerably

THE PUBLIC LIBRARY MOVEMENT

exceeded in the near future when the libraries grow older and the stocks of books become worn out and need replacement, and when effect is given to the schemes now under consideration in a number of counties for extending the service to those centres of larger population which have hitherto not been served at all, or not adequately served, by the local county library scheme.[1] Demands are likely to be made in those more populous areas for permanent buildings to house reference collections as well as general lending libraries. The Carnegie Trustees have offered to some twenty-two counties a grant towards the cost of extending the service to their populous areas, and have asked these counties to prepare a programme which may be carried out within the quinquennium 1931–35, the Trustees to meet one-third of the cost of the capital expenditure.

In Scotland the county library system is administered under the provisions of the Education (Scotland) Act, 1918, Section 5, which empowers county education authorities, as an ancillary means of promoting education, to provide collections of books which shall be available not only to scholars in the schools, but also to adult persons within their areas. It should be noted that there is no limit imposed on the amount that education authorities may spend in this direction, so that Scottish county libraries have been organized untrammelled by the penny-rate limitation which

[1] E. Salter Davies in *Library Association Record*, 1931, pp. 398–99.

COUNTY LIBRARIES

for so long hindered the progress of library work in the burghs. The question of co-operation between county education authorities and the smaller burghs which have already established libraries under the Public Libraries Acts was discussed at a special Conference held at Dunblane in March 1931, which we have dealt with under the section on the Scottish Library Association.

CHAPTER XVII

COMMERCIAL AND TECHNICAL LIBRARIES

Commercial Libraries

The objects of commercial libraries may be defined to be the collection, indexing, arrangement, and distribution of such information as may be serviceable to those who are engaged in the business of manufacturing and mercantile affairs. That is to say, to supply the manufacturer with information regarding the sources and nature of raw materials, means of transport, methods of management, cost of production, markets and agents for distribution, tariffs, and all other particulars incidental to the successful conduct of home and foreign trade.[1]

It is desirable that the mass of information collected by the Commercial Intelligence Department of the Board of Trade should be made as widely known as possible, and the public library in its commercial department affords the best means of effecting this object. Where a separate building cannot be secured for this purpose, a section of the reference department should be organized as a commercial library in which should be collected directories, gazetteers, atlases, and maps, telegraphic code books, tariff lists, postal, shipping, and railway guides, parliamentary papers relating to trade and commerce, dictionaries of

[1] S. A. Pitt's Memorandum, *Library Association Record*, 1917, p. 175.

COMMERCIAL AND TECHNICAL LIBRARIES

technical terms in several languages, Acts of Parliament, trade catalogues of all sorts—in short, every item whether in book, pamphlet, or scrap-book form that is likely to be of value to the commercial man. The need for such information was clearly demonstrated during the Great War, and the want of it acutely felt both during and after that terrible calamity. Since then most manufacturing towns have risen to the occasion and have supplied the want by establishing commercial libraries.

Mr. Pitt, in his article above mentioned, has indicated two important adjuncts to the commercial library which are in use at Glasgow, viz. a Register of Business Firms, arranged alphabetically by names of articles produced or dealt in, and a Register of Translators, including a list of printers equipped for printing catalogues and trade lists in foreign languages.

The Interim Report on the provision of technical and commercial libraries[1] gives a list of the type of material which should be included in a commercial library, and mentions that useful lists of books for such a library are to be found in Mr. Bernard Kettle's *Directories and Codes in the Guildhall Library*,[2] and in Mr. Pitt's *The Purpose, Equipment, and Methods of the Commercial Library*, published by the Glasgow Public Libraries in 1916.

[1] *Library Association Record*, Vol. 19, 1917, pp. 551–57.
[2] Ibid., pp. 203–9.

THE PUBLIC LIBRARY MOVEMENT

TECHNICAL LIBRARIES

During the Great War the need for better technical libraries was as acutely felt as that for the establishment of commercial libraries. At a meeting of the authorities of scientific and technical societies and institutions in Glasgow, held in the Royal Technical College on June 27, 1916, and attended by representatives of fourteen societies, along with the City Librarian, it was resolved that with a view to mobilizing the resources of these institutions, a joint catalogue of the technical books in their libraries should be compiled, and a Committee was appointed to carry out the work, the City Librarian undertaking to act as editor.

In the same year Mr. E. A. Savage moved for the appointment of a Technical and Commercial Libraries Committee "to prepare a Report upon the ways and means of strengthening public technical and business libraries in industrial centres." The Committee was formed, with Mr. Savage as Hon. Secretary. He at once set to work to collect information, and requested members of the Association to send him any information or publications which would be useful to the Committee, and, in particular, to state the needs of their own districts. The Committee held a number of meetings and much information was forthcoming. An Interim Report was prepared and after approval was submitted to the Department of Scientific and Industrial Research in April 1917.

COMMERCIAL AND TECHNICAL LIBRARIES

After drawing attention to the great need for developing scientific and technical libraries, the Report submitted a number of recommendations, including, in the first place, the removal of the rate limitation, second, the formation of a national lending library of scientific and technical literature for research work; closer union between State and copyright libraries, on the one hand, and municipal public libraries, on the other, so as to make available for technical students the books in the former class of libraries. Other recommendations were that local authorities should be more generous in the provision of scientific and technical literature; that there should be co-operation in issuing union catalogues of technical books; that a State scientific or technical library should publish periodically a descriptive list of selected books in science and technology; that a more extended use of periodical literature should be made possible by the increased provision of current indices and digests (*Library Association Record*, 1917, pp. 551–57).

In the May issue of the *Library Association Record* there were published two Reports which were provisionally approved by the Committee. The first, on Trade Catalogues, indicated the purposes served by such catalogues and detailed the methods of collecting them, arranging, binding, and shelving them, and recommending that proposals should be made to the leading professional societies and trade journals for the organization of this class of literature on standardized lines. The second Report dealt with Patent Libraries, giving particulars of their contents as to specifications, abridgments, subject indices, etc., and the methods of their supply by the Patent Office.

At the annual meeting of the Association in London, in October 1917, a resolution was moved by Mr. E. Wyndham Hulme urging the necessity for these technical libraries being established as departments of public libraries in all important manufacturing towns, with a special organization, including a librarian trained not only in library methods but possessing also a sufficient technical knowledge to enable him to act as a medium of information to inquirers. The resolution was carried unanimously. In his paper Mr. Hulme stated that the foundation of a technical library should be a collection of modern standard text-books, encyclopædias, dictionaries, and tables, to which should be added a collection of polyglot technological dictionaries, not only for the use of the staff but to attract the translator class to the library.

In February 1918 Mr. Savage read a paper before the Institution of Automobile Engineers on the "Utilization of the Accumulated Data of the Automobile Industry," and in the discussion which followed it was brought out that the arguments used in favour of an information bureau for one industry exclusively would apply equally to all industries, and a good deal of overlapping would occur in the case of analogous industries. Much of the data collected would be common to more than one industry; it would be necessary, therefore, for each individual industry to collect only the vitally essential material and to look to a central bureau of information for scientific and industrial research, the formation of which was advocated by the Library Association. A resolution was moved in favour of the provision of a National Central Reserve Library or Libraries, and copies of said resolution and of Mr. Savage's paper were sent to the Department of Scientific and Industrial Research.

In March 1918 the Engineers' Club, Manchester, requested the Manchester Library Committee to provide a Technical Department in the Municipal Library. The request was supported by practically every scientific and technical association and institution in the city. This request, which was acted upon, shows the urgent need for such libraries.

In the course of a discussion at the Faraday Society on the co-ordination of scientific publication it was suggested that there should be established a College of Librarians, a body of young men, well-educated, well-trained, and well-paid, who could read and index all published papers and records of researches for the use of researchers and translators.

In a Memorandum on the future work of the Technical Libraries Committee by Mr. Savage, it was shown that the demands of technical men were for (*a*) A central applied-science library; (*b*) the collection, organization, and dissemination of information by specially trained bibliographers; (c) better co-ordination between London and provincial libraries; (d) works libraries. In order to accomplish the above work, Mr. Savage recommended that the Committee should include more representatives of science and industry, and that adequately remunerated secretarial assistance should be provided by the Association to give effect to the Committee's decisions, and to carry on the necessary propaganda.

At the Conference called by the Northern Counties Library Association in October 1918, important papers were read on technical libraries. Mr. R. H. Clayton, Manchester Oxide Company, Ltd., in defining what is a technical library, said that to be complete it must contain all that information which a firm or individual does not possess in the private libraries belonging to them, and, in particular, complete sets of all English and foreign technical journals. Such libraries were necessary and should be found in every large manufacturing and industrial centre. The Government should support them as it does education. Having voted money for industrial research, it must supply the means to that end, namely, libraries. Municipalities should support them, as doing so would lessen their own library expenses on technical matters. Private firms should support them for the same reason.

Mr. J. G. Pearce, Research Department, British Westinghouse Electric and Manufacturing Company, Ltd., spoke of the works library in its rela-

COMMERCIAL AND TECHNICAL LIBRARIES

tion to the public technical library. While the latter did the work of collecting, classifying, and cataloguing of information, the former dealt with the preparation of abstracts and bibliographies, and maintained a translation service. The advantage of the works library over the public technical library lay in this, that the works library had information from many sources closed to the public library from allied concerns, from the manufacturers' association, from technical societies, etc. Its needs are highly specialized and cover strictly limited fields. The public library has to cover the whole field and consequently cannot specialize sufficiently to meet the needs of the specialist. Intimate co-operation between the two should be the aim.

In speaking of the functions of technical libraries, Mr. Savage said: "It would be too costly to form in every locality a general technical reference library, but with a local technical library and a National Central Lending Library of technology all demands could be met."

With reference to the recommendations of the third Interim Report of the Adult Education Committee in the matter of providing technical libraries, Mr. Savage, at the annual meeting at Southport in 1919, said that the Library Association differed from that Committee as to their policy of the organization of technical libraries for each separate industry by that industry. His contention was that instead of setting up a new parallel series of libraries, the existing libraries should be improved and extended, and in the larger industrial towns, such as Birmingham and Glasgow, they should be developed beyond the needs of the city itself, so that they might become provincial technical libraries on the scale of the Patent Office, with power to lend books in the surrounding district, and a central general lending library of scientific and technical books should be organized as the final resource of the searcher.

CHAPTER XVIII

LIBRARIES FOR THE BLIND—HOSPITAL LIBRARIES—CHILDREN'S LIBRARIES—SCHOOL LIBRARIES

LIBRARIES FOR THE BLIND

At the annual meeting of the Association in 1886, the late J. Potter Briscoe, of Nottingham, gave an account of the efforts that had been made by public libraries prior to that date to provide reading matter for the blind in their neighbourhood. With the exception of eleven libraries, in Liverpool, Halifax, Salford, Nottingham, and seven other towns, very few libraries possessed any books for blind readers. The cost of books embossed in the Braille system averaged about four shillings a volume, those in the Moon type about half a crown, so that the cost was not prohibitive. He pleaded for the purchase of a collection of books in both types by all public libraries. The system devised by Dr. William Moon, of Brighton, was largely in favour by the older blind readers, as the characters were formed to a considerable extent on the lines of Roman characters; the Braille system, which was invented by Louis Braille in 1829 and perfected in 1834, was preferred by others because it can be written by the use of a machine as well as read.

The Incorporated National Lending Library for the Blind (now the National Library for the Blind) was originated by Miss Martha Arnold in 1882. A grant of £25 was obtained from Gardner's Trust for the Blind for its foundation, a number of friends subscribed and the library started, with Miss Arnold as librarian, in a little back room at Hampstead, where books were lent out to the blind people of the neighbourhood. The library, now housed at 18, Tufton Street, Westminster, contains many thousands of volumes in the Braille and Moon types, with several thousand volumes of embossed music. The books are sent out to the readers by post, being carried at a cheap rate, and readers exchange their books once a month and pay the postage. Some libraries have formed separate collections of books for the blind, but it has been found, at least in the smaller towns, that they are apt to lie on the shelves unused when all the blind readers in the neighbourhood have read them. The better plan seems to be to have one central library for every blind person to draw upon, either directly or through the local library. In some towns the local representative of the National Institute for the Blind borrows and returns the books on behalf of those unable to come to the library themselves.

Hospital Libraries

Sir Alfred Davies, at a meeting of the Public Health Congress in 1930, said that the place of the book in the ministry of healing was not yet adequately realized, although a striking and unexpected result of the war had been a new conception

HOSPITAL LIBRARIES

of human duty in the supplying of books to people who, through circumstances beyond their control, were unable to get access to them. The three main needs for the development of the library system in hospitals were:

1. Adequate recognition of the value of books for healing.
2. The provision in every hospital of a library of its own under the care of a qualified librarian, assisted by a staff of voluntary workers.
3. The placing of the Red Cross library in the position of the central organization.

Negotiations were opened by the Red Cross and Order of St. John Hospital Library with the Library Association, and at the annual meeting of the Library Association at Cambridge a session was devoted to the question of hospital libraries. Sir Humphrey Rolleston took the chair. It was stated that the Hospital Library Service originated during the war with Mrs. Gaskell's scheme for supplying the wounded with books. After the first six months the system she had organized was financed by the Joint Committee of the British Red Cross Society and the Order of St. John, her staff ran it, and the public helped with gifts of books. At the end of the war £25,000 were given to enable the work to be carried on primarily for ex-service men.

The Council of the Library Association afterwards appointed a Hospital Libraries Committee to explore the position and to report. The Committee elected Miss M. Frost, Librarian of Worthing, as Chairman, and Mr. H. Farr, Librarian of

Cardiff, undertook the duties of Secretary. The Committee considered the question very fully at several meetings, having had the co-operation of Mr. E. A. Bedwell (House Governor, King's College Hospital), Mr. R. H. P. Orde (Central Bureau of Hospital Information), Dr. Charles Porter (Society of Medical Officers of Health), and Mrs. M. E. Roberts (Organizing Secretary, British Red Cross Hospital Library). A Report was drawn up embodying the following recommendations:

1. That a hospital library service should be established in voluntary and public assistance hospitals; these to be a responsibility of the public library authorities.

2. That the British Red Cross Hospital Library should confine itself to the supply of books to special hospitals not otherwise dealt with.

3. That the distribution of books to patients should be made individually by, or under the supervision of, a competent librarian responsible not only for book selection and service, but also for the recruitment and training of the voluntary helpers.

4. That all library authorities be circularized as to the desirability of organizing a hospital library service in their district.

5. That a Joint Standing Committee of members of the Library Association and representatives of the hospital and medical services should be appointed to co-operate in helping and guiding the movement.

The Report was submitted to the Council on August 31, 1931, approved, and its recommendations adopted.

An important Bibliography on "Hospital Libraries and Bibliotherapy," by W. J. Bishop,

CHILDREN'S LIBRARIES

Assistant Librarian, Royal College of Physicians, appeared in the *Library Association Record* in June, July, and August 1931, pp. 198–200; 231–32; 274–75.

CHILDREN'S LIBRARIES

In addition to the provision of libraries for children in schools, and in towns where such provision has not been found practicable, many library authorities have established separate departments or sections of the lending library for young readers of the ages of seven to fourteen or thereby. The Report on Public Libraries already quoted advises that it is highly desirable that this separate accommodation should be provided for young readers of school age in order that their presence may not inconvenience adults, and deter them from coming to the library.

Admirable provision for a children's library was provided at Nottingham in 1882 when Mr. Samuel Morley, M.P., a manufacturer of Nottingham, presented a sum of £500 for the purpose. A separate building was acquired, and the children's library was installed therein. Mr. J. Potter Briscoe, in *The Library Chronicle*, Vol. 3, pp. 45–48, gives a full account of the establishment of the library, which has the distinction of being the first children's library to be housed in a separate building with a staff and catalogue of its own. In the same article Mr. Briscoe indicates the lines on which, in his view, a children's library should be formed.

THE PUBLIC LIBRARY MOVEMENT

In the days before open access to libraries was known provision for young readers coming to the public library took the form of a separate section of bookshelving for children's books, and a separate counter for the issue and return of books by young readers. In those days the indicator formed an efficient barrier between the reader and the books he desired to borrow. Nowadays the more enlightened policy introduced by Mr. James Duff Brown at Clerkenwell in 1894 is practically universal, and children as well as adults are admitted to the shelves to choose their reading matter. Separate rooms for children are provided which in the matter of attractiveness, so far as heating, lighting, and decoration are concerned, leave little to be desired.

School Libraries

The establishment of lending libraries for scholars in public elementary and secondary schools through the agency of the public library is no new development. In several towns the school library has been treated as a branch of the main public library, and its scope enlarged to meet the needs of adult borrowers as well.

Edward Edwards, in his evidence before the Select Committee on Public Libraries in 1849, spoke strongly in favour of school libraries. "I do not believe," he said, "that a more prudent or a more wise subsidiary measure could be taken with

SCHOOL LIBRARIES

reference to education than to connect with schools lending libraries of a good kind."

In 1877, at the International Conference of Librarians in London (*Transactions*, p. 26), Mr. W. H. K. Wright, Librarian of Plymouth, suggested that the Board Schools might be utilized by being opened in the evenings as reading-rooms and lending libraries for the district in which they were situated. Two years later he returned to the subject in a paper on "The Public Library and the Board School" (*Transactions of the Library Association*, Vol. 2, pp. 38–41), in which he advocated that in each district school there should be deposited a small collection of 100 selected books from the main library stock, the selection to be approved by both library and school authorities. The collections should remain in each school for a period of six months, and should then be returned for overhaul to the central library, to be sent out again to the different schools in rotation. By this plan the distribution of the library stock would be spread over the whole area covered by the library to the advantage of the borrowers and the relief of congestion at the central building.

At the annual meeting of the Library Association in Glasgow in 1888 he gave details of the working of his plan (*The Library*, Vol. 1, p. 166) in a paper on the subject.

It should be noted that the cost of Mr. Wright's plan was met out of the ordinary penny library rate, and that he expressed the hope that since

THE PUBLIC LIBRARY MOVEMENT

co-operation between the Library Committee and the School Board had thus been established, it might be possible for the School Board to devote some of its funds to the provision of books for these branch libraries, although he feared that it was too much to expect that the library rate would ever be supplemented by State aid as was done with respect to schools.

In 1878 the London School Board established a system of school lending libraries for the use of teachers and scholars (*The Library Chronicle*, Vol. 4, pp. 169–71). The various schools were divided into groups of from six to eighteen schools, so that the aggregate accommodation of each group should be for 10,000 children. To each group books to the same value were apportioned, divided into as many libraries as there were schools in the group. Each school kept its library for six months, at the end of which time the library of A was sent to B, and so on, the last library in the group going to A. Each group kept its own libraries at first, but in the course of a year or two the group system was abolished, and each library was then sent into a central store, overhauled, replenished, and sent out to a different school. The books borrowed by the children were frequently read by their parents, and served as propaganda for the establishment of public libraries in London.

Many other library authorities, for example, Bootle, Leeds, Norwich, etc., early established libraries in Board Schools, which were administered

SCHOOL LIBRARIES

gratuitously by the teachers in the schools. In several places, however, these efforts to provide reading for the children through the schools had failed for want of funds when financed out of the public library rate, limited as it was then to one penny in the pound.

In 1898 Mr. J. J. Ogle, of Bootle, contributed an important report on "The Connection between the Public Library and the Public Elementary School," which was published in volume two of the Special Reports on Educational Subjects issued by the Education Department in London. The Report showed what had been accomplished up to that date.

At the Leeds Conference of the Library Association in 1903 a session was devoted to the subject of "The Relations between Public Education and Public Libraries." Delegates representing the principal educational associations in Great Britain had been invited by the Library Association, and took part in the reading of papers and subsequent discussions. Dr. Richard Garnett, of the British Museum, moved, and Mr. John Ballinger, Cardiff, seconded, "That a Committee consisting of the Council of the Library Association and the delegates of other bodies present should be appointed to prepare and publish a report on the subject they had under discussion." This was carried unanimously.

This Committee presented an Interim Report to the Newcastle Conference in 1904, which it was decided to print and distribute for further con-

THE PUBLIC LIBRARY MOVEMENT

sideration at the Cambridge Conference in 1905. On that occasion the Report (*Library Association Record*, Vol. 7, pp. 611–17) was introduced by Mr. Henry R. Tedder, with a very clear summary of its conclusions and with comments upon the Resolutions which it embodied. The Report was adopted unanimously, the first Resolution, which concerned children's libraries, being as follows:

"In order that children from an early age may become accustomed to the use of a collection of books, it is desirable (*a*) that special libraries for children should be established in all public libraries, and (*b*) that collections of books should be formed in all elementary and secondary schools."

Since the passing of the Education Act of 1902, library authorities throughout the country have been active in endeavouring to carry out the objects embodied in the foregoing Resolution. Their efforts have been ably seconded by education authorities which were given power under that Act to spend money on the provision of school libraries.

As to the best methods of conducting the school libraries, Mr. Ballinger, in his paper on "Library Work with Children in Great Britain," contributed to the St. Louis Meeting of the American Library Association in 1904 (*Papers and Proceedings*, pp. 46–9, 1904), gave it as his opinion that the most satisfactory way of reaching children is through libraries deposited in the schools, the books being distributed by the teachers to the children for home reading. The teacher, knowing the capabilities and tasks of the individual child, can get into closer contact with

SCHOOL LIBRARIES

them than a librarian can. But there is need of the librarian's special qualifications in the selection, purchase, organization, and supervision of the school libraries.

The Report of the Departmental Committee of the Board of Education on Public Libraries in England and Wales (1927) is emphatic on the point that it lies with education authorities to be responsible for the supply and use of books in the schools under their control. At the same time, the Report urges that the active co-operation which exists in many places between Education Committees and Library Committees in the selection of books for the schools and the maintenance of school libraries is greatly to be commended. Statistical Table XII of the Report shows that in 1924 there were 113 public library authorities actively co-operating in supplying schools with books. "It was generally recognized that the supply of books through the schools should not be restricted to the supply of text-books to be used in class, but must cover much of the home reading of the pupils, both of a recreational and of a more instructional character. We are strongly of opinion that every school, elementary or secondary, should have a well-equipped library in proportion to its needs, furnished by means, either of fixed libraries or of circulating stocks of books, or of a combination of these methods, as may seem best to the Education Committees" (par. 107).

The Report (par. 109), in recommending co-

THE PUBLIC LIBRARY MOVEMENT

operation between the Library Committee and the Education Committee, instances the cases of Cardiff, Blackburn, Nottingham, Halifax, Coventry, and Tottenham, where such co-operation in various forms has been in operation with highly satisfactory results. In almost every case a joint committee of the two Committees, on which teachers are represented, is responsible for the selection of the books in consultation with the librarian of the public library.

An example of such co-operation is afforded by the action of the Public Library Committee of Kendal in organizing, in 1903, the distribution of stocks of books from their library to schools in Westmorland, the funds being provided by the Westmorland Education Committee. The scheme was subsidized by the Carnegie Trustees in 1915, on the understanding that books for adult readers were included in the distribution.

CHAPTER XIX

PROMINENT WORKERS AND BENEFACTORS

THOMAS CHARLES ABBOTT (1851–1927)

Alderman Abbott (J.P., Manchester) became a member of the Library Association in 1899, and took a prominent part in the agitation for the abolition of the restriction on the rating powers of library authorities. At the Leeds meeting in 1903 he read a paper on "The Matter of the Rate Limitation: the Practical Steps." He served as Chairman of the special legislation committee appointed by the Council, and did all in his power to secure the passing of the Association's Bill for the removal of the rate limitation by frequent speaking at annual meetings in its support, by attendance at Westminster to interview Members of Parliament and in securing their support for the Bill. He was elected a Vice-President of the Association in 1906–20, President in 1921, and subsequently an Hon. Fellow. He was a member of the Manchester Public Libraries Committee for the long period of thirty-six years, holding the office of Vice-Chairman, and afterwards Chairman. He took an active interest in the formation of commercial and technical libraries in Manchester, and formed one of a deputation from that city to America, which, on its return, published an important Report on American Public Libraries. He was for several years a Governor of the John Rylands Library. He was a member of the Council of the Workers' Educational Association, and did much good work as an organizer and lecturer to Working-Men's Clubs and the Oxford University Extension Lectures movement. He was a Vice-President of the Manchester Playgoers' Club and other local associations. He died on January 26, 1927, at the age of seventy-five.

THE PUBLIC LIBRARY MOVEMENT

FRANCIS THORNTON BARRETT (1838–1919)

F. T. Barrett was born at Liverpool in 1838, and after leaving school was engaged in bookselling and printing in Lancashire and the Midlands. He was appointed an assistant in the Birmingham Public Libraries, and rose to the position of sub-librarian in the reference library. In January 1877 he was appointed Librarian of the Mitchell Library, Glasgow, on its establishment. By November 1, 1877, when the library was opened in Ingram Street, Mr. Barrett had collected about 15,000 volumes, a well-selected collection. The library under his fostering care rapidly grew, and by 1889 the collection numbered 89,000 volumes, and had an annual issue of about 500,000. The Ingram Street premises soon became too small and the library was removed to 21, Miller Street in October 1891. These premises also soon became congested, and the present handsome building in North Street was erected, and formally opened by the Earl of Rosebery in 1911.

The adoption of the Public Libraries Acts by the city of Glasgow was thrice rejected, notwithstanding Mr. Barrett's constant efforts in support of it. A special Act, however, was obtained in 1899 authorizing the Corporation to establish public libraries. Mr. Barrett prepared a scheme under which each district of the city was to be supplied with either a branch library or a reading-room. When Mr. Andrew Carnegie's magnificent offer of £100,000 to defray the cost of buildings was received this scheme was amended and enlarged, and by 1915 there were twenty-two separate libraries containing about half a million volumes and issuing over three million volumes per annum. Mr. Barrett was very successful in securing many valuable gifts and bequests to the libraries under his charge, the Mitchell Library, in particular, having been enriched with many special collections, notably the Jeffrey Library, which is housed in a separate room. There are special collections on Burns, Scott, Scottish poetry, and early Glasgow printed books.

PROMINENT WORKERS AND BENEFACTORS

Dr. Barrett was an original member of the Library Association, and his attendance at its meetings was unfailing. He was elected to the Council in 1879, made a Vice-President in 1886, and elected to fill the presidential chair in 1907 on the occasion of the Glasgow meeting. His contributions to the *Transactions* of the Association were numerous and valuable, and his wise counsel and clear judgment were much valued by his colleagues. Ever ready to lend a helping hand to the younger members of the profession, whom he took special care to know individually, he was frequently requested for testimonials, and many of his staff and others in whom he took a fatherly interest rose to important positions in the library service—James Duff Brown, Thomas Mason, his own son (Franklin T. Barrett), and the present City Librarian of Glasgow being among the number.

He took a prominent part in the foundation of the Scottish Library Association in 1907–8, was its first President for three years, and continued a member of Council till his death on January 21, 1919.

He was a well-known member of most of the literary and scientific societies of Glasgow, and for several years was President of the Glasgow Bibliographical Society. In 1913 the University of Glasgow conferred upon him the honorary degree of LL.D. in recognition of his many public services. He retired from the city librarianship in 1914, full of years and honours, while his eye was not dim nor his natural force abated.

SIR EDWARD AUGUSTUS BOND (1815–1898)

Sir Edward Augustus Bond, Principal Librarian of the British Museum, was born at Hanwell on December 31, 1815. He was educated at Merchant Taylors' School, and entered the Record Office as an assistant in 1833. The knowledge of the handwriting of the national records which he there obtained under Sir Thomas Duffus Hardy and Rev.

THE PUBLIC LIBRARY MOVEMENT

Joseph Hunter stood him in good stead when he was transferred to the British Museum in 1838, where he speedily became an accomplished palæographer. In 1850 he was made Egerton Librarian, and in 1854 Assistant Keeper of MSS. On the retirement of Sir Frederic Madden in 1866, he succeeded him as Keeper. The work of the department was considerably in arrears, and Bond set himself to remedy this state of affairs, and speedily accomplished the task. He was appointed Principal Librarian in 1878, succeeding J. W. Jones, and held the office until 1888, when he retired. In his post as Principal Librarian he displayed the same energy and reforming spirit as he had shown in the department of MSS. He succeeded in procuring the introduction of electric light into the building. He was ever ready to adopt new ideas, and quick to carry them into effect. The plan for printing the catalogue which Dr. Garnett had brought forward was taken up by him, and successful negotiations with the Treasury concluded to provide the necessary funds. He at once adopted Dr. Garnett's idea of the sliding press, a plan which saved a vast sum of money.

Apart from his work at the Museum, Bond's greatest service was the founding of the Palæographical Society along with Sir E. Maunde Thompson, whose publications of facsimiles have raised palæography to the rank of an exact science. He was made C.B. in 1885 and K.C.B. in 1898. The University of Cambridge conferred upon him the degree of LL.D.—(DR. GARNETT in *D.N.B.*)

JOHN POTTER BRISCOE (1848–1926)

John Potter Briscoe, City Librarian of Nottingham, was born at Lever Bridge, near Bolton, on July 20, 1848. He was the eldest son of John Daly Briscoe, by whom he was educated. For some years he was engaged in teaching in Bolton, afterwards becoming Assistant Librarian in the Public Library there from 1866–69. In 1869 he was appointed to Nottingham Public Library, where for forty-

PROMINENT WORKERS AND BENEFACTORS

seven years he was the honoured Chief Librarian, and on his retirement in 1916 was made Consulting City Librarian.

He was an original member of the Library Association, member of its Council from 1881–90, and a Vice-President from 1891–20. He was also a member of the Council of the Thoroton Society.

His contributions to the *Transactions* were numerous, and included the following: "Subscription Libraries in connection with Public Libraries" (1878); "Libraries for the Young" (1885); "Libraries for the Blind" (1886); "Book Music in Public Libraries" (1888); "Notes on Swedish Libraries" (1889); "Half-hour Talks about Books" (1894); "How to extend the Public Library Movement" (1895); "Bergen Public Library" (1897); "Tim Bobbin: a Lancashire Humorist" (1897); "Public Libraries and Emigration" (1898); "Libraries and Reading Circles" (1902).

Among his other publications were the following: *Bypaths of Nottinghamshire History; Chapters of Nottinghamshire History; Concise History of Nottingham Castle; Curiosities of the Belfry; Gleanings from God's Acre: Epitaphs; Nottinghamshire and Derbyshire at the Dawn of the Twentieth Century; Nottinghamshire Facts and Fancies; Old Nottinghamshire*, 2 vols.; and with S. J. Kirk, *Contributions to a Bibliography of Hosiery and Lace* (1896).

He edited the *Bibelots Series*, 29 vols.; *The Sportsman's Classics*, 3 vols.; *Nottinghamshire and Derbyshire Notes and Queries*, 6 vols.; and was the antiquarian editor of the *Nottinghamshire Guardian* for twenty-one years.

He was instrumental in founding the North Midland Library Association in 1890, and was its first President. In the same year he instituted a series of Half-hour Talks at his library about books and book-writers, which pioneer work he carried on for many years. He lectured at the London Summer School in 1895 on the selection of books and the best means of assisting readers. On the occasion of his twenty-first anniversary as Librarian of Nottingham, and again on his completion of fifty years' connection with the

Library, his staff in 1919 made well-deserved presentations to him in token of their esteem and affection for their chief.

He was a pioneer in the establishment of children's libraries, and his foresight led him to secure a separate building in Nottingham for a children's library, the first of its kind. He died in the seventy-eighth year of his age on January 7, 1926. In an obituary notice of him in the *Library Association Record*, Mr. Jast paid the following just tribute to his memory:

"His was a completely genial and lovable nature, and it is good for us and for the city he so faithfully served that he lived—more and better cannot be said of any of us, when we, too, come to close the volume of our doing."

JOSEPH BROTHERTON (1783–1857)

Joseph Brotherton was born on May 22, 1783, at Whittington, Chesterfield. His father had a cotton mill in Manchester, and Joseph became his partner when still a young man, retiring from business in 1819. He was a keen vegetarian, and a total abstainer. He belonged to the sect of Bible Christians, and became the pastor of the local church. He became M.P. for Salford at the passing of the Reform Bill of 1832, and remained member for that constituency till his death. He was a keen supporter of the Free Trade movement, and when twitted with the "enormous fortune" which he had amassed by the factory system, he retorted that "his riches consisted not so much in the largeness of his means as in the fewness of his wants," a phrase which was inscribed upon his statue in the Peel Park, Salford, erected to his memory in 1858. He died suddenly in an omnibus on January 7, 1857.

Brotherton was instrumental, along with William Ewart, in promoting and passing the Museums Act of 1845, and those two, along with George A. Hamilton, introduced the Act of 1850 establishing public libraries. In supporting the Bill in the House, Brotherton laid stress upon the enormous

PROMINENT WORKERS AND BENEFACTORS

sums which the punishment of crime annually cost the country, and yet Members of Parliament were objecting to a measure which would allow communities to tax themselves, to the extent of a half-penny in the pound, the effect of which would be to prevent crime. In his opinion it was of little use to teach people to read unless they were provided with books to which they might apply the faculty so acquired. Mr. Brotherton's early advocacy of the public library movement is fittingly kept in mind by a sum of money for the purchase of books for Salford Public Library out of the "Brotherton Memorial Fund," and by his statue in Peel Park, already mentioned.

JAMES DUFF BROWN (1862–1914)

James Duff Brown was born in Edinburgh in November 1862. After serving an apprenticeship to the publishing trade for a short time in Edinburgh, then in Glasgow, he joined the service of the Mitchell Library, Glasgow. He was Senior Assistant in this library for ten years, and became Librarian of Clerkenwell Public Library in 1888. Here the experimental introduction of the safeguarded open-access system brought about a new era in public library method. As the question whether he owed his ideas to America has been in debate, we may quote his own words on the point. "It has been stated that the adoption of the safeguarded open-access system arose out of a visit I paid to the United States in 1893. This is entirely erroneous, as my ideas on the subject were formulated as far back as 1891, when they were first published in *The Library* in the form of a paper entitled 'A Plea for Liberty to Readers to help themselves.' There was no such thing as proper safeguarded open-access as now understood in existence anywhere in America, when I was there." In 1905 he accepted his final post, that of Borough Librarian at Islington. His work in organization there was the admiration of many. Throughout his career he took a deep interest in the labours of the Library Association, holding various offices in the Council until his resignation in 1911. To numerous library workers, especially the young men of the profession, he was a source of inspiration, help, and cheer.

Although best known as the pioneer of open-access, his name would have been of high repute in the library world even without that special claim to fame. The Clerkenwell Public Library *Quarterly Guide* (a periodical library bulletin with annotated entries) was the first of its kind in Great Britain. Systematic annotated catalogues owe much to him; library workers to-day still use appliances invented or perfected by him; the student who eagerly claims his non-fiction ticket has Duff Brown to thank. The adjustable and subject schemes of classification, although they did not supersede the schemes produced by Dewey and the Library of Congress, were interesting and valuable contributions to library science. In 1897 he planned and edited the *Greenwood's Year Book*; in 1898 he founded (and for some time edited) *The Library World*. His *Manual of Library Economy* and his *Manual of Practical Bibliography* are in constant use for library examinations.

His chief recreation, in addition to reading, was music. On this subject, too, he published several volumes, of which the *Guide to the Formation of a Music Library* was for many years the only practical manual of the kind. Better known is *Characteristic Songs and Dances of all Nations*, produced in conjunction with Alfred Moffat.

He died in March 1914. In the *Library Association Record* of May 1914, tributes from far and near are paid to his memory by friends and opponents alike, with a warmth which proves sufficiently that good work is not always so unappreciated as pessimists suppose.—(E. A. S.)

ANDREW CARNEGIE (1835–1919)

The romantic story of Andrew Carnegie's rise from a poor Dunfermline boy to a multi-millionaire philanthropist has

PROMINENT WORKERS AND BENEFACTORS

often been told. Suffice it to say here that having emigrated to the United States with his parents in 1848, he took up whatever work he could find to do, and ultimately in the service of the Pennsylvania Railroad Company rapidly rose to the important position of Superintendent of the Pittsburg division of the company's lines. A fortunate investment in oil lands brought him money which he used to establish rolling mills at Pittsburg, which developed into the largest system of steel works in the world ever controlled by one man, and brought him great wealth.

It is with his career as a benefactor of libraries that we are more immediately concerned here. He himself has told us that when he was a boy in Pittsburg he and other lads there were befriended by Colonel Anderson, of Alleghany, who gave them the run of his library. This kind action was so appreciated by him that he there and then resolved that, should wealth ever come to him, he would use it to establish free libraries that other poor boys might have opportunities similar to those for which he had been indebted to Colonel Anderson. How fully he carried out this resolve will be appreciated when it is stated that more than half of the towns in the United Kingdom which possess rate-supported libraries have been recipients of his generosity. Of the 437 towns in England and Wales possessing public libraries, 213 have received grants in aid; in Scotland 50 out of 77, and in Ireland 47 out of 58 have been so favoured. Prior to 1913 Mr. Carnegie had given or promised a sum of £1,946,579 for the erection of public libraries, and at the time of his death 380 separate buildings in the United Kingdom were associated with his name, and between fourteen and fifteen hundred if we include the Dominions and Colonies and the United States. (Article by A. L. Hetherington in *Library Association Record*, 1919, p. 284.)

His gifts for buildings were always accompanied by the condition that a free site should be provided by the community accepting the gift, and that an undertaking should be given to maintain the library from local funds by the

THE PUBLIC LIBRARY MOVEMENT

adoption of the Public Libraries Acts. He deemed it a privilege to help those who were willing to help themselves. Unfortunately, many of the recipients of his bounty were more concerned to seize the opportunity of erecting a handsome building which would be an ornament to the neighbourhood than to go into the question of the cost of its upkeep and administration as a library, concerning which a lamentable amount of ignorance seems to have prevailed. The result has been that in too many cases the cost of maintenance of the building has left very little indeed for the provision of the library itself. Particularly was this the case before 1919, when the amount that could be spent upon libraries was limited to the sum produced by a rate of one penny in the pound of assessable rental.

In addition to giving building grants, Mr. Carnegie founded a number of separate Trusts of an educational nature. In 1901 he established a Scottish Universities Trust for the better equipment of the Universities in their various faculties, and for the payment of the fees of Scottish students whose parents would otherwise have been prevented from giving them a university education. In the following year the Carnegie Institution of Washington, for the promotion of education and research, was founded with the like capital of two millions sterling. In 1905 he gave the same sum for providing pensions to American university and college teachers. The Carnegie Corporation of New York was founded with a capital of 25 million pounds, and with wide powers. It has been calculated that before his death his benefactions had amounted to over 70 million pounds.

So far as libraries are concerned, his last, and perhaps his most far-reaching benefaction, was the creation of the Carnegie United Kingdom Trust in 1913 to carry on his grants for libraries and other schemes for the well-being of the masses of the people. Under this Trust the Trustees established the system of county libraries which has covered the kingdom with a network of libraries, and brought a supply of books to readers in the remotest districts. Under

PROMINENT WORKERS AND BENEFACTORS

the enlightened policy of the Trustees the National Central Library in London and similar central libraries in Scotland and Ireland have been established. Quite recently a building has been acquired by the Trustees in the Bloomsbury district of London, which will adequately house the National Central Library, and provide much needed headquarters for the Library Association.

RICHARD COPLEY CHRISTIE (1830–1901)

Richard Copley Christie, scholar and bibliophile, born July 22, 1830, at Lenton, Nottinghamshire; son of Mr. Lorenzo Christie, a Manchester mill-owner; studied at Lincoln College, Oxford, graduated B.A. in 1853 (M.A. 1855), taking a first class in law and history. He entered Lincoln's Inn in 1854, and was called to the Bar in 1857. He practised his profession in Manchester, and became leader of the Equity Bar there.

On the foundation of the Owens College (now Manchester University), he was one of the first professors appointed; and as there were more chairs than professors at that time, he was called upon to fill the chairs of ancient and modern history, political economy and commercial science, and jurisprudence and law, in addition to teaching evening classes. His legal work had so increased by 1866 that he was obliged to resign his chairs of political economy and history, and in 1869 that of jurisprudence.

When Owens College was reconstituted he was appointed a governor and member of the executive, and Manchester University, in 1895, granted him the degree of LL.D.

In January 1872 the Bishop of Manchester conferred upon him the Chancellorship of his diocese, an office which he held until 1894. Chancellor Christie was one of the three legatees under the will of Sir Joseph Whitworth, who left an estate of over half a million. Lady Whitworth and Mr. R. D. Darbishire were his co-legatees. It was bequeathed to them "in equal shares for their own use, they being each of

THE PUBLIC LIBRARY MOVEMENT

them aware of the objects to which the testator would have applied these funds." Out of the share falling to him Christie built the Whitworth Hall at a cost of over £50,000. He also bequeathed his library of over 70,000 volumes to the University (Owens College).

Chancellor Christie took a very keen interest in libraries and in bibliography. He was a member of the Committee of the London Library, Governor, and Chairman of Committee of the Library of the Royal Holloway College, and a Vice-President of the Bibliographical Society. He became a member of the Library Association in 1879, when it met in Manchester, on which occasion he was a prominent member of the Reception Committee. For years he took an active part in the discussions at the annual meetings, held office as Vice-President for a long period, and was elected President in 1889. His presidential address was on the work and aim of the Library Association, and formed an excellent critical survey of the work done. His other contributions to the *Transactions* were "The Catalogues of the Library of the Duc de la Vallière" (1885); "Elzevier Bibliography" (1888); "A Dynasty of Librarians" (1889), dealing with the Bignon family, and the librarianship of the Bibliothèque du Roi (now the Bibliothèque Nationale).

He edited the final volume of the *Diary of Dr. John Worthington* for the Chetham Society, and compiled a *Bibliography of Worthington*. His work on *The Old Church and School Libraries of Lancashire* was published in 1884 by the Record Society of Lancashire and Cheshire. *Etienne Dolet*, published in 1880. New edition, 1899. *Selected Essays and Papers*, 1902. He edited for the Record Society *Annales Cestrienses* in 1887. At his death, which occurred on January 9, 1901, he generously left a legacy to the Library Association of £2,000.

EDWARD EDWARDS (1812–1886)

The Father of the Public Library movement was born in London on December 14, 1812. His father, Anthony

PROMINENT WORKERS AND BENEFACTORS

Turner Edwards, was a builder living in Idol Lane. Little is known of his early years, but in 1836 he began to write on subjects of public interest, notably on the British Museum, at that time undergoing investigation by a Select Committee. His pamphlet *Remarks on the Minutes of Evidence taken before the Select Committee*, had attracted the notice of the authorities, and he received an appointment as a supernumerary assistant in the Museum on cataloguing work. He was one of the co-adjutors of Panizzi in framing the ninety-one rules for the formation of the catalogue, along with John Winter Jones, afterwards Principal Librarian, and the first President of the Library Association; Thomas Watts, afterwards Keeper of the Printed Books; and Serjeant Parry, another supernumerary assistant. Edwards catalogued the Thomason collection of Civil War tracts, a work which occupied him for several years. About 1846 he began to devote great attention to library statistics, collecting returns from foreign librarians and other sources, and the results were published in *The Athenæum*. His statistics were called in question as to their accuracy by Mr. Watts in a series of letters to *The Athenæum*, signed "Verificator," but, notwithstanding, he was asked to give evidence before the Select Committee established by William Ewart in 1849, which led to the passing of Ewart's Act, the first Act for the setting up of public libraries in Great Britain.

His engagement at the Museum having been terminated, he accepted, in 1850, the librarianship of the first public library to be established, namely, that of Manchester (opened in 1852). He organized the library on sound lines, throwing himself into its management with characteristic energy and zeal. Being taxed with an indifference to economy in his management of the institution, his natural impatience of temper led to his having to resign his appointment in 1858.

He devoted his leisure to literary work. In 1859 his *Memoirs of Libraries* was published, followed in 1864 by its complement, *Libraries and Founders of Libraries*. *Lives of the Founders of the British Museum* was issued in 1870, and contains the history of the national library up to that period. He was responsible for the article on "Libraries" in the eighth edition of the *Encyclopædia Britannica*, edited the "Liber Monasterii de Hyda" in the Rolls Series, and wrote a life of Sir Walter Raleigh (1865). He catalogued the Library of Queen's College, Oxford, and afterwards went to reside at Niton in the Isle of Wight, where he occupied himself with a new edition of his *Memoirs of Libraries*. He did not live to complete this, but Volume One was published posthumously and presented to members of the Library Association by Thomas Greenwood. His works will always remain a mine of information for the historian.—(DR. GARNETT in *D.N.B.*).

JOHN PASSMORE EDWARDS (1823–1911)

Born at Blackwater, near Truro, on March 24, 1823, son of a working carpenter, Edwards was apprenticed to a lawyer in Truro at the age of twenty, but left that employment at the end of eighteen months to take up journalistic work in Manchester. In 1845 he went to London, maintaining himself by lecturing and journalism. He actively promoted the early closing movement, and although in sympathy with the Chartist movement he deprecated the use of physical force. He was sent to the Continent by the London Peace Society to attend the Peace Conferences in 1848, 1849, and 1850. In the latter year he started a number of weekly newspapers, writing, printing, and publishing them single-handed, but his projects ended in bankruptcy. In 1862 he bought the *Building News*, which he succeeded in bringing to a flourishing condition, and was thereby enabled to pay his old creditors in full although he had been legally discharged. For this honourable action he was presented by his former creditors with a watch and chain at a banquet given in his honour in 1866. In 1869 he acquired the *Mechanics' Magazine*, and in 1876 the *Echo*, which he himself edited as an advocate of social reform. He was a continuous and active supporter of all progressive movements, such as the abolition of capital punishment, of taxes on knowledge, of flogging in the Army and Navy, etc., etc. He entered Parliament in 1880 as Liberal member for Salisbury, but did not stand again after 1885.

He then devoted himself to philanthropic work, mainly in connection with public libraries and hospitals. He established reading and lecture-rooms, a school, a literary institute, and a mechanics' institute at villages near his birthplace. He established hospitals and convalescent homes, epileptic homes and homes for boys at various places in the South of England.

His benefactions included gifts for the erection of the public libraries of Whitechapel, Shoreditch, Hoxton, Edmonton, Walworth, Hammersmith, East Dulwich, St. George's in the East, Acton, Poplar, Limehouse, Nunhead, East Ham, Plaistow, North Camberwell, Newton Abbot, Truro, Falmouth, Camborne, Redruth, St. Ives, Bodmin, Liskeard, and Launceston. He also founded an art gallery for the Newlyn colony of artists, near Penzance, and technical schools at Truro, the West Ham Museum, the Passmore Edwards Settlement, Tavistock Place, of which Mrs. Humphry Ward was Hon. Secretary, University Hall, Clare Market, and the Sailors' Palace, Commercial Road, London.—(*D.N.B.*)

WILLIAM EWART (1798–1869)

Born in Liverpool on May 1, 1798; son of a Liverpool merchant; educated at Eton, and Christ Church College, Oxford, where he had a distinguished career, carrying off the Newdigate prize, Ewart graduated with second-class honours in Classics in 1821. He studied law and was called to the Bar at the Middle Temple in 1827, and became M.P. for Bletchingley in 1828. He afterwards sat for Liverpool from 1830 to 1837. Two years later he was elected for Wigan, and in 1841 began his long connection with Dumfries burghs which ended with his retirement in 1868. He died at Broadleas, near Devizes, on January 23, 1869.

To the unflagging zeal and tenacity of purpose of William Ewart in the conduct of the Public Libraries Act of 1850 through Parliament was due the start of the public library movement in Great Britain, which has done so much for the advancement of adult education, and the enlightenment and recreation of the masses of the people.

Ewart's parliamentary life was one long struggle for social betterment. He was a supporter of the repeal of the corn laws, carried Bills for doing away with hanging in chains, capital punishment for horse, cattle, and sheep stealing, and for removing the prohibition on prisoners being defended by Counsel in cases of felony. He drew the Report of a Committee which he had obtained on the connection between arts and manufactures, which led to the establishment of the Schools of Design at Somerset House in 1837. He moved for the examination of candidates for the Civil Service (1845), for the Army (1847), and for the Diplomatic Service (1852), which measures were subsequently adopted.—(*D.N.B.*)

RICHARD GARNETT (1835–1906)

Richard Garnett was born in Beacon Street, Lichfield, on February 27, 1835. He was the elder son of Richard Garnett (1789–1850), Assistant Keeper of Printed Books, British Museum. He was educated at home and at a private school in Caroline Street, Bedford Square. He had all his father's faculty for acquiring foreign languages, and all his life he was a student not only of the classics, but of French, German, Italian, and Spanish literature. In 1851 he became an assistant in the British Museum, and was employed in cataloguing work. He was promoted to the position of Assistant Keeper of Printed Books and Superintendent of the Reading Room, the duties of which he discharged with characteristic courtesy, placing at the disposal of readers all his immense

PROMINENT WORKERS AND BENEFACTORS

stores of knowledge. In 1881 the printing of the general catalogue of the Museum was entered upon to relieve the pressure on the available space occupied by the volumes of the manuscript catalogue in use by the public. To this task he devoted himself heart and soul, and to enable him to do so he retired from his service in the Reading Room in 1884, and carried on the work of seeing the catalogue through the Press up to 1890, when he was appointed Keeper of Printed Books.

To Garnett was due the idea of the sliding press, the value of which was apparent to the Principal Librarian, who took it up at once, with the result that valuable space was economized. He retired from the Museum service in 1899, and on that occasion was presented with his portrait painted by the Hon. John Collier.

After his retirement he devoted himself almost entirely to literature. He had been from his early days a wooer of the muse, and had published several volumes of his poems and translations from the Greek. He was a frequent contributor to periodicals and published lives of Milton, Carlyle, and Emerson in the Great Writers Series. To the *Dictionary of National Biography* he contributed many memoirs, as well as to the *Encyclopædia Britannica*.

He discovered among Shelley's MSS. and notebooks a small collection of unpublished verse, which he issued as *Relics of Shelley* (1862). His *The Twilight of the Gods* was published in 1888, and reprinted in 1903, and was well received on its second appearance. His *History of Italian Literature* (1897), a subject in which he was keenly interested, is a useful manual. He wrote Volumes One and Two of the *Illustrated Record of English Literature*, which he and Edmund Gosse compiled in 1903–4. The "Three Hundred Notable Books" purchased for the Museum during his keepership was privately printed, with a portrait, in 1899 in honour of his services.

The University of Edinburgh in 1883 conferred on him the honorary degree of LL.D., and he was made C.B. in

1895. He died at his home, 27 Tanza Road, Hampstead, on April 13, 1906.

Dr. Garnett was an original member of the Library Association, and was annually elected to the Council from the beginning until his election as President in 1893. For many years Dr. Garnett rarely failed to make some contribution to the *Transactions* on a topic of practical importance, many of them relating to the affairs of the British Museum and the improvement of its service to the public. His presidential address at Aberdeen was a succinct account of the work done by the Association since its beginning, with interesting reminiscences of the men who guided its destinies in its early years.

Mr. G. K. Fortescue, his successor at the Museum, in an obituary notice of him (*Library Association Record*, 1906, pp. 201–3), thus speaks of his work there: "From the day of his appointment and of his sudden introduction to the thronging crowd of questioners and seekers for light in the Reading Room his reputation was made. There seemed to be no subject which he had not studied, and few which he had not mastered, and to all who asked he distributed information as practical as it was accurate and critical. There was a kindliness and cordiality in his manner, a vivacity and energy in his speech, a constant half-suppressed humour in his conversation, combined with a total absence of red tape, or of the insolence of office, which attracted all who came within his influence."

THOMAS GREENWOOD (1851–1908)

Thomas Greenwood was born at Woodley, near Stockport, on May 9, 1851. He was educated at the village school, and early came under the influence of the Rev. William Urwick, of Hatherlow, who greatly encouraged his passion for knowledge. He was a constant reader at the Manchester Public Library, and it was the help he obtained there in his early studies that made him so warm an advocate for public

PROMINENT WORKERS AND BENEFACTORS

libraries. He entered on a business career, but served for about three years as librarian of a branch library in Sheffield. He then went to London to a post on the staff of the *Ironmonger*. In 1875, realizing the great need for more technical literature, he co-operated in the establishment of the firm of Smith, Greenwood & Co., which gained a high reputation as publishers of technical works. His son, Mr. Edward Greenwood, was taken into partnership, and the firm became Scott, Greenwood & Co.

Mr. Greenwood was a strong believer in the value of education, and realized the importance of the public library as a factor in the after-education of the masses by self-culture. The movement for the establishment of public libraries found in him one of its most enthusiastic supporters. He corresponded with the promoters of the movement in every part of the country, and addressed meetings throughout the United Kingdom. He did not take much part in the proceedings of the Library Association, but was keenly interested in the efforts for the removal of the rate limitation, although in this matter he was of opinion that a rate of twopence in the pound would be found sufficient for libraries everywhere, and that a Bill to raise the limit to that figure would have more chance of being passed by the legislature than one calling for complete abolition of the rate limit.

His published works were a powerful aid to the library movement. *Public Libraries*, first published in 1886, ran through several editions; *The Library Year Book* (1897), and *The British Library Year Book* (1900–1901) were indispensable tools for the librarian. He also published *Sunday Schools and Village Libraries* (1892), *Museums and Art Galleries* (1888), *Edward Edwards, the Chief Pioneer of Municipal Public Libraries* (1902). He gathered all the items he could find concerning Edwards, and presented them to the Manchester Public Library. He erected a monument to Edwards over his grave in Niton Churchyard, being assisted in this pious work by Dr. Garnett, Mr. C. W. Sutton, Mr. J. J. Ogle, and Mr. W. E. A. Axon.

THE PUBLIC LIBRARY MOVEMENT

He collected at great pains and expense a library of books dealing with librarianship, bibliography, and the production of books, amounting to some 12,000 volumes, and presented it to Manchester Public Library, "The Thomas Greenwood Library for Librarians," and in his will left an endowment of £5,000 for its maintenance and augmentation. It is available for borrowing to all members of the Association on the payment of carriage.

He presented a library to Hatherlow, in honour of the Rev. W. Urwick, whose kindly interest in his early struggles he never forgot.

In 1907 he visited Japan, but an illness which he contracted there he was unable to shake off, and he died on November 9, 1908.

ROBERT HARRISON (1820–1897)

Robert Harrison was born in Liverpool on November 28, 1820. He came of a good Lancashire family, and began life as an assistant to a Holborn parliamentary bookseller. He became tutor to the family of Prince Demidoff, and a lecturer in St. Anne's School, St. Petersburg. He lived in Russia until the outbreak of the Crimean War, and on his return published his *Notes of a Nine Years' Residence in Russia, 1844–1853* (1855). He obtained the librarianship of the Leeds Library, and made that important subscription library a flourishing concern. He then became Secretary and Librarian of the London Library in succession to Mr. Bodham Donne, a post which he held until 1893, when he resigned. He died on January 4, 1897.

He was an original member and one of the founders of the Library Association, being appointed its first Treasurer, an office which he filled with distinction until January 1889, when, owing to ill-health, he was obliged to resign. On that occasion he was specially thanked for his services by the Association, and presented with a gold watch and chain as a mark of appreciation. He regularly attended the meetings of

PROMINENT WORKERS AND BENEFACTORS

the Association, was a member of several special committees, and took a prominent part in the discussions, besides contributing the following papers to the *Transactions*: "The Salaries of Librarians" (1877); "On the Elimination of Useless Books from Libraries" (1881); "Charles Nodier" (1883); "County Bibliography" (1886); "Etienne Gabriel Peignot" (1888).

In addition to these technical papers, he wrote, along with Joseph Gostwick, *Outlines of German Literature* (1873; 2nd ed., 1883); edited Mackenzie's *Dictionary of Universal Biography*; and assisted Captain Hozier in his history of the Franco-Prussian War. He also contributed a number of biographies to the *Dictionary of National Biography*.

He was elected President of the Association in 1891, and presided at the Nottingham Conference in that year. He was a ready and agreeable speaker, a man of a genial temperament, and his memory was cherished by his friends with affection and esteem.

MINNIE STEWART RHODES JAMES

Miss M. S. R. James became a member of the Library Association in 1889. She was appointed, in 1887, Librarian of The People's Palace, London, Sir Walter Besant's Palace of Delight, then recently founded. Here she served until 1894, when she went to the United States to take up a position in the Library Bureau at Boston, Mass. After six months' preparatory work there, she came back to England to assist in the establishment of a branch office in London. She returned to Boston in 1897 to fill a position in the library department at the head office of the Bureau, a post which she occupied until her death.

While in this country she took a very prominent part in the work of the Library Association, attending the meetings regularly, reading papers, and contributing to the discussions. She was a zealous supporter of the employment of women in librarianship, and was a whole-souled advocate of the need

THE PUBLIC LIBRARY MOVEMENT

for the education and training of assistants. She took the keenest interest in the affairs of the Library Assistants' Association, particularly in the establishment of their library, to which she gave both money and books.

At a monthly meeting of the Library Association in 1892, Miss James gave a most interesting, historical, and amusing account of the People's Palace Library and her experiences with readers in it (*The Library*, 1890, pp. 341–51). It was an entirely free library, not supported by the rates, but managed by a body of Trustees, of whom Sir Edmund Hay Currie was Chairman.

Miss James contributed a paper at the Association's meeting at Paris in 1892 on "Women Librarians," showing that there is no hindrance to their employment if only they will undergo the necessary training (*The Library*, 1892, pp. 217–24). At the same meeting her "Plan for Providing Technical Instruction for Library Students and Assistants" (*The Library*, 1892, pp. 313–18) was proposed. Her paper was read again at a meeting in Liverpool later in the year, and a full discussion took place (*The Library*, 1893, pp. 161–66).

At the Aberdeen meeting of the Association in 1893 Miss James returned to the question of women in libraries, with a paper on "American Women as Librarians" (*The Library*, 1893, pp. 270–74), indicating the conditions of service, the remuneration, and the training classes provided.

In 1898 Miss James wrote to *The Library* (Vol. 10, pp. 88–91) an interesting account of a typical meeting of the Massachusetts Library Club, showing how American librarians conducted their meetings.

She again dealt with "Women Librarians and their Future Prospects" (*Library Association Record*, 1900, pp. 291–304) in a paper read before the International Conference of Women, London, June 1899, with a bibliography appended.

She communicated an account of the Public Libraries of Nassau, N.P., and the Bahama Islands to the *Library Association Record* in 1901 (pp. 368–70), and an appreciation of Sir Walter Besant to the same volume (pp. 416–20), paying a glowing tribute to his kind-heartedness, his great love for London, and his hard work for the dwellers in the East End, his common sense and practical views of the purpose of education, and the important part played by libraries therein.

Miss James's interest in the Library Association and its work was clearly shown by her undertaking to index the first two volumes of the *Library Association Record*, and carrying out the work in a manner so thorough as to put to shame the compilers of the indexes to some at least of the volumes of our Journal. The same thoroughness and sincerity were shown in all her work, and her wit and vivacity were equalled by her personal charm. In the spring of 1903 her friends noted that she was struggling against illness, and an attack of measles, upon which typhoid supervened, proved too much for her to struggle through. She died at St. Botolph Hospital, Boston, on June 5, 1903.

SIR JOHN LUBBOCK, BARON AVEBURY (1834–1913)

The Right Hon. Sir John Lubbock, 4th Bt., created 1st Baron Avebury in 1900, was born in London on April 30, 1834. He was educated at Eton and privately at home. He early evinced an interest in public libraries, and took a prominent part in introducing legislation concerning them. In the year of the foundation of the Library Association he introduced a Libraries Bill, along with Mr. Mundella and others, but the Bill was dropped. A similar fate befell another measure which he introduced on January 7, 1881, owing to opposition to certain of its features by the municipalities of Birmingham and Manchester. The Bill was re-introduced in 1882 and 1883, but was blocked on both occasions. He again brought forward an amended measure in March 1887, which gave power to metropolitan districts to adopt the Acts. The amending Bill of 1890 bore his name, and became law on August 18th in that year. He acted as one of the adjudicators on the prize Bill drafted by Messrs. Ogle and Fovargue, and he introduced, and carried through the House of Commons the Act of 1892, the principal Act for England and Wales. His services were frequently in request on the occasion of the laying of the foundation-stones of public libraries, and his addresses on those occasions did much to further the library movement. He may rightly be regarded as the successor to William Ewart in the parliamentary leadership of the movement, nearly every Bill being backed by him and receiving his hearty support. He held the presidentship of a great number of scientific societies and sat on numerous Royal Commissions, and was a member of many foreign scientific societies and international associations, contributing to their transactions and proceedings. He was elected President of the Library Association on the occasion of the Second International Library Conference in London in 1897. He died on May 28, 1913.

THOMAS WILLIAM LYSTER (1855–1922)

Thomas William Lyster, Librarian of the National Library of Ireland, was born at Barraghcore, Co. Kilkenny, on December 17, 1855; the eldest son of Thomas Lyster, Rathdowney, and Jane Smith, Roscrea. He was educated at the Wesleyan School, Dublin, from which he went to Dublin University, where he graduated M.A., with a first senior moderatorship. He was appointed Assistant Librarian of the National Library of Ireland in 1878. On the retirement of William Archer in 1895, he succeeded to the librarianship, which he continued to hold until his retirement in 1920. He acted as Examiner in English under the Intermediate Education Board in 1880 and several subsequent years. His literary output was not extensive, but of rare quality. His translation of Düntzer's *Goethes Leben*, which he published in 1883, was much more than a translation, for he supplied references to all the authorities for the author's statements, involving much research and a first-hand knowledge of German sources. He edited an anthology of *Select Poetry for Young Students* in 1893 (5th ed., 1904, *English Poetry for Young Students*), an admirable selection of choice pieces carefully edited. He contributed critical papers to the *Academy*, the English Goethe Society, and *Hibernia* (a short-lived review which he helped to found). For some years before his death he was engaged on a study of Burke, with a view to the publication of a new edition of his complete works, which unfortunately was not destined to see the light.

Lyster became a member of the Library Association in 1895, and at once became a frequent and valuable contributor to its transactions. He was an enthusiastic advocate of the Dewey Decimal Classification, and at the Buxton Conference in 1896 read a paper, "Observations on the Dewey Classification and Notation," illustrating the notation on the blackboard. In the following year, at the London Conference, he contributed "Notes on Shelf Classification by the Dewey System." Again in 1899 he read a paper, "On Shelf Classification," published in the *Library Association Record* in 1900. A lecture which he delivered in Dublin in 1900 on "The Characteristics and Work of the Modern Public Library" was published in the *Record* in 1901. In 1902 he gave his "Idea of a Great Public Library: an Essay in the Philosophy of Libraries" (*Library Association Record*, 1903). He contributed a "Brief List of some of the more important Historical Publications of 1902," with a prefatory note, and this was followed by "The Best Books of 1903: History" and "The Best Books of 1904: History" in the two following years (*Library Association Record*, 1904 and 1906). A lecture to the Cork Literary and Scientific Society, entitled "Ireland and Public Libraries," was printed in the *Library Association Record* in 1906. In 1913 a paper entitled "An Index to Periodicals Wanted" (*Library Association Record*, 1914, pp. 39–47), pleading for co-operation between English and American librarians in the publication of a continuation of Poole's Index paved the way for the

Subject Index to Periodicals, for the support of which by librarians he appealed in a letter to the editor (*Library Association Record*, 1915, p. 223).

Lyster was elected as a country member of the Council in 1895, a Vice-President in 1899, an office which he held until his death, which occurred on December 12, 1922. The abrupt cessation of his contributions to the *Transactions* is explained by a serious illness which overtook him during a visit to his sister in Kent, in 1914, an operation having to be performed from which he never fully recovered, although he was able to return to duty, and bravely struggled on in the face of much pain and suffering. Loving tributes to his memory were paid in the pages of *The Record* in 1923, accompanied by a fine portrait.

SIR JOHN YOUNG WALKER MACALISTER (1856–1925)

John Young Walker MacAlister, born in 1856, was the son of Donald MacAlister, Tarbert, Kintyre. He was educated at the High School of Liverpool, proceeding thence to Edinburgh University, where he studied for three years in the Medical Schools, but owing to ill-health he was unable to go farther with a formal course of medicine. He turned his attention to library work, becoming Sub-Librarian of Liverpool Library, subsequently Librarian of Leeds Library, and, in 1887, first Librarian of the Gladstone Library (National Liberal Club). Shortly after, he was appointed Librarian of the Medical and Chirurgical Society. While in the North he found time, in the midst of his many duties, for contributions to the *Leeds Mercury* and the *Yorkshire Post*—a foundation for the professional journalism of his later years. The two main lines, medicine and librarianship, ran steadily side by side throughout his life. From 1887 to 1898 he held the position of Honorary Secretary to the Library Association, founding in 1889 the periodical entitled *The Library*, which he edited for many years, at first alone, then jointly with Professor Pollard. His

PROMINENT WORKERS AND BENEFACTORS

strenuous and enthusiastic efforts were instrumental in the consolidation of the various Libraries Acts resulting in the Act of 1892. As one of the Legislation Committee at that time, he haunted the House of Commons so persistently that it was said police and officials regarded him as a Member of the House, permitting him various privileges. In 1897 he had a heavy task as Honorary Secretary-General and Organizer of the Second International Library Conference. During the difficult years of 1914–1919 he was President of the Library Association.

This record might well be deemed sufficient for one man's achievement; but since all along he was doing as much for medicine as for librarianship, it is no marvel that the only form of recreation he could report to *Who's Who* was "sleeping." It is evident, too, from records remaining that at times of crisis the work of the day overflowed into the night. Besides acting as commissioner or member of various important committees on medicine and hygiene, in 1905 he formulated the scheme for amalgamating the Medical Societies of London, which culminated in the union of all the leading societies, with a new charter under the name of the Royal Society of Medicine. As Sir John Ballinger has written of him, "He was full of great ideas, and knew how to get them accepted and realized." While President of the Library Association, he was also Secretary of the War Office's Surgical Advisory Committee, as well as organizer and Honorary Secretary, Emergency Surgical Aid Corps for Admiralty, War Office, and Metropolitan Police. In 1919 His Majesty conferred recognition of these numerous invaluable services in a knighthood. Sir John also received the Order of the British Empire. He did not, however, live long to enjoy his richly-deserved honours, for in December 1925 he succumbed to failing health.

MacAlister was, without any doubt, the best friend the Library Association has had so far. He was an eager fighter on its behalf; he first suggested an official Manual of Librarianship; he gave the Association and librarianship far and away the liveliest and most stimulating journal it has ever had; he was a warm friend of young librarians, and offered many prizes for competition among them; and, last but not least, he obtained for the Association its Royal Charter. With more than his share of the Scot's high spirit and pugnacity, he was a gay and "bonnie fechter," and whenever he found the Council of the Association to be slack he fought relentlessly for reform, as at the memorable Conference at Plymouth, when he routed the Conservative diehards on the Council in a single witty speech.—(E.A.S.)

THOMAS MASON (1857–1914)

Thomas Mason, son of Thomas Mason, Librarian at Arbroath, was born in Aberdeen in 1857, educated in Arbroath, and began work as a mechanic, but afterwards obtained a post as an assistant in the Mitchell Library, Glasgow, in 1877, where he soon rose to be Assistant Librarian. He became a member of the Library Association in 1880, and read a paper at the Edinburgh Conference in that year on "The Free Libraries of Scotland" (*Transactions*, 1880, pp. 49–57), published separately in Glasgow, 1880. In 1881 he was appointed Librarian of Stirling's Public Library, Glasgow, and in 1885 published his *Public and Private Libraries of Glasgow*.

In 1886 he was elected to the Council of the Library Association, and became Joint Hon. Secretary with J. Y. W. MacAlister in 1890, serving for three years in that capacity. At the Glasgow Conference in 1888 he acted as Joint Local Secretary along with the Librarian, F. T. Barrett, and read a paper entitled "A Bibliographical Martyr—Dr. Robert Watt, author of the *Bibliotheca Britannica*" (*The Library*, Vol. 1, pp. 56–63). When he left Glasgow in 1889 to become the first Librarian of St. Martin-in-the-Fields Public Library, London, he received a substantial token of the regard in which he was held in Glasgow. His novel, *Adam Dickson: or, sae sweet, sae bonnilie*, published in

PROMINENT WORKERS AND BENEFACTORS

Glasgow in 1888, was reviewed in *The Library*, Vol. 1, 1889. At a monthly meeting of the Association at Gray's Inn in May 1889 he was presented with an album of photographs of members who had been present at the Glasgow meeting, in appreciation of his services as Joint Hon. Secretary. At the annual meeting in London in 1889 he opened a discussion on the value of fiction in public libraries with an interesting paper entitled "Fiction in Free Libraries."

Other papers contributed to the *Transactions* by Mr. Mason were: "An Alphabetical List of Places where the Acts have been adopted, with dates of adoption" (1890); "A New Method of arranging a Lending Library," with illustrations of his "star" plan—a plan of open access with card charging system (1893); "Lecture to the London Summer School on the Fitting and Equipment of a Library" (1895); "Local Prints and Records of a London Parish (St. Martin-in-the-Fields)" (1897).

The library of the Royal Historical Society was housed for some years in the St. Martin's Library, and Mr. Mason acted as librarian and clerk. When the passing of the London Government Act necessitated the amalgamation of St. Martin's parish with others to form the City of Westminster, Mr. Mason retired on a pension in 1905. He entered the service of Messrs. W. Stevens, Ltd., and devoted his energies to journalistic work. He died on March 30, 1914.

Mr. Mason was an enthusiastic Freemason, a member of the Order of Oddfellows, and Hon. Librarian of the Savage Club in succession to J. Y. W. MacAlister.

EDWARD WILLIAMS BYRON NICHOLSON (1849–1912)

Born on March 16, 1849, at St. Helier, Jersey, only son of Edward Nicholson, R.N., educated at Llanrwst Grammar School, Liverpool College, and Tonbridge School, Nicholson entered Trinity College, Oxford, in 1867, where he took a high place in Classics, gaining the Gaisford

Prize for Greek verse (1871), and the Hall-Houghton Junior Greek Testament Prize (1872), graduating B.A. in 1871 and M.A. in 1874. After taking his B.A. degree he taught for a short time until his appointment as Librarian of the London Institution in 1873, a post which he held until 1882, when he succeeded the Rev. Henry Octavius Coxe as Bodley's Librarian.

Dr. Garnett has told us that Nicholson more than any other man has the right to be considered the founder of the Library Association, for, as we have already stated (p. 163), it was on his initiative that the International Conference of Librarians was convened in 1877, at which the Association was inaugurated. He and H. R. Tedder were Joint Hon. Secretaries of the Conference and of the Association in the first two years of its existence; but on May 23, 1878, he wrote to the Council stating that his many and increasing duties compelled him, much against his will, to resign his joint secretaryship. The Council were extremely loth to part with so admirable a co-adjutor, and passed a resolution to that effect, trusting that his valuable assistance might continue to be given in other ways. For the next few years he attended the annual Conferences of the Association and took a prominent part in the proceedings, but after his appointment to the Bodleian his new duties absorbed the greater part of his energies. This will readily be understood when the Report to the Curators which he published in 1888 is examined. In it he details the chief events of the Bodleian history since his appointment. Among these were: an increase in the staff, the introduction of boy labour, a new code of cataloguing rules, the development of a subject catalogue of the whole library and of the shelf classification of printed books, improvements in the methods of binding books, MSS., and music, the incorporation of minor collections, and the discorporation of certain donation-collections, much increase in the facilities for readers, and the establishment of a course of instruction in palæography.[1]

[1] H. R. Tedder in *Library Association Record*, 1913, p. 100.

PROMINENT WORKERS AND BENEFACTORS

Nicholson apparently was constitutionally unable to delegate any of his duties to subordinates, and supervised everything personally. He was in frequent conflict with the University authorities over such details as the parking of bicycles in the Proscholium, the honour and dignity of Bodley on all occasions finding in him a zealous champion. The provision of the underground storeroom, which was not opened until after his death, was due to his planning. His Staff Calendar, which detailed the hour-to-hour duties of each member of the staff, gave rise to much amused criticism.

As to his literary work, his interests were very varied. He published no great work with which his name can be associated, but many pamphlets on such diversified subjects as celtic antiquities, athletics, biblical criticism, comparative philology, folk-lore, music, numismatics, palæography, vivisection, etc. Curiously enough his contributions to library literature are confined to two articles on the binding of books in which he took a very keen interest. At the 1877 Conference he read a paper on buckram binding, which he had experimented with and which he praised highly. In 1880, when he had had further experience in the wearing qualities of that material, he issued a warning against its use for books subject to much handling, in an article contributed to the Edinburgh Conference, entitled "Buckram: a Palinode."

Like all forceful characters, Nicholson was not without enemies. He was impatient of opposition, but even those who were most opposed to him recognized his unselfish aims, his thorough zeal for his duty, his restless energy, and his untiring efforts on behalf of the institution over which he presided. He died practically in harness on March 17, 1912, and it has been recorded of him by one who knew him intimately that he never heard him say an unkind word about any man, not even about those whom he considered to be his enemies. He was a great librarian, and one who deserves an honoured position in the history of the Library Association.

THE PUBLIC LIBRARY MOVEMENT

JOHN JAMES OGLE (1858–1909)

J. J. Ogle was born at Carlton, near Nottingham, in 1858. He obtained his first library appointment at Nottingham Public Library under Mr. J. Potter Briscoe, and was the first library assistant to win a certificate under the Library Association's scheme of examinations. He and Mr. Butcher, of Welling, obtained second-class certificates at the first examination in 1885. While an assistant at Nottingham, Mr. Ogle availed himself of the opportunity of studying at the University College there, his studies being mainly in languages, literature, and science, especially botany, physics, and mathematics. He matriculated at London University, but did not take a degree.

In 1887 he became the first Librarian and Curator of Bootle Public Library and Museum. In June 1891 he added to his duties by accepting the post of Organizing Secretary for Technical Instruction, and held the three offices until 1900, when he was appointed Director of Technical Instruction at the opening of the new Technical School at Bootle. It was with considerable regret that he severed his connection with library work, in which he took the keenest interest.

Mr. Ogle joined the Library Association in 1883, and in 1885 there appeared the first of a long series of valuable practical papers contributed by him to the *Transactions*. This was an "Outline of a Scheme of Classification applicable to Books." In the following year he won the prize, given by E. M. Borrajo, for the best essay "On the Extension of the Free Libraries Acts to Small Places" (*Library Chronicle*, Vol. 4, 1887, pp. 17–23). He contributed a letter to the Editor of *The Library* (1889, p. 247), entitled "A Plea for Papers on Bibliology," suggesting that members who had special knowledge of particular subjects should prepare lists, with critical notes, of the best books on those subjects for the guidance of their fellow-librarians and the general public.

PROMINENT WORKERS AND BENEFACTORS

He was the winner, jointly with H. W. Fovargue, of the prize of £10 presented by Mr. MacAlister in 1889 for the best draft of a Consolidating Libraries Bill. This draft afterwards formed the basis of the Bill which became the Public Libraries Act, 1892. The essay was afterwards expanded and published in 1893 in the Library Association Series, under the title *Public Libraries Legislation*.

At a monthly meeting in London in 1891 he read a paper on "The Selection of Geological and Biological Books for a Public Library," which he afterwards repeated at a meeting of the librarians of the Mersey District. At the annual meeting at Nottingham in the same year he contributed a paper on "The Place of the Free Public Library in Popular Education" (*Library*, Vol. 3, pp. 401–7), reprinted by Bale & Sons, 1891.

In 1892 there appeared his plan for "A Summer School of Library Science" (*Library*, Vol. 4, pp. 319–23). This gave rise to the successful summer schools (for which he was the first Hon. Secretary) which were held in London and elsewhere. In the same year appeared, as Part I of the Public Library Manual, *Library Legislation, 1855–1890*, by H. W. Fovargue and J. J. Ogle.

In 1893 he put forward a "Proposal for the Establishment of District Public Libraries on an Economical Basis" (*Library*, Vol. 6, pp. 42–44).

In 1894 "The Relationship of the Public Library Committee to Other Educational Bodies" was dealt with (*Library*, Vol. 7, pp. 129–34).

In 1895 he supplemented the 1894 paper with one on "The Public Library and the Public Elementary School—a Note on an Experiment" (*Library*, Vol. 8, pp. 93–95). This gave the result of his experience at Bootle and included a set of "Rules for the School Delivery" for the use of the voluntary teacher librarians. In the same year he lectured to the London Summer School on the formation of a public library after the adoption of the Acts.

In 1896 he spoke of "Some Pitfalls in Cataloguing"

(*Library*, Vol. 8, pp. 150–156), and in 1897, at the International Conference in London, he dealt with "Hindrances to the Training of Efficient Librarians." In this year he published his work on *The Free Library*, its history and present condition, one of the volumes in The Library Series edited by Dr. Richard Garnett, published by George Allen.

In 1898 he commenced a "Library Assistants' Corner" in the pages of *The Library*, which he continued to edit with much advantage to candidates for the Library Association examinations, until, in 1900, the pressure of his new duties at Bootle compelled him to hand it over to Dr. Guppy, who maintained it for some time longer as "Our Junior Colleagues' Corner." In this year also appeared the important Report which he prepared for the Education Department (now the Board of Education), "On the Connection between the Public Library and the Public Elementary School," which was based on an Inquiry addressed to the public libraries of England and Wales and certain American public libraries. It was published in Volume 2 of the special *Reports on Educational Subjects*, pp. 232–65, with a select list of papers bearing on the subject at the end.

Mr. Ogle was a striking example of the value of public libraries as factors in the self-education of those who are willing to take advantage of the opportunities they afford, but he had none of that arrogance which the self-made man so often displays. He was the most modest of men, and his withdrawal from active participation in the affairs of the Association was a great loss. The Association showed appreciation of this in making him an Hon. Fellow in the year preceding his death. In 1909 he had to undergo an operation from which he seemed to be recovering satisfactorily when a relapse came, and he passed away on December 19, 1909.

FRANK PACY (1862–1928)

Born at Wishaw, Lanarkshire, on May 26, 1862, son of John Pacy, a Civil Servant, Frank Pacy removed with his parents to Wigan in Lancashire while he was still of school age. He became a pupil at the Wigan Grammar School, and on leaving school was appointed to the staff of Wigan Public Library at the age of sixteen. He quickly rose to be Sub-Librarian, and his experience gained on the work of the important printed subject catalogue of the Wigan Library led to his appointment on the cataloguing staff of the Birmingham Public Libraries in 1883. In the following year he succeeded Mr. Alfred Cotgreave as Librarian of Richmond, Surrey. While there he acted as Secretary of the Richmond Athenæum, a very vigorous literary and debating society, to the published *Transactions* of which he contributed a number of articles.

He remained at Richmond until 1891, when the parish of St. George, Hanover Square, adopted the Public Libraries Act and he was called to fill the office of First Librarian. Again in 1905, when the passing of the Local Government of London Act necessitated the regrouping of the library authorities of the Metropolis, and the city of Westminster was revived to form a library district, Pacy was chosen to be Chief Librarian of the city, with his headquarters at the Public Library in Buckingham Palace Road. Here he spent the rest of his library career, retiring in 1928. He was not fated, however, to enjoy his retirement for long. For several years it was evident to his colleagues that his health was far from good. He had purchased a house at Richmond, and had only just entered on its occupancy when he had to undergo an operation which in his frail state of health he was unable to recover from. He passed away on June 24, 1928, and was laid to rest in Richmond Cemetery, the service being attended by many librarians and friends, including a number of members of the Council.

Mr. Pacy became a member of the Library Association in 1880. He contributed a number of papers to its *Transactions*, including the following: "Town Libraries and Surrounding Districts," dealing with subscription libraries and individual subscribers in connection with public libraries

THE PUBLIC LIBRARY MOVEMENT

(1887); "Borrowing and Rating Powers under the Public Libraries Acts" (1888); "Notes on the Richmond Library" (1891); "On the Library Movement in St. George, Hanover Square" (1895); "On the Exemption of Public Libraries from Income Tax and Local Rates" (1897); "The Reference *versus* the Lending Department" (1901); "The New Opportunity," dealing with the question of control of public libraries by a central authority, and the rural library movement (1920); "On the Possibility of Mutual Arrangements between County Schemes and (*a*) Borough Libraries and (*b*) Special Libraries" (1920).

It was in 1898 that he first took office as Hon. Secretary, following on the resignation of Mr. MacAlister. He did not serve long on this occasion, feeling obliged to resign in 1901, owing to dissensions in the Council on the occasion of the Plymouth meeting. He took over the duties again on the resignation of Mr. Jast in October 1915, and continued to hold the office until his death in 1928.

HENRY RICHARD TEDDER (1850–1924)

H. R. Tedder, son of William Henry Tedder and Elizabeth Ferris, was born on June 25, 1850, at South Kensington. He was educated privately and in France, and became Librarian to the 1st Lord Acton in 1873, on whose recommendation he was appointed Assistant Librarian in the Athenæum Club, London. In 1874 he succeeded Spencer Hall as Librarian, and in 1889 became Secretary as well as Librarian, holding both offices until his retirement in 1922. He was requested by the Committee of the Club to write its history, but his illness supervened and the work was never completed. Before he died, however, he contributed to *The Times* of February 16, 1924, an article entitled "The Athenæum, 1824–1924: a Centenary Record," which was reprinted as a souvenir pamphlet and presented to his fellow-members of the Club by Nicholas Murray Butler, President of Columbia University.

PROMINENT WORKERS AND BENEFACTORS

Mr. Tedder was an original member and one of the founders of the Library Association. He was one of the organizers of the first International Conference of Librarians in 1877, and along with E. B. Nicholson, acted as Joint Secretary and Editor of its *Transactions*. At this Conference the Library Association was formed, and he and Ernest C. Thomas, who had succeeded Nicholson as Joint Secretary, edited the *Transactions* of the first and second annual meetings. He was elected Hon. Treasurer in 1889, an office which he held until his death on August 1, 1924, with the exception of the year 1897-8, when he was elected to the office of President.

He acted as Treasurer and Secretary to the Metropolitan Free Libraries Committee appointed by the International Conference to endeavour to secure the adoption of the Public Libraries Acts by the vestries of London, and presented their Report in 1878. The Committee was afterwards enlarged to form the Metropolitan Libraries Association, Mr. Tedder continuing to act as Secretary, but the apathy of the vestries was such that the efforts of the Association ended in failure. Mr. Tedder was Organizing Secretary to the Pope Commemoration Committee, Twickenham, in 1888; Honorary Treasurer of the Second International Conference of Librarians, London, 1897; Treasurer of the Robert Proctor Memorial Fund; Honorary Treasurer and Secretary of the Advanced Historical Teaching Fund from 1902 till his death; Honorary Treasurer of the Royal Historical Society from 1904; Secretary to Herbert Spencer's Trustees, and Editor of Sections 9 and 10 of Spencer's *Descriptive Sociology* for the Trust. He was a member of the Royal Commission on Public Records, 1910-1919.

Mr. Tedder took the keenest interest in the training of library assistants. It was on his motion that a Committee, of which he was a member, was appointed to consider and report how best such training might be carried out. He read a paper on "Librarianship as a Profession" at the Cambridge meeting in 1882, and an examination scheme was shortly afterwards put into operation. Mr. Tedder held the office of Chairman of the Education Committee from 1902 until 1924.

Mr. Tedder contributed many papers to the *Transactions*, notably "Librarianship as a Profession" (1882); "Women as Librarians" (two papers, 1882 and 1897); "The Librarian in Relation to Books" (1907); "The Place of Bibliography in Education" (two papers, 1912 and 1913); "Public Records and the Reports of the Royal Commission" (1920). He was the joint-author, along with J. D. Brown, of the admirable article on "Libraries," with its accompanying bibliography, in the 11th edition of the *Encyclopædia Britannica*. He wrote a number of lives for the *Dictionary of National Biography*, and contributed many articles to Palgrave's *Dictionary of Political Economy*, as well as assisting the editor in seeing the dictionary through the press.

ERNEST CHESTER THOMAS (1850–1892)

Ernest Chester Thomas, bibliographer, was born on October 28, 1850, at Birkenhead; was educated at Manchester Grammar School, and Trinity College, Oxford, where he graduated B.A. in June 1875. He studied law at Gray's Inn, and won the Bacon Scholarship of that Inn in May 1875. In 1876 appeared his treatise on *Leading Cases in Constitutional Law*, a second edition of which was published in 1885. He studied in the Universities of Jena and Bonn, and translated Lange's *Geschichte des Materialismus*, 1877–81. In 1878 he published *Leading Statutes Summarized for the Use of Students*. He was called to the Bar at Gray's Inn on June 29, 1881.

When, in 1878, E. W. B. Nicholson resigned the Joint Hon. Secretaryship of the Library Association, Thomas was appointed in his stead, and held that office for twelve years, at first jointly with H. R. Tedder until the resignation of the latter in July 1880, and again jointly with Charles Welch, then Sub-Librarian of the Guildhall, from October

1880 till September 1882, afterwards alone until 1887, when he obtained the valuable co-operation of Mr. J. Y. W. MacAlister, who gradually assumed the entire burden of the administrative work. At the Reading meeting in 1890, Thomas finally resigned from his secretarial duties, and was elected one of the Vice-Presidents of the Association.

Thomas's editorial work for the Association was a labour of love excellently performed. Along with his co-adjutors, Tedder and Welch, he edited the *Transactions* of the first three Conferences, and by himself the fourth and fifth Conferences. He succeeded Mr. William Brace as editor of *Monthly Notes* of the Library Association in 1882, and in the concluding number in December 1883 he announced that the plan of the periodical would be followed and enlarged in a somewhat more ambitious journal. This was *The Library Chronicle*, the first number of which was issued in January 1884. Thomas established the *Chronicle* and carried it on at his own expense until 1888, when he was obliged to discontinue it, partly through his having undertaken the translation of a work on Japan from the German of Professor Rein, and partly owing to the commercial worries of his own venture.

Apart from his work for the Library Association, it had long been his wish to bring out a critical edition of Richard de Bury's *Philobiblon*, of which the printed text was very faulty. This work appeared in 1888, and established his reputation for scholarship. The new text is based upon personal examination of a large number of different manuscripts, and the translation is exact and well written, with a full bibliography of the different editions.

For a year or two before his death Thomas took up business in the city, but his health, greatly undermined by an attack of typhoid fever, gave way, and he passed away at Tunbridge Wells on February 5, 1892. An *In Memoriam* article, with a complete bibliography of his books and periodical articles from the pen of H. R. Tedder, appeared in *The Library*, Vol. 4, 1892.

THE PUBLIC LIBRARY MOVEMENT

WILLIAM HENRY KEARLEY WRIGHT (1844–1915)

W. H. K. Wright, Librarian of Plymouth, was born in Plymouth on September 14, 1844. He was appointed Librarian of his native city in 1876, and held the office until his death on April 27, 1915.

He attended the first International Conference of Librarians in 1877, and his paper "On the Best Means of Promoting the Free Library Movement in Small Towns and Villages" was the first to be read. He was an original member of the Library Association, and was present at every annual meeting from the first to the thirty-sixth inclusive. He contributed many papers and took part in a great many discussions, in which his experience and sound commonsense were highly valued. His principal contributions were: "Special Collections of Local Books in Provincial Libraries" (1878); "The Public Free Library and the Board School" (1879); "An Indicator-Catalogue and Charging System" (1879); "Librarians and Local Bibliography" (1882); "Municipal Libraries and Suburban Districts" (1886), dealing with the question of extending the use of public libraries to residents beyond the rating area on payment of a subscription equivalent to the rate imposed by the Act—a plan which he favoured; "Lending Libraries and Board Schools" (1888); "The Library Association; 1877–97: a Retrospect" (1897), in which he gave interesting recollections of prominent members of the Association; "Literary and Artistic Associations of Plymouth and Devonport" (1901); "Local Collections: what should be collected and how to obtain materials" (1904).

For a long series of years he was an active member of the Council, and served as a Vice-President on several occasions. He attended both the International Conferences in London and took part in the proceedings.

He was the founder of the Ex-Libris Society and edited its *Journal*. He took a prominent part in all the social move-

PROMINENT WORKERS AND BENEFACTORS

ments of Plymouth, and received a presentation in acknowledgment of his services in connection with the National Armada Memorial in 1888. He was President of the Plymouth Institution in 1898, and of the local branch of the Dickens Fellowship. He was a Fellow of the Royal Historical Society, and editor of numerous local publications, e.g. *West Country Poets*, *Blue Friars*, *The Western Antiquary*, etc. He published an edition of Gay's *Fables*, and of the *History of Okehampton*.

Mr. Wright was the possessor of a powerful bass voice, which he often used with great effect at meetings of "The Executive" in reciting the "Ballad of the *Revenge*," or at our annual dinners, when he led off the National Anthem at the close. His tall, handsome bearded figure, usually accompanied by his faithful helpmeet, was sadly missed from our annual gatherings when he passed away.

APPENDIX I

LIST OF SOME BOOKS CONSULTED

Acts of Parliament Relating to Public Libraries, 1845 onwards.

Baker, Ernest A. The Public Library. 1922.

Board of Education. Public Libraries Committee. Report, 1927.

Brougham, Henry, Lord. Practical Observations upon the Education of the People. 1825.

Brown, Samuel. Itinerating Libraries and their Founder. 1856.

Brown, William. Memoir relative to Itinerating Libraries. Circa 1830.

Burns, C. Delisle. History of Birkbeck College. 1924.

Cannons, H. G. T. Bibliography of Library Economy, 1876–1920. 1927.

Carnegie U.K. Trust.
    Adams, W. G. S. Report on Library Provision and Policy. 1915.
    Mitchell, J. M. The Public Library System of Great Britain and Ireland, 1921–1923: a Report. 1924.

Chambers's Encyclopædia. Various articles, Andrew Bell, Library, etc.

Church of Scotland, General Assembly Acts, 1704–1740.

Clark, J. W. The Care of Books. 1901.

Edwards, Edward. Memoirs of Libraries. 2 vols. 1859.
    Libraries and Founders of Libraries. 1864.

Encyclopædia Britannica. Article "Libraries." Various editions.

Garnett, Richard. Essays in Librarianship and Bibliography. 1899.

Godard, J. G. George Birkbeck. 1884.

Grant, James. Old and New Edinburgh. 3 vols. *n.d.*

THE PUBLIC LIBRARY MOVEMENT

Gray, Duncan. County Library Systems. 1922.
Greenwood, Thomas. Public Libraries. 4th ed. 1894
    British Library Year Book, 1900–1901. 1900
Hammond, J. L. and B. The Age of the Chartists. 1930.
Hansard's Debates.
Hole, James. Essay on Literary and Scientific and Mechanics' Institutions. 1853.
Kirkwood, James. Overture for Founding Bibliothecks. 1699.
Library Association (of the United Kingdom):
    International Conference of Librarians. Transac. and Proc. 1877. Second ditto, 1897; Third ditto, 1927.
    Monthly Notes, 1880–1883.
    Transactions and Proceedings, 1878–1885.
    The Library Chronicle, 1884–1888.
    The Library, 1889–1898.
    The Library Association Record, 1899 to date.
    Year Books, 1892 to date. *v.y.*
Macleod, Robert D. County Rural Libraries. 1923.
The Mechanics' Magazine, 1823, etc.
Ogle, J. J. The Free Library. 1897.
Papworth, J. W. and W. Museums, Libraries, and Picture Galleries. 1853.
Savage, Ernest A. The Story of Libraries and Book Collecting. 1908.
Select Committee on Public Libraries: Reports, 1849–1852.
Statistical Account of Scotland: Haddington. 1845.
Wodrow, Robert. Analecta. 1843

APPENDIX II

CONSPECTUS OF THE VARIOUS ACTS OF PARLIAMENT RELATING TO PUBLIC LIBRARIES, MUSEUMS, AND GYMNASIUMS

Compiled for the purposes of the Summer School of Library Service, Aberystwyth.

By JAMES HUTT M.A. F.L.A.

THE PUBLIC LIBRARY MOVEMENT

ENGLAND AND WALES

DATE	NAME	SPECIAL FEATURES	REPEALED
1708 *7 Anne, c. 14.*	Dr. Bray's Act.	For the better preservation of parochial libraries in that part of Great Britain called England.	
1845 *8 & 9 Vict. c. 43.*	Museums Act.		by Act of 1850.
1850 *13 & 14 Vict. c. 65.*	Public Libraries Act, 1850.	Public Libraries & Museums. Municipal Boroughs only. Rate limited to ½d. in £.	by Act of 1855.
1855 *18 & 19 Vict. c. 70.*	Public Libraries & Museums Act, 1855.	Extends provisions to towns, to parishes, and to the City of London (§24). Rate limit raised to 1d.	portions by Acts of 1866, 1887, §13 (*re* meetings) by Act of 1889; rest by Act of 1892.
1861 *24 & 25 Vict. c. 97.*	Malicious Injuries to Property (England & Ireland).		
1866 *29 & 30 Vict. c. 114.*	Public Libraries Amendment Act, 1866 (England & Scotland).		as to Scotland by Act of 1867; rest by Act of 1892.

APPENDIX II

1871 34 & 35 *Vict. c. 71*.	Public Libraries Act, 1855, Amendment Act, 1871.	Extends powers to Local Boards.	by Act of 1892.
1877 40 & 41 *Vict. c. 54*.	Public Libraries (Amendment) Act, 1877.	Adoption by Ratepayers' Meeting, or by Voting Paper.	by Act of 1890.
1884 47 & 48 *Vict. c. 37*	Public Libraries Act, 1884.	Explains *re* Schools of Science & Art. Also buildings in Ireland & Scotland.	by Act of 1892.
1887 50 & 51 *Vict. c. 22*.	Public Libraries Acts Amendment Act, 1887.	Library authority may provide Lending Libraries without providing a separate building. Parishes partly without any borough or district. Metropolitan Districts (excluding City of London).	by Act of 1892.
1889 52 & 53 *Vict. c. 9*.	Public Libraries Acts Amendment Act, 1889.	*Re* Meetings and voting; Joint Libraries.	by Act of 1892.
1890 53 & 54 *Vict. c. 68*.	Public Libraries Acts Amendment Act, 1890.	*Re* Voting, etc.	by Act of 1892.
1891 54 & 55 *Vict. c. 22*.	Museums & Gymnasiums Act, 1891.	England & Wales, not London.	Administrative county of London by Act of 1901.
1892 55 & 56 *Vict. c. 53*. Principal Act.	Public Libraries Act, 1892.	The consolidating Act.	small portions by Act of 1901. Rate limitation by Act of 1919.

347

ENGLAND AND WALES—*continued*

DATE	NAME	SPECIAL FEATURES	REPEALED
1893 56 *Vict. c. 11.*	Public Libraries Amendment Act, 1893.	Urban districts; co-operation.	Rate limit by Act of 1919.
1898 61 & 62 *Vict. c. 53.*	Libraries Offences Act, 1898.		
1901 1 *Edw. VII, c. 19.*	Public Libraries Act, 1901 (England & Ireland).	To amend the Acts relating to Public Libraries, Museums, and Gymnasiums, and to regulate the liability of Managers of Libraries to proceedings for libel.	§12 (extension to Ireland) by Act of 1902. §10 (repairing of damage by subsidence) by Act of 1919.
1919 9 & 10 *Geo. V, c. 93.*	Public Libraries Act, 1919.	Power to County Councils. Education Committees. Repeal of rate limitation. If limit set, it must be adhered to.	
1925 15 & 16 *Geo. V, c. 90.*	Rating and Valuation Act, 1925.	Parish Library Authorities to raise the library rate as an item of the general rate.	

APPENDIX II

IRELAND

DATE	NAME	SPECIAL FEATURES	REPEALED
1853 16 & 17 Vict. c. 101.	Public Libraries Act (Ireland and Scotland).	Extends Act of 1850 to Ireland (Municipal boroughs) and to Scotland.	by Act of 1855.
1854 17 & 18 Vict. c. 103.	Town Improvements Act (Ireland) 1854.	Paving, lighting, draining, cleansing, etc. Sect. 99 incorporates Acts of 1850 & 1853.	by Act of 1855.
1855 18 & 19 Vict. c. 40. Principal Act.	Public Libraries Act (Ireland) 1855.	Consolidating Acts of 1853 and 1854.	
1861 24 & 25 Vict. c. 97.	Malicious Injuries to Property (England & Ireland).		
1877 40 & 41 Vict. c. 15.	Public Libraries (Ireland) Amendment Act, 1877.	Powers extended to Schools of Music.	
1884—See E. & W.			
1894 57 & 58 Vict. c. 38.	Public Libraries (Ireland) Act, 1894.	Modification as to adoption.	
1901 1 Edw. VII, c. 19.	Public Libraries Act, 1901.	Amends 1892 and 1893, and applies certain provisions (byelaws, etc.) to Ireland.	§10 (repairs of damage by subsidence) by Act of 1919. §12 (Extension to Ireland) by Act of 1902.

IRELAND—continued

DATE	NAME	SPECIAL FEATURES	REPEALED
1902 2 *Edw. VII, c.* 20.	Public Libraries (Ireland) Act, 1902.	Rural districts.	§§ 2, 3, 4, 6 by Act of 1924 (Northern Ireland).
1911 1 & 2 *Geo. V, c.* 9.	Public Libraries (Art Galleries in Co. Boroughs) (Ireland) Act, 1911.	Amending Act of 1855.	
1920 10 & 11 *Geo. V, c.* 25.	Public Libraries (Ireland) Act, 1920.	Rate limit raised to 3d., but in County Boroughs may be raised another 3d., with consent of Local Government Board.	
1924 15 & 16 *Geo. V, c.* 10	Public Libraries Act (Northern Ireland), 1924.	County Councils may adopt. Rate limit 1d., except in urban districts or towns, where, by consent of Ministry, it may be exceeded by not more than another 2d.	
1925 *c.* 25.	Irish Free State Local Government Act, 1925.	Rural District and Urban Councils (except Co. of Dublin) relinquish powers to County Councils, who may adopt Acts of 1855 to 1920.	

APPENDIX II

SCOTLAND

DATE	NAME	SPECIAL FEATURES	REPEALED
1853 16 & 17 *Vict. c. 101.*	Public Libraries (Ireland and Scotland).	Extends Act of 1850 to Ireland and Scotland (Royal and Parliamentary Burghs).	by Act of 1855.
1854. 17 & 18 *Vict. c. 64.*	Public Libraries (Scotland) Act, 1854.	Amends Act for Scotland, allowing 1d. rate.	by Act of 1867.
1866 29 & 30 *Vict. c. 114.*	Public Libraries Amendment Act (England and Scotland), 1866.		as to Scotland by Act of 1867; rest by Act of 1892.
1867 30 & 31 *Vict. c. 37.*	Public Libraries (Scotland Act), 1867. Amendment.	Amending and consolidating.	§§7 & 8 (borrowing) by Act of 1871; rest by Act of 1887.
1871 34 & 35 *Vict. c. 59.*	Public Libraries Act (Scotland, 1867) Amendment Act, 1871.	Adds facilities.	by Act of 1887.
1884—*See* E. & W.			
1887 50 & 51 *Vict. c. 42.* Principal Act.	Public Libraries Consolidation (Scotland) Act, 1887.	Consolidating Acts, 1867 to 1884.	

SCOTLAND—continued

DATE	NAME	SPECIAL FEATURES	REPEALED
1894 57 & 58 *Vict.* c. 20.	Public Libraries (Scotland) Act, 1894.	Modification as to adoption.	
1899 62 *Vict.* c. 5.	Public Libraries (Scotland) Act, 1899.	Combination of burghs or parishes.	
1918 8 & 9 *Geo. V*, c. 48.	Education (Scotland) Act, 1918.	Provision of County Libraries by Education Authorities.	
1920 10 & 11, *Geo. V*, c. 45.	Public Libraries (Scotland) Act, 1920.	Rate limit raised to 3d.	
1929 19 & 20 *Geo. V*, c. 25.	Local Government (Scotland) Act, 1929.	Rating of burghs by County Education Authorities. Library Estimates to be submitted to Town Councils.	

ISLE OF MAN

DATE	NAME	SPECIAL FEATURES	REPEALED
1885 July 6.	H. K. Public Libraries Act.	Modelled on the English Acts.	by Act of 1886.
1886 December 14.	H. K. Isle of Man Local Government Act, 1886.	Incorporates the above in §§220–26.	by Act of 1916.
1916	H. K. Isle of Man Local Government Consolidation Act, 1916.	§§334–35.	

INDEX

L.A. = Library Association.

Abbott, Ald. Thomas Charles, urges removal of the rate limit for libraries, 128, 163, 251; member of Net-Book Committee, 268; Life of, 301

Aberystwyth Summer Schools, 219–21

Acts of Parliament relating to libraries, etc., 80–144; 345–52

Adams, W. G. S., Report on library provision, 137, 275.

Addison, *Dr.*, Minister of Health, 136; backs Library Bill (1919), 138

Adult education, 36–7; Interim Report on, 134–6

Advocates' Library, Edinburgh, 51, 59–61

Agricultural libraries, 70

American Library Association, 163, 261

American Library Journal, 168

Anderton, Basil, President, N. Counties L.A., 244–5

Arnold, Martha, Libraries for the Blind, 290

Associated Booksellers: net-books, 266–71

Association of Assistant Librarians, 189, 205, 236–8

Association of Special Libraries and Information Bureaux (ASLIB), 203–4; Conferences, 254–5; Publications, 255–6

Atkins, J. W. H., lectures, 220

Axon, W. E. A., original member, L.A., 168; on legislation for Public Libraries, 127, 176

Bailey, Ernest (South Shields), 245

Bailey, *Sir* William H., 163

Baker, *Dr.* E. A., Hon Secy., L.A. Education Committee; Director, School of Librarianship, 224, 226

Ballinger, *Sir* John, on the rate limit, 128; interviews Sir Herbert Lewis, 136; proposes registration of librarians, 190; member of Departmental Committee, 1927, 193; Aberystwyth Summer School, 219–20; staff association at Cardiff, 232; on net books, 268; on library work with children, 297–8

Banbury, *Lord*, opposes Library Bills, 129; 139

Barker, W. R., Member of Departmental Committee, 193

Barrett, Francis Thornton, original member of L.A., 168; First President of Scottish L.A., 247; Life of, 302–3

Barrett, Franklin T., Hon. Secy., Cataloguing Rules Committee, 188; Lecturer for Education Committee, 225

Barwick, G. F., Editor of *Aslib Directory*, 255

Beccles parochial library, 25

Bedwell, E. A., on Hospital Libraries Committee, 292

Beetlestone, G., Hon. Secy., Birmingham and District L.A., 240

Belgian libraries, 55

Bell, *Rev.* Andrew, educational work, 16–17

Bentley, *Councillor* F., 250

Best Books, Lists of, 260
Beveridge, W. Storrie, Treasurer, Scottish L.A., 248
Bibliothèque Nationale, Paris, 57
Birkbeck, George, founder of Mechanics' Institutes, 41–5
Birkbeck College, London, 45
Birmingham and District L.A., 240–3; Scholarship, 242
Birmingham Circulating Library, 39
Birmingham Summer School, 221–2
Bishop, W. J., Bibliography on Hospital Libraries, 292
Blades, William, 165
Blind, Libraries for the, 289–90
Board of Education Report on Public Libraries, 1927, 299–300
Bond, Sir Edward A., Life of, 303–4
Bonser, Dr. W., lectures, 221
Book Production Committee, 261
Book supply in libraries inadequate, 155
Books consulted, list of, 343–4
Books, no powers for purchase of, 81, 83, 94
Books to Read, 262
Books, value of, in healing, 291
Brace, William, 169
Bradshaw, Henry, President of L.A., 177, 211
Braille system for blind readers, 289
Bray, Thomas, and his Associates, libraries founded by, 24–5, 68, 272
Bridle, W., President, Soc. of Public Librarians, 239
Bright, John, supports Libraries Bill, 85, 90
Brighton Pavilion Act, 1850, 97
Briscoe, John Potter, President, N. Midland L.A., 235–6; on libraries for the Blind, 289; on children's libraries, 293; Life of, 304–6
Briscoe, Walter A., 235–6; on library publicity, 262–3
Bristol and Western District Branch, L.A., 246–7
Bristol City Library, 1615, 23
Bristol Museum and Library, 1772, 39
British and Foreign School Society, 16
British Museum Library, accessibility and administration, 50, 67–8, 77; catalogue, 166; duplicates, 73–4
Brittain, *Alderman*, 163
Brotherton, Joseph, on Salford Library, 65, 70; supports Libraries Bill, 84–5, 89; Life of, 306–7
Brougham, Henry, Lord, *Practical observations upon Education*, 41, 45
Brown, James Duff, correspondence courses, 230; on library appliances, 152; open access, 152, 294; Life of, 307–8
Brown, Reginald W., Hon. Secy., N. Midland L.A., 236
Brown, Samuel, itinerating libraries, 33–5, 272
Buckinghamshire libraries, 274
Bullen, George, original member of L.A., 168
Burgoyne, F. J., lectures, 225
Burns, John, M.P., 128
Burton, G. L., lectures, 222
Business Firms, Register of, 281
Butcher, Albert, 211
Byers, G. W., President, N. Counties L.A., 245

Callander, T. E., 238
Carlyle, Thomas, and the London Library, 40

INDEX

Carnegie, Andrew, benefactions of, 109, 161–2, 274; Life of, 308–11

Carnegie U.K. Trustees, letter to library authorities, 134; their county library scheme, 137, 274–6; policy of, 161; grants to Library Association and National Central Library, for headquarters, etc., 202–4; for School of Librarianship, 226

Cashmore, H. M., Birmingham Summer School, 223

Catalogues of libraries, 69–70

Cataloguing, co-operative, 166

Cataloguing Rules Committee, 186–9

Cathedral libraries, 25; 69

Central Library for Students. *See* National Central Library

Chambers, R. W., lectures, 226

Chambers, Wm., on Peebles Library, 70

Chambers's Journal and other publications of the firm, 18–19

Chatterton, *Col.* (Cork), 93

Chennell, Frank E., President, Soc. of Public Librarians, 239

Chetham Library, Manchester, 23; 51

Children's libraries, 293–4

Christie, Richard Copley, 114, 163; Life of, 311–12

Chubb, Leonard, Birmingham Summer School, 222–3

Church libraries, 25; 69; 272

Church of Scotland libraries, 25–6; 68–9; 272

Clark, James T., Advocates' Library, 164, 167, 174

Clay tablets, collections of, 13

Clayton, R. H., on technical libraries, 286

Cleave, John, Chartist, publications, 20

Coats, James, of Ferguslie, 273

Cockerell, Douglas, lectures, 225

Colles, E. R. P., on Dublin libraries, 65–6

Commercial libraries, 280–1

Conference of Librarians (1877), 163

Convention of Royal Burghs and rate limit, 133

Cook, Eliza, publications, 19–20

Co-operation between borough and county authorities, 195, 249

Co-opted members on library committees, 196

Copyright libraries, 52, 71

Correspondence courses, 230

Cotton Library and British Museum, 52

County Councils as Library Authorities, 137, 194–5

County Libraries, 272–9; in N. Ireland and Irish Free State, 142–3; in Scotland, 122

Coventry Grammar School library, 22–3

Cowell, Peter, original member of L.A., 168, 211

Coxe, *Rev.* H. O., Vice-President, L.A., 167, 171

Craigie, James, Hon. Secy., and Treasurer, Scottish L.A., 248

Crestadoro, Andrea, original member, L.A., 168

Crowther, Wm., President, N. Midland L.A., 235

Curry, Eugene, on Irish libraries, 64

Davies, *Sir* Alfred, on hospital libraries, 290

Davies, E. Salter, member of Departmental Committee, 194

Davies, W. Ll., Hon. Secy., Welsh Branch, L.A., 258

Davis, Cecil, lectures, 225

Dawes, Annie J., on library work with children, 242

355

Dawson, George, evidence on libraries, 57–9
Decimal Classification, 256
Dent, R. K., founder of Birmingham and District L.A., 240-1
Dewey, Melvil, 164; joint-code on cataloguing rules, 188
Dickens' works imitated and pirated, 20–1
Dorset County Library, 274
Doubleday, Wm. E., spokesman for deputation to Board of Education on rate limit, 1919, 132; Hon. Secy. and Lecturer to L.A. Summer Schools, 225; on net-books, 265–6, 270
Douie, C. O. G., Secy. to Departmental Committee, 194
Dublin libraries, 65–6
Dublin Society Library, 51
Dublin, University College Library School, 229
Duckworth, T., lectures, 221
Duff, David, Treasurer, Scottish L.A., 248
Dunblane Conference (1931), 249, 279
Durability of Paper Committee, 256, 261
Durham College of Science, 232

East Lothian Itinerating Libraries, 33–5; 63; 67; 272
Edinburgh Circulating Library, Ramsay's, 38–9
Edinburgh Mechanics' Institution, 44; Subscription Library, 45
Edinburgh School of Arts, 43
Edinburgh training school for assistants, 248
Education Act, 1902, 298
Education (Scotland) Act, 1918, 122, 278
Education and Public Libraries, 263

Education Authorities may delegate powers to Education Committees, 141
Education Committees and libraries, 196; rating powers, 121-4
Education, Parliamentary grants in aid, 17
Education, spread of, 15–21
Edwards, Edward, evidence before Select Committee on libraries, 48 *et seq.*; specially thanked, 76; on British Museum Library, 67–8; on school libraries, 294–5; Life of, 312–14
Edwards, John Passmore, gifts of libraries, 161–2; Life of, 314–15
Elgin, *Earl of*, President, L.A., 194; Presidential address, 200–2
Eliza Cook's Journal, 19–20
England and Wales, Library Acts, 346–8
Esdaile, Arundell, Editor, L.A. Record, 170; Lecturer on Bibliography, 220, 226; on Dr. Johnson, 221; Chairman of University and Research Section, L.A., 257
Ewart, William, M.P., moves for Select Committee on libraries, 48; appointed Chairman, 48; introduces Libraries Bill, 1850, 80–2; Life of, 315–16
Exhibitions of library appliances, books, etc., 259

Family Herald, 19
Farmers' clubs, 70
Farr, Harry, Lecturer on library work with children, 220; Chairman of Welsh Branch, L.A., 258; Secy. of Hospital Libraries Committee, 291
Fegan, Miss Ethel S., lectures, 220
Fiction in public libraries, 179–80
Fisher, H. A. L., receives depu-

INDEX

tation, 131; backs Library Bill (1919), 138

Flack, G. E., lectures, 223

Fortune, W. W., Secy., Library Assistants, Association, 236

Foskett, Edward, 180, 239

Fovargue, H. W., Prize Bill, 114; Hon. Solicitor, L.A., 207; drafts Library Bill, 128; lectures on library law, 226

Fraser, G. M., President, Scottish L.A., 247

"Free" Libraries a misnomer, 100, 167

French libraries, 55, 66, 69

Frost, B. J., President, Soc. of Public Librarians, 239

Frost, *Miss* M., Chairman, Hospital Libraries Committee, 291

Frowde, John, President, Soc. of Public Librarians, 239

Furnish, A. H., President, N. Counties L.A., 245

Gaelic sacred and popular literature, 33

Garnett, *Dr.* Richard, original member of L.A., 168; on printing British Museum Catalogue, 177; Chairman of L.A. Education Committee, 210, 224; on public education and public libraries, 297; Life of, 316–18

German libraries, 63

Glasgow Branch libraries gifted by Mr. Carnegie, 109

Glasgow Mechanics' Institution, 42

Glasgow Public Libraries Association, 109

Glasgow Royal Technical College, 43

Glasgow Training School for Assistants, 248

Godding, C., Hon. Secy., Soc. of Public Librarians, 239

Goldsbrough, J. B., Chairman, N. Ireland L.A., 253

Gorrie, Thomas, on library co-operation, 253

Goss, C. W. F., Hon. Secy., and President, Soc. of Public Librarians, 239

Goulbourn, H., opposes Libraries Bill, 84

Government grants to libraries recommended, 74

Green, Edward, Hon. Secy., N. Central Branch, L.A., 250

Greenwood, Thomas, Life of, 318–20

Griffiths, D. G., lectures, 220

Guizot's evidence on French libraries, 55

Guppy, Dr. Henry, Editor of *L. A. Record*, 170, 213; lectures on cataloguing, 220, 225; President N. Central Branch, L.A., 250

Guthkelch, A. C. L., lectures, 231

Haddington School of Arts, 44

Haddington Town Library, 44

Hall, *Sir* B. (Marylebone), 91

Hall, Hubert, lecturer on palæography, 220

Hamilton, G. A., on libraries and education in Ireland, 70; supports Libraries Bill, 85

Hand, T. W., President, N. Counties L.A., and N. Central Branch, L.A., 245, 250

Hanson, C., lectures on bookbinding, 220

Hanson, J. C. M., Editor of Cataloguing Rules, 188–9

Harkness, T., on agricultural libraries, 70

Harrison, Robert, moves foundation of L.A., 164; Hon.

Treasurer of L.A., 167; on Examination Committee, 210; Life of, 320–1
Harrison, Sydney E., on library work with children, 242
Hatcher, S. (Canning Town), 239
Hawkes, A. J., lectures, 220
Headicar, B. M., lectures, 226
Hentsch, *Miss*, lectures, 225
Heriot-Watt College, Edinburgh, 44
Hewitt, H. J. (Chiswick), 239
Heywood, J., supports Libraries Bill, 87
Highland libraries, 29–33; 68–9
Hill, B. R., Hon. Secy., N. Counties L.A., 244
Hill, R. H., Hon. Secy., University Section, L.A., 257
Hill, Rowland, founder of Sunday Schools, 15
Hole, James, *Essay on Mechanics' Institutes*, 40–1
Hopwood, H. V., Editor of *Best Books*, 260
Hospital libraries, 290–3
Howard, P. H., *Baron*, opposes Libraries Bill, 87
Hudson, Baker, President, N. Counties L.A., 245
Hulme, E. Wyndham, on cataloguing rules, 188; on technical libraries, 284
Hume, J., supports Libraries Bill, 85, 92
Hurford, W. E., Hon. Secy., N. Counties L.A., 245
Hutt, James, lectures, 220; Chairman, Education Committee, 224; Hon. Secy., N.W. Branch, 244; Conspectus of Libraries Acts, 345–52
Hynes, W., President, Soc. of Public Librarians, 239

Imray, John, on Scottish libraries, 66–7
Income tax exemption for libraries, 197
Indicators, 152
Inkster, Lawrence, Hon. Secy., L.A., 207
International Library and Bibliographical Committee, 200
International Library Conferences (1877), 171; (1897), 181–2; (1927), 199–203
Ireland, Library Acts, 349–50
Irish Free State libraries, 143, 145–6
Irish libraries, 64–6, 70
Irish Library Association, 252
Isle of Man public libraries, 147; Library Acts, 352
Isle of Wight libraries, 274
Italian libraries, 55
Itinerating libraries founded by Samuel Brown, 33–5; 67; 272

Jackson, C., lectures, 222
James, *Miss* M. S. R., on training library assistants, 178; on forming an assistants' library, 237; Life of, 321-3
Jast, L. Stanley, articles on cataloguing, 187; on registration of librarians, 190; Hon. Secy., L.A., 207; lectures, 220–1; Hon. Secy., and President, N. Central Branch, L.A., 250; Chairman, Publicity Committee, L.A., 263
Jenkinson, Hilary, lectures on business handwriting, 231; on palæography and archives, 222, 226
Jesson, Charles, M.P., introduces deputation to Mr. Fisher, 131
Jevons, W. Stanley, 166
Johnson, Charles, lectures on palæography and archives, 220

INDEX

Johnston, H. E., Hon. Secy., N. Counties L.A., 244

Joint Advisory Committee on Net Books, 270–1

Jones, George, lectures on printing, 220

Jones, Gurner P., on Publicity Committee, 263

Jones, Herbert, Kensington, 232, 253

Jones, John Winter, First President, L.A., 164, 167, 170

Jones, Wm., evidence on R.T.S. libraries, 64–5

Juvenile libraries recommended, 155

Keay, *Ald.* H. W., President, Associated Booksellers, 268

Kederminster, *Sir* John, 23

Keeling, Guy W., Secretary, L.A., 205, 207

Kemp, T. C., lectures, 222

Kenyon, *Sir* Frederic G., Chairman of Committee on Libraries, 1927, 193–4

Kettle, Bernard, Hon. Treasurer, L.A., 207; *Directories in Guildhall Library*, 281

Kirkwood, *Rev.* James, *Overture for founding bibliothecks*, 26–9; 'Father of free libraries,' 27; Letter anent erecting libraries in Highland Counties, 29

Knight's Penny Magazine, 19

Kroeger, Alice B., Hon. Secy., A.L.A. Catalog Rules Committee, 188

Kyte, Ernest C., Secy., L.A., 207

Labouchere, H., supports Libraries Bill, 85

Lakin, Julius T., Hon. Secy., Birmingham, etc. L.A., 241

Lancaster, Joseph, 16–17

Langley, J. B., evidence, 64

Langley Marish parochial library, 23

Law, C. E. (Cambridge Univ.), opposes Libraries Bill, 93

Leather for libraries, 260

Lectures, value of, 73; lectures in libraries, 197

Leeds Library, 1768, 39

Leicester City Library, 1632, 23

Lewis, *Prof.* Henry, lectures, 220

Lewis, *Sir* Herbert, secures passing of Libraries Act, 1919, 136–40; receives deputation from Carnegie U. K. Trustees, 138

Librarians' College suggested, 285

Librarians of the Mersey District, 234

Librarians, qualifications necessary for, 183; 197–8; registration, 189; training and remuneration, 198–9

Librarianship, training for, 208–33

Libraries, British compared with European, 49–50; cathedral and church, 25, 69; copyright, 52; earliest public, 13; early municipal, 22–4; Egyptian, 13; evening opening of, 54; French provincial, 66; German, 63; Government grants to, 74; Inspection desirable, 53–4; Irish, 52, 64–5; Itinerating, 33–5, 63, 67, 272; Lending, 75; Monastic, 52; Parochial, 24–33, 68–9, 272; Scottish, 52, 66–7; Should be fireproof, 76; Special, 70, 74; Subscription, 37–40; United States of America, 51, 61

Libraries. *See also* Children's Libraries; Hospital Libraries; Blind, Libraries for the; Public Libraries; School Libraries

Libraries Offences Act, 1898, 119–

20; extended to Museums, etc., 121
Library (The), 169
Library Acts, adoptions of, 160–1
Library Advertising: Briscoe, 263
Library Assistant, 237–8
Library Association, Annals, 260; annual meetings, 170–80; byelaws, 191–2; campaign for removal of rate limit, 135–44; correspondence courses, 230; educational work, 158, 208–33; examinations, 210–16; exhibitions, 259; foundation and history of, 162–207; headquarters, 202–3; history, 1877–97, 182; officers, 1877–date, 206–7; professional register, 158; publications, 260–2; publicity, 262–4; Royal Charter of incorporation, 169, 183–5; summer schools, 216–33; syllabus of examinations, 157–8, 214
Library Association of Ireland, 252
Library Association Record, 170
Library Associations, amalgamation of, 203
Library Chronicle, 169
Library Committees, composition of, 159–60
Library Extension Work: McColvin, 264
Library Journal, 168–9
Library property vested in town councils, 70; 74; 81
Library service, reforms needed, 159
Library staffs, standard of education, 156–7
Libri, W., evidence on Italian libraries, 55–7, 78
Lindsay, *Dr.* A. D., presidential address, Blackpool, 36–7
Lineker, Arthur, Hon. Secy., N. Midland L.A., 236

Liverpool Lyceum founded 1758, 39
Liverpool Mechanics' Apprentices Library, 45
Lloyd, Edward, publications, 21
Local Government Act, 1929, 117–18
Local Government Board, library powers and duties of Treasury transferred to, 108
Local Government (Scotland) Act, 1929, 123; rating powers, 146
London and Home Counties Branch, L.A., 240, 253
London, City of, a library district with no rate limitation, 117
London, early circulating library, 39
London coffee-houses, 65
London Library, 40
London library authorities and rate limit, 130–2
London Mechanics' Institution, 45
London School Board libraries, 296
London School of Economics Classes, 218; 225
Lovett, Wm., evidence, 65
Lubbock, *Sir* John, Baron Avebury, introduces Library Bills, 114–15, 174; Chairman of Second International Conference, 1897, 181–2; aids in obtaining Royal Charter, 184; Life of, 323–4
Lyster, Thomas William, 128; Life of, 324–6

MacAlister, *Sir* John Y. W., founded and edited *The Library*, 169; presented many prizes for students, 114, 212–13, 217, 219; Hon. Secy., L.A., 1887–98; Secy., International Conference of Librarians, 1897, 182; ob-

INDEX

tained Royal Charter for L.A., 183–5; President, L.A. and member of School of Librarianship Committee, 226; Life of, 326–8

McColvin, L. R., 223; on publicity, 262, 264

McDougall, D., Plaistow, 239

Macfarlane, J., lectures, 225

Mackenzie, W. Munro, Dunfermline, 248

McKnight, Edward, Secy., N.W. Branch Summer School, 244

Maclauchlan, John, outlined scheme for county libraries, 175

Macmillan, H. P., *Baron*, 207

Macray, *Rev.* W. D., 166

Madeley, Charles, Warrington, 234, 243

Madras Orphanage, experiment in education at, 16

Maitland, Thomas (Lord Dundrennan), evidence on Advocates' Library, 59–61

Malet, *Dr.* J. A., Vice-President, L.A., 167

Malicious injury to libraries, 103

Manchester Conference, 1918, 129; Public Library opened, 1852, 97; Technical Library, 285

Manners, *Lord* John, supports Libraries Bill, 85

Mansbridge, Albert, 194; founded Central Library for Students, 202

Marsh, J. F., 61–2

Mason, Thomas, on Scottish libraries, 174; joint Hon. Secy., L.A., 206; Life of, 328–9

Mathews, E. R. Norris, 246

Mechanics' Institutes, 40–46; Libraries of, 64

Metropolitan Free Libraries Committee, 171, 174

Meyer, Charles, on German libraries, 63

Millar, Alex. H., President, Scottish L.A., 247

Minto, John, Hon. Secy., Cataloguing Rules Committee, 187–9; lectures on Reference Books, 220; *Reference Books* published, 262; President, Scottish L.A., 247

Mitchell, *Lieut.-Col.* J. M., Secy. to Carnegie U.K. Trustees, Member of Departmental Committee on Libraries, 194; 199–200

Monastic libraries, 52

Monthly Notes, 169

Moon, William, system for Blind readers, 289

Moon, Z., President, Soc. of Public Librarians, 239

More, Hannah, and Sunday Schools, 15

Morley, Henry, 166

Morley, Samuel, M.P., 293

Morrison, Hew, President, Scottish L.A., 247

Mullins, J. D., original member of L.A., 168; on training assistants, 175, 211

Municipal libraries, early, 22–4

Munro, R. (*Lord* Alness), receives deputation, 133

Murphy, Gwendolen, lectures, 220

Museums Act, 81–2, 346; extension desirable, 53–4, 74

Museums & Gymnasiums Act, 1891, 113, 347

Museums transferred to library authorities, 141

National Central Library, 195; Royal Charter, 202

National Hall, High Holborn, classes and library, 65

National Library of Wales, Summer School, 219

361

National Society for the Education of the Poor, 16–17
Net-Book Agreement, 264–71
Newcombe, *Lieut.-Col.* L., on regional co-operation, 223; Chairman, London Branch, L.A., 254
Newspapers, stamp duty on, 19–20
Nicholson, Edward W.B., founder of L.A., 163, 173; Hon. Secy., 164, 168, 206; Life of, 329–31
Nicholson, Frank C., President, Scottish L.A., 248
North Central Branch, 250–2; Conference in Manchester, 250
North Midland L.A., 205, 234–6
North Western Branch, L.A., 243–4; Summer School, 218
Northern Counties L.A., 244–6; conference, 1918, 286
Northern Ireland libraries, 145
Northern Ireland L.A., 252–3
Norwich, early municipal library, 23

Ogle, John James, first certificated assistant, 211; prize for draft Library Bill, 114; paper on training assistants, 178; conducts Library Assistants' Corner, 212; Director of Technical Instruction, Bootle, 213; Report on the Public Library and the Public Elementary School, 297; Life of, 332–4
O'Neill, J. J., Irish L.A., 252
Open access in libraries, 152
Orde, R. H. P., 292
Orr, Ryrie, President, Scottish L.A., 247
Osler, *Sir* Wm., *Bt.*, 219
Oswald, A., opposes Libraries Bill, 87, 89
Overall, W. H., original member of L.A., 168, 211

Owen, Joseph, *H.M.I.*, 194
Oxfordshire County Libraries, 275

Pacy, Frank, member of Departmental Committee, 1927, 194; Hon. Secy., L.A., 207, 226; Life of, 334–6
Pafford, J. H., lectures, 222
Palmer, Roundell (*Lord* Selborne), opposes Libraries Bill, 86, 90
Panizzi, *Sir* A., evidence, 78
Paper, durability of, 256, 261
Parochial libraries, 24–33; 68–9; 272
Parsons, Edgar H., Hon. Secy., Scottish L.A., 248
Pattison, Mark, 166
Pearce, J. G., on works' libraries, 286–7
Peddie, R. A., President, Library Assistants' Assoc., 236
Peebles Library, 70
Penny Magazine and *Penny Cyclopædia*, 19
Percival, *Dr.*, circulating libraries at Hereford, 274
Peto, *Sir* Henry, Book Lending Association at Dorchester, 274
Picton, *Sir* James, 114
Pierce, Miss Kate E., Hon. Secy., N. Midland L.A., 236
Pitt, S. A., member of Departmental Committee, 1927, 194; on commercial and technical libraries, 220, 242, 251, 280–1; President, Scottish L.A., 248
Plant, W. C., President, Soc. of Public Librarians, 239
Plummer, *Ald.* H., Manchester, 268
Pollard, A. W., lectures, 231
Poole's Index to periodicals, 172
Popular literature, circulation of, 18–19
Porter, *Dr.* Charles, 292

INDEX

Powell, Walter, lectures, 220; paper on libraries and reconstruction, 242

Prideaux, W. R. B., on professional education and registration, 189; lectures on cataloguing and library routine, 226

Pritchett, *Ald.* J. S., Hon. Legal Adviser, L.A., 207

Public Libraries and the People, 263

Public Libraries Act, 1850 [England only], Early adoptions, 96–8; extended to Scotland and Ireland, 99; P.L. Act, 1855, 99; Amended, 1871, 106; Again amended, 1877, 107; Amendment Act, 1887, transferred powers of Treasury to Local Government Board, 108; P.L. Act, 1889, 112; Amending Act, 1890, gave power to libraries to combine, 113; P.L. Act, 1892 (the Principal Act), 116; Amended, 1893, 117; P.L. Acts Amendment Act, 1901, 120; P.L. Act, 1919, removed rate limitation, 125–41, 276–7

Public Libraries [England and Wales], Departmental Committee's Report, 1927, 193–9, 275

Public Libraries Act (Ireland) 1855, 99; Amended, 1877, 110; P.L. Act (Ireland), 1902, 216; Amended, 1911, 122; P.L. (Ireland) Amendment Act, 1894, 118–19

Public Libraries (Northern Ireland) Act, 1924, 142, 145; Public Libraries in Irish Free State, 143

Public Libraries in Isle of Man, 147–8

Public Libraries (Scotland) Act, 1854, 99; Repealed, 104; P.L. (Scotland) Act, 1867, 104; Amended, 1871, 105; Amended, 1884, 107; P.L. Consolidation (Scotland) Act, 1887 [Principal Act], 110–12; P.L. (Scotland) Act, 1894, 118; P.L. (Scotland) Act, 1899, gave powers to burghs and parishes to combine, 120; Estimates of Scottish Committees subject to approval, 147

Public Libraries and Public Education, 297; Control of, 136, 196; Methods of service, 152; Powers of library authorities, 197; Progress and policy, 149–61; Statistics, 133; Use of term 'Free,' 100–3

Public Libraries Select Committee: Reports and Evidence, 47–79

Public Library Rules, Code adopted, 254

Publishers' Association: Net-book agreement, 266–71

Purves, J. W. C., President, N. Counties L.A., 244–5

Quinn, J. H., Hon. Treasurer, L.A., 207; lecturer on Books of Reference, cataloguing, etc., 220, 225, 226; Chairman of London, etc., Branch, 254

Radford, John T., Hon. Secy., N. Midland L.A., 235

Ragged Schools and libraries, London, 67

Raikes, Robert, founder of Sunday Schools, 15

Rameses II, library at Thebes, 14

Ramsay, Allan, founded circulating library in Edinburgh, 38

Rate limit for Irish and Scottish libraries raised, 141; for England removed, 1919, 125–44

Rating and Valuation Act, 1925, and public libraries, 146

Rating for Scottish libraries, 122–3; double rating in Scottish burghs, 146

Rawson, *Ald.* Harry, 163, 182

Reading matter, demand for, 17

Red Cross Hospital Libraries, 291

Reference Books: guide, 262

Reference Department, stocking of, 155

Reilly, *Mrs.* Kate, Asst. Secy., L.A., 207

Religious Tract Society's libraries, 64–5

Report on Public Libraries, 1927, 98

Riddle, Charles, lectures, 220

Ridley, A. F., lectures, 222

Roberts, F. Meaden, 236

Roberts, Henry D., Hon. Secy., L.A. Summer School, 217; Paper on Education of the Library Assistant, 223; Hon. Secy., L.A. Education Committee, 224–5; instituted courses of study at Newcastle, 232

Roberts, *Mrs.* M. E., 292

Robinson, Lennox, Library Conference, Dublin, 252

Roebuck, G. E., Walthamstow, 130–3, 264

Rogers, *Rev.* Charles, 166

Rolleston, *Sir* Humphrey, 291

Rowlatt, H., Chairman, London Branch, L.A., 254

Roy, A. Stewart, Hon. Secy., N. Ireland L.A., 253

Royal Dublin Society's library, 65–6

Royal Society's Library, 67

Rutherford College, Newcastle, 232

Sainte-Geneviève, Library, Paris, 54

Salford Library, 65, 81

Sanderson, C. R., lectures, 220

Saturday Magazine, 19

Savage, Ernest A., Memorandum on public libraries, 153–9; Hon. Secy., L.A., 206–7; Lecturer on classification, bibliography and book-selection, 220; Papers on Technical Libraries, 242, 282–3; On Data of the Automobile Industry, 284; President, Scottish L.A., 248; Compiled Annals of L.A., 260

Sayers, W. C. Berwick, on registration of librarians, 190; Lecturer at School of Librarianship, 226; Member of Publicity Committee, 263

School Libraries, 294

School of Librarianship, London, 158, 198, 226–9

Scotland Education Act, 1918, and county libraries, 133

Scottish libraries, 66–7

Scottish Library Acts, 351–2

Scottish Library Association and rate limit, 133; Amalgamated with Library Association, 205; History of the Association, 247–9; Scholarship founded, 248

Seligman, Leopold, 172

Seymour, *Lord*, 77

Shaw, G. T., Secy. of N.W. Branch Summer School, 244; Broadcasts on libraries at Liverpool, 263

Sibthorp, *Col.*, opposes Libraries Bill, 83, 88, 91–3, 150

Signet Library, Edinburgh, 51

Simpson, D. J. H., Belfast, 253

Singleton, J. W., Secy., N.W. Branch, L.A., 244; Member of Publicity Committee, 263

INDEX

Sion College Library, 52
Small, John, original member of L.A., 168
Smiles, Samuel, evidence, 62–3
Smith, H., Bishopsgate, 239
Smith, *Lady* Mabel, 194
Smith, Sydney, founder of Sunday schools, 15
Society for Promoting Christian Knowledge, founded, 24; publications, 19
Society for the Diffusion of Useful Knowledge, publications, 19
Society for the Propagation of the Gospel founded, 25
Society of Public Librarians, 238–40
Soper, H. Tapley, Hon. Treasurer, L.A., 207
Sound Leather Committee, 260
Southern, *Alderman*, 163
Southport Conference, Memo. on control of public libraries, 135
Southward, John, lectures, 225
Spooner, Richard (Warwickshire), opposes Libraries Bill, 85–6, 88
Staffordshire County Libraries, 275–6
Stamp duty on newspapers, 19–20
State aid for libraries, 167
Stephen, Geo. A., on Publicity Committee, 263
Stevens, Henry, of Vermont, 164, 166, 172; evidence on U.S. libraries, 61
Stewart, James H., Treasurer, Scottish L.A., 248
Strassburg Library, 54
Subject Index to Periodicals, 261
Subscription libraries, 37–40
Summer schools of library training, 216–18
Sunday schools, 15–16
Sutton, C. W., 211

Taylor, L. Acland, Hon. Secy., Bristol Branch, L.A., 246
Technical libraries, 282–8
Technical and Commercial Libraries Committee, 261
Tedder, Henry Richard, jointsecy., Librarians' Conference, 1877, 164; and of L.A., 168, 206; on the training of library assistants, 176; on librarianship as a profession, 177; treasurer of Conference, 1897, 182; President of L.A., 182; Chairman of Cataloguing Rules Committee, 188; Member and chairman of L.A. Education Committee, 210, 224, 226; Chairman of Conference on Net-Books question, 267; Report on school libraries, 298; Life of, 336–8
Tenison's (*Abp.*) Library, 52
Tennant, H. J., *M.P.*, introduces Library Bill, 128
Thacker, Francis J., Birmingham Summer School, 222, 241
Thomas, Ernest C., Hon. Secy., L.A., 169, 206, 210; editor of *Monthly Notes* and *The Library Chronicle*, 169; Life of, 338–9
Thomas, Henry, lecturer on bibliography, 220
Thorne, W. Benson, 254
Topley, W. W., Croydon, 267
Town Councils, Library property vested in, 70, 74, 81, 95; purchase of books not sanctioned by 1850 Act, 81, 83
Town Improvements Act (Ireland), 1854, 99
Translators, Register of, 281
Twentyman, A. E., on Departmental Committee, 194; on School of Librarianship Committee, 226

Ulster library authorities conference, 253
Union Catalogue of London Libraries, 256
University and Research Section, L.A., 257
University Matriculation standard a minimum requirement, 198
University of London, School of Librarianship, 226–9
Unwin, Stanley, 271
Ure, Andrew, lectures to Glasgow mechanics, 41–2

Vatican Library, restricted access to, 55–6
Vaux, W. S. W., original member of L.A., 168
Village libraries, 75, 166–7

Waley, S. W., on French provincial libraries, 66
Walford, Cornelius, 166
Walls, *Ald.* John, 246
Walthamstow conferences, 1919, 130–1
Ward, *Ald.* D. S., Harrogate, 245
Warrington library, 1760, 39; Museum and Library established, 1848, 39, 61, 81
Watt Institution, Edinburgh, 44
Welch, Charles, Paper on public library movement in London, 178; Hon. Secy., L.A., 206, 210; Chairman, Summer Schools Committee, 217
Weld, C. R., on Royal Society's Library, 67
Welsford, P. S. J., Asst. Secy., L.A., 205, 207
Welsh Branch of L.A., 258
Westmorland school libraries, 300
Weyer, Van de, evidence on Belgian libraries, 55
Wheatley, Benjamin R., original member of L.A., 168
Whitwell, C., West Ham, 239
Williams's (*Dr.*) Library, 52
Williams, W., lectures, 220
Wilson, William, Darlington, 244
Wodrow, *Rev.* Robert, on Allan Ramsay's circulating library, 38
Wood, Butler, President, N. Counties L.A., 245
Woodbine, H., lectures, 222
Woolston, W. P., Nottingham, 236
Wright, W. H. K., on promoting village libraries, 166, 175; on school libraries, 295; Life of, 340–1
Wyld, J., supports Libraries Bill, 87, 92

Yates, James, original member of L.A., 168
Yorkshire Union of Mechanics' Institutes, 62
Yorkshire Village Library, 273

For Product Safety Concerns and Information please contact our EU representative GPSR@taylorandfrancis.com
Taylor & Francis Verlag GmbH, Kaufingerstraße 24, 80331 München, Germany

www.ingramcontent.com/pod-product-compliance
Lightning Source LLC
Chambersburg PA
CBHW052141300426
44115CB00011B/1467